D0891821

On Broken Glass

LOVING AND LOSING JOHN GARDNER

Susan Thornton

CARROLL & GRAF PUBLISHERS, INC.
NEW YORK

Carroll & Graf Publishers, Inc.
A Division of Avalon Publishing Group
19 West 21st Street
New York, NY 10010-6805

Library of Congress Cataloging-in-Publication Data is available.
ISBN: 0-7867-0774-7

Manufactured in the United States of America

Contents

Contents

DIED. John Gardner, 49, prolific author of stylistically adventuresome fiction, enthusiastic teacher and, sometimes, messianic literary critic, of injuries sustained when he lost control of his motorcycle and crashed; near his home in Susquehanna, Pa., four days before he was to have married for the third time.

—*Time* magazine, September 27, 1982

John Gardner's many books include *The Resurrection, The Wreckage of Agathon, Grendel, The Sunlight Dialogues, Nickel Mountain, The King's Indian, October Light, The Life and Times of Chaucer, The Poetry of Chaucer, On Moral Fiction, Freddy's Book, The Art of Living and Other Stories, Mickelsson's Ghosts, On Becoming a Novelist,* and *The Art of Fiction: Notes on Craft for Young Writers.*

Preface

———

A man is lying on a gurney in a hospital room. A woman is cradling his head in her arm. She runs her hand down his torso. Through the opening in the torn shirt, she touches the warm skin of his belly. He doesn't respond, doesn't turn to her. She traces the line of his nose, paints his eyebrow with the tip of her finger, pushes the resilient skin against the solid cheekbone. She wraps her fingers in his silky hair, teases his scalp with her nails. He doesn't respond, doesn't turn to her. The room is much too bright; why is he lying on this gurney? She palms his cheek, runs the pads of her fingers over his lips, hovers with her warm, lambent breath over his mouth. She wants to lie down with him, press her body to his, wake his face with kisses—why will he not speak to her? Why does he not respond?

A man is lying on a gurney in a hospital room. A woman is cradling his head in her arm. At last a nurse pulls on the woman's arm, leads the woman away, and orderlies take the body to the morgue.

The full taffeta skirt of my wedding dress rustled as Mother lifted it from its paper wrappings, smoothed the hem, checked the alterations and the stitching. She ran her long tapering fingers delicately over the fitted bodice, embroidered with tiny seed pearls. Satisfied, she adjusted the puff sleeves on the padded hanger and hung the dress in my closet. Downstairs the oval mahogany dining room table was crowded with boxes of paper napkins, monogrammed in gilt script: Susan and John, September 18, 1982. *Other boxes wrapped in white paper and silver ribbon spilled out over the formal chairs and onto the Oriental rug.*

Across town in a fragrant shop, bending to his work over a table scattered with blooms, the florist sang to himself as he wreathed my bridal headpiece; the owner of the neighborhood liquor store whistled as he boxed for delivery the champagne my father had ordered; in a quiet studio outside the city, one of John's oldest, dearest friends sounded a note on his piano, bent over his score, wrote and erased, wrote and erased, composing the music John had commissioned for the service. We were to have a church wedding and a garden reception with 150 guests; my godmother was telephoning the restaurant with her final instructions for our rehearsal dinner; John's mother was planning what to wear.

On my way home on the afternoon of Tuesday, September 14, 1982, I stopped for one or two items at the local grocery. As the clerk rang up my few purchases he smiled at my shining face. "You look happy," he remarked.

"I am," I replied, and touched the diamond solitaire on my left hand. "I'm getting married on Saturday."

As I opened the car door, an ambulance siren rose from the distant, narrow road that wound through the dark, surrounding hills of Pennsylvania's Endless Mountains. I stopped for a moment to listen. I didn't know it at that moment, but the accident had already happened and my wedding to John Gardner would never take place.

John's death shattered me. Recovery has been slow. I attempted to rebuild my life and followed John's footsteps into academia. However, I wouldn't talk about the past. I clung to John's friends; they knew what had happened. When I met new people I froze out questions, pretended nothing unusual had happened in my life. If strangers mentioned John's name, I left the room. Five years later, in 1987, I married, but the foundation of my marriage was shaky, threatened by my belief that John's accident had robbed me of my perfect and only love.

When my daughter, a much-wished-for child, was born in 1993, I was puzzled by my severe depression. A therapist suggested I had unresolved grief issues involving John's death. I took a maternity leave and began to write the story of my life with John.

I planned it as a love story, a poignant story of loss; I visualized a filmy, romantic image of myself on the back flap of the book with the haunting statement, *Ms. Thornton still lives not twenty-five miles from where John Gardner died.* I intended not to mention my changed circumstances, my marriage, our child; I planned a portrait of a Victorian heroine, still mourning her perfect love.

The story wouldn't write itself that way.

The first draft had a hole in the middle: the account of John's and my day-to-day life together. I couldn't tell it. Why not? Gradually I realized I would have to think thoughts I was unable to think before, look clearly at what had happened, tell stories I didn't want to tell. In the end the book that came to be written was a much different book from the one I had planned.

Indian poets sing the legend of a Moghul prince of the fourteenth century. Bored with his dancing girls, he wanted to know the depth of their love for him. His prime minister took him aside, spoke low into his ear. "My lord, break a glass carafe and see which girl, if any, will dance on the broken glass. That will surely tell you which of them loves you most dearly." The prince thought it over, summoned his harem; at a signal, his minister dashed the bottle to the marble floor. "His majesty wishes to test your loves. Which of you girls will dance?"

The prince watched and waited, his index finger pressed to his chin, his dark eyes hooded. The girls, dressed in jeweled costumes and transparent veils, stood silent, waiting, until one stepped forward. As if casually, she stepped onto the marble floor and began to dance on the broken glass, her fingers graceful, her face serene, tears pouring down her cheeks, blood pouring from her feet. The other girls turned away so as not to watch, and the prince, smiling, knew which of his dancing girls loved him the best.

To love John was to walk a difficult path. I am no longer the young woman who loved so deeply and so passionately, who lost her beloved on the eve of her wedding. I have been profoundly changed by my life's experience. John remains a complex character: an obsessed writer, a passionate lover, a gifted and generous teacher, a devoted son, a witty and charming raconteur, and an abusive partner who took chances, both with his life and with mine. He was multiply motivated, his demons as large or larger than his gifts. This story illuminates the day-to-day life of this driven author in his last months; it sheds light on the events just before his nearly inexplicable motorcycle accident; and it traces the arc of a love story that began in joy, moved through desolation and loss, and rose again to hope.

1

"Only One in a Galaxy of Stars":
Bread Loaf Writers' Conference, 1979

I first read about John Gardner in July of 1979, in *The New York Times Magazine.* The cover showed a striking closeup of his face, scrutinizing the viewer with a wry, guarded look. He had straight white hair, not well combed, unruly, that fell to his collar, almost in the style of a woman's pageboy cut. He wore a blue-jean jacket over a blue flannel shirt; just at the margin of the photograph one could see the curving stem of his pipe. His face filled the cover of the magazine: the chin thrust forward, the eyes accessible yet hidden, holding a look that was a cross between an invitation and a dare. I couldn't stop looking at that face. Beside it the smaller inset photos of John Updike in a fur-collared coat, John Barth in beret and horn rims, and Saul Bellow in a suit jacket and tie looked negligible, boring. In yellow type a quote from John—"Almost all modern fiction is tinny, commercial and immoral"—in white type the title of the article, "The Sound and Fury Over Fiction," and under each other author's photo a quote in biting answer to John's remark.

I turned at once to the article. Here was another photograph: John in a leather motorcycle jacket astride a Honda, just coming off a bridge, his square hands gripping the controls, his eyes hidden by opaque glasses, his hair curling out underneath his motorcycle helmet and over his collar. Then other photos, less flattering, one showing him with longer hair, wearing a suit jacket, holding a drink and a pipe, posing with Kurt Vonnegut, Bernard Malamud, and John Barth, all smiling for the camera. I flipped the page. John smoking, quite obviously fat, hunched before an IBM Selectric typewriter and a desk strewn with papers, tins of tobacco, a telephone to his left. I began to read.

I discovered this extraordinary man was forty-five. His work had gone unpublished for fifteen years because "no one would have him." He was now publishing fast and furiously, both his fiction, which was admired, and his criticism, which made people angry. He had grown up in Batavia, a small farming community outside Rochester, New York, where I had grown up. In this article I first encountered his voice in a series of lively quotes: confident, unusual, interesting remarks. At the very end of the text, John was quoted speaking about art and about joy. Art, he said,

> made my life and it made my life when I was a kid, when I was incapable of finding any other sustenance, any other thing to lean on, any other comfort during times of great unhappiness. Art has filled my life with joy and I want everybody to know the kind of joy I know—that's what Messianic means. . . . I work all the time on my own fiction. I work hard and I work critically because I want to be part of that joy. I want to be a piece of the great conversation.

Much later I realized that the writer of the article had meant to be unflattering, describing John in his black leather jacket crossing the campus at the State University of New York as "something like a pregnant woman trying to pass for a Hell's Angel." I read right past that to find a man who would speak openly, candidly about emotional topics—his love for his mother and father, his failed first marriage, his girlfriend—a man who could find joy in reading and contemplating literature. I encountered his direct and engaging voice: art had saved him when he was "a kid." I knew what he meant by "the great conversation," that dialogue begun by great minds of the past and carried on by thinkers of the present. I knew he was going to be at the Bread Loaf Writers' Conference in August of that year, and I was suddenly excited to be going there too.

I had recently been accepted at the conference as a paying contributor. In 1971, I had graduated from Middlebury College, which sponsors the conference. Because my undergraduate education had been in British literature, I had read very few contemporary American authors and none I'd really liked. I knew I had to play catch-up if I was going to be serious. I was then living on a narrow tree-lined street in Cambridge, Massachusetts, and, like a good student, I took the brochure that came from the Writers' Conference and trotted off to the bookstores surrounding Harvard Square. I scoured the shelves until I had one book by each fiction writer represented at the conference. My shopping list included Gail Godwin, John Irving, David Madden, Tim O'Brien, Lore Segal, Nancy Willard, Hilma Wolitzer, and John Gardner.

Swinging my bag of books, I returned to my one-bedroom apartment and spent all my spare hours that summer on my front porch, sitting in an Adirondack chair, my feet up on the porch railing facing my landlady's crabapple tree, methodically reading one book after another.

The pile of books next to my chair dwindled until I got to *October Light*, John's book, which had won the National Book Critics Circle Award for Fiction in 1976. I still have my dog-eared paperback copy, emblazoned at the top of the front cover with the announcement "10 weeks a *New York Times* bestseller!" As I read, I felt something different than I had in reading the other books, well done as they were. Here was an intriguing mind at work; here was evidence of an unusual sensibility.

"Corruption? *I'll* tell you about corruption, sonny!" The old man glared into the flames in the fireplace and trembled all over, biting so hard on the stem of his pipe that it cracked once, sharply, like the fireplace logs. You could tell by the way he held up the stem and looked at it, it would never be the same.

As soon as I read the first words I was hooked. James Page, the protagonist of the novel, leapt from the text, and I shared both his anger and his disappointment. This book aroused feelings, not just ideas. This angry, miserly old man who had blown his TV screen "to hell" with his twelve-gauge shotgun was as real to me as one of my own relations.

I read and read, losing myself in the story as I had lost myself in the treasured books of my childhood. I was intrigued by the characters as they developed, pleasantly surprised when John won me over with his image of a vital, energetic woman and then startled me with the detail that she was over eighty and used a walker. His description of physical landscape rang true; I had lived in Vermont and knew the land and people he was talking about. While I had been at Middlebury and he was writing about Bennington, I knew the "locking-in" season he wrote about; I could picture James Page's childhood memories of traveling by sleigh up over the hill and down into town before electric lights; I knew the townspeople and their Yankee frugality, their distrust of the college in their midst. The book has an odd structure, containing a novel within a novel. I enjoyed the inner novel, with its wild parody and outlandish plot. I decided the author had a puckish sense of humor; he was clearly poking fun at much of contemporary fiction.

As I read, the book seemed to stick to my hands; I could not put it down. At the climax of the novel, when the reasons for the tragedy of James Page's life are revealed in all their stark, fatal inevitability, I felt my head was beginning to come apart. The story's denouement mixed the rational and the irrational. James Page's life came together in my mind like a puzzle, completely logical and understandable, but the last pages of the story opened up a mysterious and mystical reality. James Page is working with his beehives when he is surprised by a huge black bear, which ignores him and begins to eat his honey. The old Yankee farmer lifts his gun to shoot, but something strange happens.

> As he was about to pull the trigger, something jerked the gun straight up—possibly, of course his own arm. He fired at the sky, as if warning a burglar. The bear jumped three feet into the air and began shaking exactly as the old man was doing, snatched up an armload of honeycombs, and began to back off.

Page's son-in-law asks later why Page did not shoot the bear, and Page realizes that he thought he had heard the bear speaking to him in the voice of his dead wife, forgiving him, loving him.

I sat still, absorbing the ending of this novel, not seeing the garden before my eyes and feeling gooseflesh rise on my arms. I filled the back page of the book with notes and immediately began to reread.

Then I put the book down and thought hard. I looked at the copies of the pages I'd sent in as my writing sample and knew I couldn't show my amateurish work to the author of a book such as this. But who should I work with?

From the time I had been in grammar school I had defined myself as a writer. In fifth and sixth grade I wrote story after story, creating and filling small booklets with writing of all types: adventures, science fiction, fables, morality plays. In seventh grade I wrote a novel, twenty chapters of a Civil War story where my heroine disguised herself as a man to join her love on the battlefield. I commissioned a classmate to do illustrations and carried the tightly folded draft pages in the pocket of my school uniform blazer like a talisman.

I was the petted and adored only child of older parents; my mother had been thirty-eight when I was born, my father thirty-nine. Dad ran a family business that provided many luxuries—private school, European travel, country club memberships, and the like—which I accepted as a matter of course. That I would become a writer was something I also took for granted. I wasn't sure how it would happen or what it would mean, but I knew writing was my life.

At Middlebury College I found a mentor, Bob Pack, who encouraged my poetry, but I found no channel for my fiction. My background prepared me for a conventional choice: to marry within my social class and build a life in the suburbs as the wife of an attorney or a stockbroker. However, I had a rebellious nature and kicked over the traces. I had read all of Hemingway and knew he had begun as a journalist; I decided to follow his lead and enrolled in journalism school at the University of Colorado, where I earned a master's degree in 1974.

I returned east to my first job as editor and writer for a weekly black newspaper, the *Bay State Banner*, in Boston. After two years there I had saved enough money to leave my job and write a novel, a detective story with a then-offbeat hero, a female private eye.

Once I'd finished the novel and submitted it to a publishing house, I veered even farther off the track. I had some money left and a taste for adventure. My role models were women in my family: a great-aunt who had traveled with her lover to the Orient in the years before World War I and an aunt who accompanied her father to Central America in the 1930s. As a young girl I had read Thoreau and taken him seriously. Like him, I did not want to die and discover that I had not lived. By the time my novel's first rejection letter arrived I had already planned a trip to Guatemala City to visit a friend of my parents, an eccentric American photographer. A pal in Boston agreed to act as an informal agent and keep submitting the book for me while I was gone, and off I went to Central America.

On that trip I discovered the truth to the adage that "fortune favors the brave"—or, in my case, the foolhardy. I traveled through Guatemala in 1977 during the most oppressive years of the military regime, seeing but not understanding the soldiers in fatigues who patrolled the capital, cradling their submachine guns. I had just enough tourist Spanish to get me from one place to the next and vacationed on the beautiful shores of Lake Atitlán with oblivious American hippies, while the peasants who made their homes along the shores of that volcanic lake died in the struggle with their government.

I left Guatemala City in February on a flight to New Orleans, right on time for Mardi Gras. I determined to watch this annual event. Did I know anyone in the city? No. Did I see that as a problem? No. My plane was delayed three hours leaving Central America, so I struck up a conversation with three American girls. "No sweat," one said. "My brother has a place right on Saint Charles. He'll put you up." With my new friends I waited at the airport in New Orleans for the limousine ordered by a boyfriend. The boyfriend turned out to be from Denver. I asked if he knew the only person I knew in Denver, a college acquaintance, and he had: they had played basketball together in high school.

Reassured by my sense of the smallness and safety of the world, I went off to meet the brother on St. Charles. He did indeed take care of me, finding me separate accommodations, driving me around the city in his compact MG. From his front porch we watched the Mardi Gras parade; we ate red beans and rice; I had a high old time.

I returned to Boston full of verve and high spirits and signed on almost immediately for a Jack London–style adventure, a summer as crew of the tall ship *Regina Maris*, sailing from Boston to the Arctic Circle and back. All this time I wrote. I drafted a new detective novel, a sequel to the first, with continuing characters, this one set in Central America. I kept a detailed journal and wrote a long nonfiction narrative about my voyage; I continued to work on my poetry. When I returned to Boston I went to work for the nonprofit organization that owned the *Regina Maris* and became their fund-raiser and public relations director.

"Keep at your writing," my mother urged. "And what about Bread Loaf?"

The Bread Loaf Writers' Conference in Vermont is the oldest and best regarded of any American writers' conference. Founded in 1926, it has included on its faculty Robert Frost, Archibald Mac-

Leish, Norman Mailer, Shirley Jackson, and many other famous names in American letters. In the late 1970s and early 1980s Bread Loaf boasted a cluster of stars: Erica Jong, John Irving, and John Gardner.

The conference was scheduled for twelve days in the middle of August. I arranged the time off, gave my apartment key to my neighbor, who promised to water the plants, and took the subway to the Greyhound bus terminal. In front of me in the ticket line stood a petite lady with long black hair, wearing a gauzy, flowing skirt. I knew before I asked that she too was going to Bread Loaf.

Arlene Walsh was a poet and lived in suburban Boston. As the bus chugged north we compared hopes and shared information we had received from the conference secretary regarding room assignments, mailing address, meals, and so forth. It felt a lot like heading off to summer camp.

At the terminal in Middlebury I saw the familiar blue of the college van. For me this was a homecoming. Our cheerful young driver made small talk as the van climbed the narrow road along the rushing creek, and soon enough, my heart beating fast, I saw the yellow buildings of the Bread Loaf Mountain campus.

Arlene and I went to the inn desk to get our keys and directions to our rooms. My room was a double in the annex; Arlene saw me off with a cheery wave, and I plunked my suitcase down on the squeaky bed.

Accommodations at Bread Loaf in that era were almost star-tlingly lacking in amenities. The beds were narrow, the blankets scratchy, the sheets mended, and the rooms cold. The heat worked only in the hall, where squatted an ancient black telephone with its heavy receiver and silver-edged rotary dial. I looked again at my information packet. Had I made the right decision?

I heard a voice at the door and turned to meet my roommate, another writer from Cambridge, who had a name suitable to a romance author, Serena Crystal, and an appearance to match, with small bright eyes and a mane of cascading blond hair, like a pre-Raphaelite model. Serena had a high-pitched voice and a nervous laugh. Together we remarked about the spare room with its matched set of functional pine dressers, unpacked our shirts and shorts, and ventured out to get some dinner.

The dining hall was bright and airy, with windows overlooking the road that went by the campus. Amid the hubbub of nervous and excited voices, the scraping of chairs, and the rattle of silverware, Serena leaned forward and asked, "Who are you working with?"

Each paying contributor had been asked to name a primary teacher with whom he or she wanted to work; the staff made the assignments and strove to keep the size of the classes manageable. The high point for each contributor was his or her half-hour conference about the written work with the chosen teacher.

While I had been reading all the Bread Loaf authors and deciding I wasn't good enough to bother John Gardner, I'd decided I *was* brave enough to work with Tim O'Brien, who was roughly my age. I knew he lived in Cambridge; his wife worked at *Sail* magazine, which had offices on Commercial Wharf in Boston, right next to the office where I worked. Tim's poetic novel, *Going After Cacciato*, had won the 1978 National Book Award. I didn't know enough to be intimidated by that; when I mailed back my packet, I had put him down as my first choice.

A writer's conference is, for some people, a step on the path leading to the dream of publication. Literary anecdotes abound. The young poet Langston Hughes, working as a waiter, slipped his poems under the plate of Richard Wright, the honored guest at the banquet. Wright stormed the kitchen, clutching the poems, and Hughes's literary career was born. The hopeful novice writer dreams of showing a pile of dog-eared, coffee-stained manuscript pages to the star of a conference—for example, John Irving or John Gardner—and hearing the star say, "This is fabulous! Do you have a quarter? Let's go call my agent."

While this may happen, it happens rarely. But the dream persists. In the meantime, the novice, the apprentice, and the accomplished writer can all sit in lectures, learn tips about "point of view," "omniscient narrators," "small press publishers," and, now, "publishing on the web." They can breathe the air breathed by those they worship and can talk about writing all day long.

I told Serena my choice and she nodded approvingly. "Can you really believe we're here?" she asked. I shook my head, still trying to take it all in.

I discovered my first night in the dining hall that the standard greeting, instead of "Hello," was "Do you write fiction or poetry?" Here lay a social reef that wrecked many friendships before they got up to full sail. If one said "I'm a poet" to a fiction writer, the response was usually a chilly "Oh" and a turned shoulder.

The first few days were difficult. I wrote in my journal at the end of the first day: *Exhausted—feels like a week long.* A day or two later, I wrote: *Feel so tense and nervous, feel I don't express myself well and there's no room to make mistakes. Slept soundly till four, then woke up cold as Serena had closed the door. Opened it to let in the heat from the hall but couldn't get back to sleep. Tense and tired.*

I was sorry I'd come but determined to stick it out. I dropped into my student mode, dutifully attending all the lectures and readings, taking notes, sounding out different people to find a friend.

I discovered that I was indeed comfortable with Tim O'Brien. Several other Bread Loaf contributors had chosen Tim as well; we became his "class." Our group had two meetings. At the first meeting, Tim praised one of the pieces of fiction I'd brought to show him and identified it as my work; at the next meeting he read a piece that didn't work and surprised the class by pointing out that I had written both pieces. His point, well taken, was that a good writer does not always produce good fiction.

At my conference with him, Tim was encouraging. "Read big books and think about big issues," he urged me. "You've got the talent; that's why I'm spending so much time with you." As we sat talking that Sunday morning we were interrupted by the church service and a deep booming voice announcing, "We are *all* sinners!" Tim made a comic jump and looked around as if startled and I giggled. "That's an audacious thing to say," Tim remarked.

There were still bad and lonely days, even though Tim was encouraging. In my journal I find: *Miserable all day. All wrong. Tried to talk to people, didn't work. Nearly started crying at lunch. So hard to relax.*

I kept trying. I sought out Arlene; Serena and I compared notes on Cambridge, hung around together, made casual connections with other contributors roughly our age, and watched as John Irving served himself salad, as Tim smoked his cigarette, holding it with two tense fingers, as Howard Nemerov crossed the street from Maple Cottage to Treman. Treman didn't look like much, a small yellow wooden house just like others on the campus, but it was the nerve center of the hive: Treman was the faculty lounge, the watering hole, the inner sanctum. This was where all the famous writers retreated when they wanted to be alone. It may have looked ordinary, but once inside those magic doors, we on the outside imagined that anything could happen.

A strict hierarchy ruled at Bread Loaf. I quickly discovered I was near the bottom—I had paid to attend. Invisible but potent barriers existed to separate the various levels of accomplishment. The very bottom were auditors: writers who paid tuition but were too scared to show their work to a teacher. Then came contributors: that was me. Lucky souls who had published one or two short stories could attend as scholars and have their tuition partially paid. Those who had a first novel or collection of stories in print were higher up the ladder and were called fellows; each helped read a faculty member's load of manuscripts and had tuition fully paid. Staff assistants had more than one book in print and were already on the faculty at a university. At the tippy top were the stars: Stanley Elkin, Linda Pastan, William Matthews, John Gardner. The brochure had bristled with honors unfamiliar to me: Guggenheim Fellow, American Academy of Arts and Letters, Lamont Award, and others. Somewhere in between were the conference support staff: waiters and waitresses, nurse, librarian, office assistants, and bookstore staff: these were all talented writers, some published, some not, but all judged good enough to earn their way at the conference.

The staff at once enhanced these invisible boundaries and tried to pretend they didn't exist. We all mingled in the common dining hall, but some mingled more than others. Did I really have the nerve to sit next to Gail Godwin as she sliced into a piece of chicken? Hardly. I sat with Serena and we watched. After dinner, after the evening readings, we walked alongside the macadam road, scuffing our feet in the gravel, looking sideways at Treman, and wondering who was there and what was happening.

Treman was strictly off limits. Admittance was carefully controlled. Contributors clustered on the porch of the inn, casting envious glances as John Irving casually crossed the lawn and Treman's screen door banged shut behind him, but most of us knew not even to try it.

I was told that John Gardner spent every afternoon in the barn, and whoever wanted could go and talk to him there. I knew I didn't have the nerve to do that. My writing wasn't nearly good enough to show him, and I wouldn't have been able to think of anything to say.

One night at eight it was time for John's reading. He stood at the podium silently, waiting for the crowd to settle down, looking at the typescript in his hands. Outside it was dark and quiet; two or three latecomers crossed the lawn surrounding the Little Theatre. The spotlight shone on John's silver hair. Every seat was taken; the room was hushed. At last, in the quiet, he opened the folder and began to read.

   I was in Madison, Wisconsin, on a lecture tour, when I first met
   Professor Agaard and his son.

I listened to the first sentence and fell into a dream, sitting, transfixed, on my hard flimsy chair.

John continued.

> I was there to read a paper, brand new at the time (since then, as you may know, widely anthologized), "The Psycho-Politics of the Late Welsh Fairytale: Fee, Fie, Foe—Revolution!" The lecture was behind me, a thoroughly pleasant event, as usual, at least for me. . . . I was now deep into one of those long, intense celebrations that put the cap on such affairs, making the audience (those who make the party) seem a host of old friends.

Now there were knowing laughs, some chuckles from his audience.

> The whole first floor of the house was crowded; a few may have drifted to the second floor as well; and from the sound of things, there was another party roaring in the basement. . . . I arrived, divested myself of hat and coat, and began my usual fumbling with my pipe.

Those at Bread Loaf who extended the party to Treman knew precisely the scene John was describing.

> I'd moved to my usual theater of action, backed against the drainboard in the large, bright kitchen, where I could be close to the ice in its plastic bag. . . . On every side of me, guests with their glasses were packed in so tightly that only by daring and ingenuity could one raise one's own and drink. There were the usual smiling students, heads tilted with interest, eyes slightly glazed. . . . So I was holding forth, enjoying myself. . . . One plays the game, follows wherever drink and inspiration lead; what harm? I was the guest celebrity, every word worth gold; but I was only one in, excuse the expression, a galaxy of stars.

John concluded his reading with the words *"Freddy's Book,"* closed his folder, and stepped back from the podium. This section of the book ends with a teaser: Professor Winesap, the narrator of the story, has gone to talk to young Freddy, the monstrous son of Professor Agaard, and Freddy hands him an enormous pile of manuscript. It is his book "King Gustav and the Devil," a retelling of Swedish history. This manuscript filled out the rest of the story, published later that year as *Freddy's Book.*

I shook my head and blinked, as if waking from a deeply involving dream. Around me the audience dispersed, except for a few who formed an informal line, jockeying for position by the door, their ankles awash in the cool night breezes rising off the lawn.

I was stunned by the experience of the reading, both the involving, intriguing story and the charisma of the reader. John's voice was hypnotic, his physical presence palpable. He had star quality, exuding the sense that he was a center of enormous energy. He embodied intriguing contradictions. With his great verbal facility, he could make words do whatever he wanted them to do, yet he chose to tell an apparently simple story rather than overwrite and show off with difficult, intricate language. He was highly learned, a great intellect, but there clung to his shoulders the wildness of the competitive motorcycle racer he had been in his youth. I could picture him in an academic robe, on a podium, nodding as he accepted a fellowship, and also as a motorcycle-riding outlaw, grinning as he tightened his hand on the throttle, as his engine roared, as he outraced the cops.

The other writers at the conference now seemed, next to John, to be only dull people who wasted their lives at their desks. John seemed to know how to *live.* I wanted to connect with that energy, and I resolved that I could not simply walk away: I wanted to shake his hand, to speak with him, to encounter him face-to-face.

I took my place in line, and when at last I reached John, I extended my hand. "That was a wonderful reading," I told him. His grip was firm, his hand warm. He looked at me for a long minute.

I couldn't think of anything else to say. There was another person at his elbow, and I moved on.

After Bob Pack's lecture the next day, I went up to speak to him and we hugged. "Susan, I'm so glad to see you up here," he said, in that sonorous voice that seemed to start way deep in his chest. "Are you still working on your poetry?" Bob was now the director of the conference. As I turned away, he touched my shoulder. "Listen, come on over to Treman any time."

Those words were the golden key in my hand, but did I dare unlock the door?

2

"The Biggest Martini I Ever Saw"

I stood on the lawn, watching figures pass back and forth before the lighted windows inside Treman. Behind me the campus was quiet. A group of contributors gathered, chatting on the porch of the inn. If I went back, I could stand around and make small talk and wonder what was going on inside. If I stepped forward, I would know. I took a deep breath, stepped up onto the porch, and pulled open the screen door.

Walking into Treman was like walking into a living, breathing, super-deluxe edition of the *New York Times Book Review*. I stepped through the swinging screen door into the most amazing literary cocktail party I'd ever seen. Here the faculty could relax and be themselves, the formal atmosphere that pervaded Little Theatre readings or classes in the barn forgotten. Stanley Elkin sat, cane at his side, in his wide-wale corduroy pants, in an upholstered chair next to the fire, listening, eyes shining, as John Irving leaned his dark, handsome head forward and imparted the punch line of his joke. Across the room towered Howard Nemerov, always wearing the same baggy blue-denim jacket, his white crew cut making him instantly recognizable. Donald Justice and Ellen Voight were talking together on a rust-colored sofa. Marvin Bell, a manic grin on his face, was in the midst of a hilarious story, intent on the telling, as Paul Mariani leaned forward so as not to miss a word. . . . It was heady company.

Tim O'Brien, baseball cap firmly in place over his thinning hair and cigarette pinched in his fingers, was passing through the hall on his way to the kitchen. "Susan, what are you doing here? You snuck in. I'll tell Bob Pack," he teased. "Come on in the kitchen. Do you want a drink?"

In the kitchen I saw the genial face of one of my favorite professors from college; we began an easy conversation about mutual friends and graduates of my class who had stayed on in Vermont.

I didn't stay long that first night; a party in the barn followed and we all trooped along the gravel road to the sounds of loud rock music and found the barn transformed into a temporary discotheque complete with long tables laden with kegs of beer, jug wine, pretzels, and chips.

The next night I tried again. This time, as soon as I walked in, I saw John.

Just as he had described his fictional Professor Winesap, he was holding forth in the living room, the center of a tightly clustered group, drinking gin, now and then putting down his glass to sweep back his unruly hair. He looked just like the cover photo in *The New York Times Magazine*—the prematurely white hair, the shrewd light-blue eyes, the generous, sensual mouth. Air seemed to get thicker around him; time seemed to speed up. He lived intently in the present moment, brooked no delay, seemed to spark himself and his listeners to a higher level of debate by the pure intellectual electricity that emanated from and crackled all around him. Argument grew more sophisticated, ideas more sharp, debate took on a holy quality; suddenly we were all guests at the Symposium, granted our opportunity to speak on the greatest issues of the day. Fragrant tobacco smoke swirled in the light; the air was supercharged, as if the very ideas expressed took on weight and substance. Excitement of all kinds—literary, sexual, intellectual— galvanized each minute, and all this was enhanced by the contents of the Treman closet: gin, whiskey, beer, wine. One breathed in adoration and intrigue like perfume.

Tim was nowhere in sight, and the bartender, who I didn't know, was watching me closely. He suspected a party crasher and quizzed me. "Who invited you?"

"Bob Pack," I answered. The bartender craned his neck, looking for Bob. Annoyed, I sought out Tim on the other side of a knot of people. The bartender saw I belonged and grudgingly fixed me a drink. I took it and went back to talk with Tim, but I wanted John—surrounded as he was. Tim saw the direction of my glance. "Want an introduction?"

"But what do I *say* to him?"

"You don't have to say anything. Just listen." Tim pushed me forward, his hand insistent in the small of my back. "John," he called.

John looked up.

"This is Susan Thornton."

He nodded, then plunged back into his debate. "But the point Chaucer was making. . . ."

I hesitated at the edge of the cluster. In my ear, Tim said, "I'm going upstairs to take a leak. I'll leave you to your own devices." With that I jumped into the enchanted circle.

A group always gathered at John's feet, its members jostling for position. Now, I was in the circle, close up, watching, listening. I scrunched up as small as I could, cross-legged, grasping my ankles, insinuating myself among the admirers, surrounded by tobacco smoke, and watched and listened but didn't say anything. John talked excitedly, jabbing the air with his pipe stem.

I leaned forward. He was speaking about this medieval author as if they were personal friends. He had the authority of one who *knows*, not one who has simply studied. And there was something more: he had the confidence, the optimism, of the man who works on a daily basis to realize the totality of his potential. He did not worry, he did not fret, he did not mince his words. He seemed to move effortlessly from success to success. It was not so much that he had published many books but that he devoted his energy to a calling he felt in his soul to be noble and worthwhile. Even when unpopular, he was not afraid to speak out. His intellectual courage drew me like a beacon.

Once I'd walked into Treman, I couldn't stay away. After Bob Pack's reading I told him, "Your puns are still atrocious." He hugged me, laughed, and said, "Susan, that makes my night." I exchanged small talk with Paul Grey, the book reviewer from *Time*, who had once sublet a house from a family friend in Princeton. I chatted with Tim in the kitchen, comparing notes about swimming pools in Cambridge. And I watched John.

In my journal I described one scene: *Gardner was talking with a Jesuit about medieval scholarship. They knew someone in common. He spoke of Chaucer studies, Greek drama.... A crazy woman with red nails was clinging to Gardner telling him how beautiful she thought he was.* John's face was patient, the veil down behind his eyes, carrying on the conversation but watchful, reserved. My diary continues: *Then she began on Ron Hansen.* Ron was tall, with dark hair, high cheekbones, and the reserve of the man who knows just how good his looks are and is slightly embarrassed at the edge this gives him over lesser mortals.

I stood in the hallway, holding my drink against my chest. Ron disengaged himself from the lady with the red nails and came toward me. "Gardner is amazing. He was saying to me that he had been looking up Newton's theology."

"Yes, Newton wrote a history of the church and also about scripture," I said.

"You knew that?" Ron was staring at me.

I had grown up with such talk. While my father had made his fortune in his family's business, he had the heart and soul of a scholar. He read voraciously and, with his eidetic memory, recalled it all in an instant. Our dinner-table conversations ranged over Greek and Roman history; he encouraged me to read the twenty-volume set of Kipling his mother had purchased, book by book, with her lunch money at Smith; we quoted Tennyson's *Idylls of the King* and Browning's "My Last Duchess" back and forth to each other over the lamb chops and Parker House rolls; now and then we switched to theology and the advantages of the King James translation of the Bible over all others.

From my journal: *Ended up at Treman at 1:30 A.M. John Gardner in the kitchen made the biggest martini I ever saw, with ice, then fished the ice out with his fingers.*

I knew all about martinis, too; my mom and dad drank them. When we stayed at our summer home, after Dad's business failed, I would hear his step on the stair, deliberate, careful, at two-hour intervals. If he went to bed at eleven, I would hear him at one, at three, and at five, coming down to the kitchen to get his measured ounces of gin. Dad never raged, never crashed a car, never publicly exhibited the signs that say with a flashing light: "alcoholic." Yet he lived in an ever-present anxiety: his hands shook; there would be scenes over misplaced keys; his doctor scolded him about his "enlarged liver."

Mom was also a quiet drinker, ostensibly only after five P.M. We had matched sets of Steuben crystal glasses, a sterling silver Tiffany cocktail shaker. Mother always maintained an elegant, mannered demeanor; she seemed to float above petty annoyances. It never occurred to me that she drank too much, but her health was undermined, she suffered from various complaints, and she was treated frequently for a heart condition I now know to be associated with alcoholism.

My parents' drinking insulated them from the world and from me. As long as they had money, their life of European travel and private clubs often excluded me. When the money began to dry up, there were no honest discussions of problems and options, only more drinking and the hope that the problems would somehow disappear. I loved my parents and they loved me, but our communication was not open and easy. Instead it was polite and restrained, characterized by evasion and wishful thinking. I was often lonely, and it was to our housekeeper, Florence Joseph, rather than to my mother that I confided secrets of my junior prom, hints about my first crush, fears about my father's drinking.

I was a drinker too. My parents had served me my first drink, wine diluted with water, when I was eight. They had observed this custom in Europe. They were wealthy, sophisticated, continental in their habits. Wine with dinner was just another nice touch, like warm milk for Mother's morning café au lait. The theory was that I would learn moderation; if alcohol was not forbidden, it would not be desired.

In practice, I learned to do what they did: to cover strong, inconvenient, or frightening emotions with a layer of alcohol, to retreat into silence and isolation; never to confront but rather to cover confusion or shyness with a wave of the hand and a request to "freshen my drink."

When I first observed John Gardner at Bread Loaf I saw his drinking and was astonished at its extent, but I was fundamentally comfortable with it—too comfortable. As I got to know him better, I learned not to look—like many people who live with alcoholics. When something frightened me, when something didn't make sense, I shut my eyes. When I got too frightened, I fixed myself a drink. I had periods of abstinence, both in my adult life and in my life with John, but alcohol was always present, the tugging current a strong swimmer ignores, until the swimmer tires, as he must, and the current pulls him under.

John Gardner in the kitchen made the biggest martini I ever saw. . . . His girlfriend left but he didn't follow.

John's girlfriend was Liz Rosenberg. I watched her leave, and I wondered what her life was like. She actually lived with this amazing man; however, she didn't seem inclined to give away any secrets. She was quite young, five years younger than I, twenty-four to John's forty-six. She was slender, handsome rather than pretty, and wore her curly dark hair almost to her shoulders. That night she wore an ankle-length denim skirt with a ruffle at the hem, flat shoes, and a peasant-style blouse. Her costume seemed at odds with her person; she dressed like a younger woman than she was but spoke with a confidence, an authority, almost an audacity that seemed older than her chronological age. Liz fought hard to create an identity for herself and had little or no patience with literary groupies. On one occasion, when trapped by an avid, gushing fan of John's work, a middle-aged lady who cornered her after a reading and glowed, "What is it like to be living with a *genius*?" Liz drew herself up and snapped, "I don't know. Why don't you ask *him*?"

She wasn't part of the late-night scene at Treman—she didn't appear to approve or to disapprove; she just removed herself and stayed in their room in Maple Cottage, across the road. I had heard they had met when she was John's student at Bennington College. I watched her leave, then turned back to listen to John.

One night he was talking about sleep and dreams and the nature of time. "They've done these experiments," he started, "at the University of California at Davis. If people are asleep under a canopy that hides a clock, and someone wakes them up while they are in REM sleep, they know the time." He'd been reading about sharks. "We think of them as primitive, right?" He pointed with the finger of the hand holding his glass. "If you put sharks in a pool and inject minute quantities, *microscopic* quantities, of blood at regular intervals, the shark will *instantly* swim to where the blood is coming into the water, and he gets there *before* the blood.

"We're just not aware what our minds can do. Once I was driving eighty miles an hour down a road, and I had a fantasy of a trooper pulling me over—right?—so I slowed down. Guess what? Around a curve was *that particular* trooper." Someone brought up Carlos Castenada and the books about Don Juan. I leaned forward; I'd read each of these as they were published. "He's an interesting guy," John said. "But there's no one Don Juan. It's a composite, a fictionalization. It's not anthropology."

I was fascinated by the scope of his interests, the authority of his pronouncements, the odd facts he seemed to know so much about. I was intrigued by the contradictions of his character. I had the sense that he was open, honest, vulnerable. He would make a statement with one breath and take it back with the next. He seemed to say, Here I am; take me or leave me. In spite of the drinking, he was aware and acute. He vibrated with energy, as if he burned the candle at both ends. To me he appeared mysterious, shamanlike.

I loved it that he was interested in psychic phenomena and ESP. Later I discovered something else interesting: to me and other women he confided his interest in these topics; when queried by male writers he pretended not to believe. For several years I'd written down my dreams each morning (when we got to know each other better he looked at me with that piercing gaze and scolded, "A great artistic imagination gone wrong"), and my friendship with Sue Watkins had led me to an introduction to Jane Roberts, the author of *The Seth Material.*

I still kept track of my dreams, and that summer of 1979 I recorded an odd one: *Dreamed about John Gardner (this after following him around tongue-tied for four days, wide-eyed and silent like a calf), dreamed he looked right at me and said, "Look here, Susan, it's all very well to be modest but you're boring as hell. Can't you just contradict me once in a while?"*

When the conference concluded I went back to my apartment in Cambridge. I had learned something; I had a new direction. At last I had found what I longed for, a community of serious writers. I looked down on my earlier work, the short stories, the formulaic detective novels. They didn't hold up to the standard I had seen at Bread Loaf. Here were men and women who worked hard at writing literature. I became determined to raise my standards, to return to Bread Loaf the following summer, and to work with John.

I made more trips to bookstores and libraries and started on a new reading list: John Gardner's books. I examined each one with interest and read them all, from the first-published (but not the first written) *The Resurrection* and *The Wreckage of Agathon* to the more well-known *Nickel Mountain* and *Grendel.* In the Cambridge

Public Library I opened the *Best Short Stories of 1978* to find his story "Redemption." This story begins:

> One day in April—a clear, blue day when there were crocuses in bloom—Jack Hawthorne ran over and killed his brother, David.

As I read this sentence I caught my breath. It didn't read like fiction. The writing drew me on.

> Even at the last moment he could have prevented his brother's death by slamming on the tractor brakes, easily in reach for all the shortness of his legs; but he was unable to think, or rather, thought unclearly, and so watched it happen, as he would again and again watch it happen in his mind, with nearly undiminished intensity and clarity, all his life. The younger brother was riding, as both of them knew he should not have been, on the culti-packer, a two-ton implement lumbering behind the tractor, crushing new-ploughed ground. Jack was twelve, his brother David, seven. The scream came not from David, who never got a sound out, but from their five-year-old sister, who was riding on the fender of the tractor, looking back. When Jack turned to look, the huge iron wheels had reached his brother's pelvis. He kept driving, reacting as he would to a half-crushed farm animal, and imagining, in the same stab of thought, that perhaps his brother would survive. Blood poured from David's mouth.

As I read this I pictured John as I had begun to know him at the conference, and the tears streamed down my face. I knew instinctively that this story was not made up. It was true. He may have changed the names, but I knew in my heart this was his life, disguised as fiction. Now that I knew him as a person I could not imagine the pain he must live with on a constant basis, having this experience in his past.

I sat, as if entranced, at the table in the public library. I could not stop reading, wiping away tears as I turned the pages. At the end of the story, Jack Hawthorne finds his redemption in the world of art, in music, and in the musical genius of his eccentric teacher, Yegudkin, "The General." John's own devotion, his vivid opinions, his messianic sense suddenly crystallized for me. I understood clearly now what I had only glimpsed as I read the article in *The New York Times*: "[Art] made my life . . . when I was a kid."

I understood all at once that writing wasn't just writing for John. It wasn't about holding a published book in his hands, seeing his work reviewed in *The New York Times*, attending literary cocktail parties and publisher's launches. It wasn't about ego and praise and being noticed. Writing was salvation for him, a devotion running as deep in his life as his own blood. I began to understand his punishing drive, his need to stay up all night and write, the energy that drove him to create such dense and complex books as *October Light* and *The Sunlight Dialogues*. Writing wasn't just writing. It was life and death.

I recalled the plot of *October Light*. In that novel, a child dies, partly because of an older brother's negligence. This is the first tragedy in the Page family. Then there is a second, when the older brother, as a man, hangs himself. The theme of responsibility for accidental death runs through all John's work. Even the last words of *Grendel*, "Poor Grendel's had an accident," resonate to this theme.

Something else came clear for me too after reading this story. While I had been in awe of John, seeing him as someone too special for me to bother, too gifted to approach, though I wanted to, I had been attracted by a sense that I didn't quite understand, that he was vulnerable. Here were more contradictions. He was charismatic, august, removed by his intellect and accomplishments, and yet accessible, honest, wounded. Anyone else who had been wounded could resonate with this hidden chord. Yet he didn't hide his vulnerability, he wore it as he wore the other aspects of his being. He was all of a piece, all the time, yet there were layers of experience that one had to be sensitive to perceive. I wanted to know him better, but I felt he was unavailable. He had a girlfriend, after all, and we hadn't yet forged a connection; I had only watched him, keeping my distance. I resolved not to be so scared the next time I had the opportunity to be in his company.

As I applied myself, with new and real devotion, to my writing, something else happened during the last months of 1979: I met a man I liked a lot. Jack was single, a consultant with a prestigious Boston firm; he'd been educated at Harvard College and Harvard Law but came, like me, from New York State. He had brown eyes, an engaging smile, and hands so beautiful they looked as though God himself had finished their details with His personal chisel. Jack and I began to date, and I decided I'd found the right man to marry. I was thirty; I'd spent my twenties accumulating experiences and adventures as I'd wished; it was time.

Jack was well-off. He owned both his home in Cambridge and a rental property on Martha's Vineyard. His work was demanding and well paid, though I understood it only vaguely and he never explained much. He made arresting remarks such as, "Do you mind if we make this an early night? I have to go to Stockholm tomorrow."

Now I was ready for the security I imagined might come with marriage. One confidante heard me out, in all my enthusiasm and said, "I don't know, Susan. That's kind of a danger signal." "What do you mean?" I demanded, impatient. "It could mean you're comfortable with him for all the wrong reasons." I didn't listen. Certain areas of Jack's life were clear: he worked hard, had political ambitions, was quite attracted to me. Other areas were less clear. I never did find out his birthday or even his exact age. From a photo on the kitchen counter I deduced that his father was old and ill, but this was a topic of conversation that was clearly off limits. And he talked way too much about his former girlfriend, an undergraduate at Wellesley College who had left him—abruptly and treacherously, he maintained—for one of his colleagues. "I came home and she was just gone," he said. I tried to console him. "How long ago did this happen?" "November," he said. We had met in

December. I pretended he wasn't just seeking me out on the rebound.

Jack and I did not communicate clearly, but this lack of clarity reminded me of the roundabout way I communicated with my parents: stretches of talk, areas of forbidden topics, a genuine sense of affection, difficult, polite conversation. My relationship with Jack felt like something I had known before, the way a relationship should be. I knew it was uncomfortable, but it felt like home. He seemed like the man I *should* love. He was available; I was the right age. Why not?

While I was hoping and dreaming about Jack, I continued to work on my writing. I joined a writers' group in Cambridge, and I applied for a Massachusetts Council on the Arts grant of $3,500. I also wrote to Bob Pack and to Carol Knauss, the Bread Loaf Conference secretary, and asked if I could work in the bookstore the following summer.

Meanwhile, I had news of John. Early in March of 1980 I went to New York to visit an acquaintance from Bread Loaf who worked as a fact checker at *The New Yorker* magazine. We were in the stairwell of his New York apartment building when he announced, "Well, Gardner's gone and married that girlfriend of his." As he said this, a wave of feeling passed over me—a sensation so strong that the hairs on the nape of my neck stood up—and I thought, *He shouldn't have done that.* This thought was immediately followed by denial. *I don't even know this man. How can I possibly have this feeling?*

3

"You're a Natural":
Bread Loaf Writers' Conference, 1980

In the summer of 1980, I went back to Bread Loaf, this time as the assistant in the bookstore, a job that paid my room and board and a small stipend. I was pleased to hear from Carol Knauss in April that I had been offered this position; it secured my membership in what I saw as an exclusive club: support staff at Bread Loaf. I was also happy to have something to do at the conference. I knew the misery I'd felt the previous summer would disappear when I had a recognized role.

The bookstore was a small ground-floor room looking out on the path to the back entrance of the inn. We stocked only volumes written by the faculty and staff. In the insular world of Bread Loaf, no other authors mattered. These books were arranged alphabetically by author, hard and soft covers jumbled together, a profusion of bright colors: fiction, poetry, essays. We also stocked aspirin, pens, pencils, small spiral notebooks. The bookstore was the perfect job, as I could close it to attend lectures, run out from the lecture at the last minute, open the store, and close it again in time to get to Treman, where, as staff, I now had unlimited entrée.

As I was arranging books on the shelves, I heard the phone ring in the adjacent office, one side of a conversation, then the click of the phone and some laughter. I stuck my head in the office. "What's up?"

"That was Liz Rosenberg on the phone. She was calling to find out when the conference started." Carol Knauss shook her head. "Today's the twelfth. They thought it started the twenty-first."

I wondered why this famous writer wasn't more organized, and why his wife didn't keep better tabs on his schedule. Isn't that what wives did? Besides, except for one year, he'd been coming up to Bread Loaf since 1974. The conference was always the middle two weeks of August. Couldn't he read a calendar? I didn't know then that Liz was busy with her own teaching, her own writing, her own publishing, and I didn't know about the disorganized quality of John's life, which all his friends had noted and many had written about. Part of it was focus; he honed in only on his writing. Part of it was an overcrowded schedule. Part of it was carelessness.

Much of my astonishment was my own investment. I now looked forward to the conference and couldn't imagine missing a day. Here was one of the faculty, and the faculty member I most wanted to see, almost missing it because he and his wife thought it started ten days later. I had worked hard on my fiction all year in order to have something to show this man. I was angry to think he might not have attended.

John and Liz did show up, the next day, August 13. On the fourteenth I was walking toward the inn for breakfast with John Bryan when Ben Reynolds, the new bartender from Treman, joined us. He leaned forward, confidential, stroking his dark mustache, and said, "The question to ask is, what famous male author got so drunk at Treman last night at three A.M. that he fell down and then had an eye-opener at the Waybury Inn?"

The answer was easy. "Was he a certain famous author with white hair?" I asked back. I knew, I saw, but I shut my eyes and made a joke.

After breakfast I went to John's fiction workshop at 9 A.M. John was ten minutes late, looked awful, and said he'd just got up. In the class he singled out one of my stories for comment; with a faked imbecilic smile on his face, he teased that the title, "The Kindest Thing," sounded like a *True Confessions* story from the 1930s. I wrote in my journal: *I want to run and grab [all the stories] back.*

Then, in my mailbox, came a note on Bread Loaf Conference stationery, written in pencil, in a spidery hand: *Susan Thornton. Can I see you at 10 a.m. (barn)? John Gardner.* The small piece of paper fluttered in my hands. This was it. Now I had to make good. This was what I had been working toward for a year. Hardly breathing, I went to the barn at quarter to ten.

The barn was a huge, echoing space, furnished with bentwood outdoor furniture. Chairs with ancient cushions stood in a semi-circle around the big stone fireplace; others were arranged for conversational groupings in the vast interior, stippled with light filtering in through the barn boards. On a bright summer morning it was cool and welcoming. Right away I saw that John was sitting before a low round table, looking at manuscripts—my manuscripts. My heart was beating fast. I walked over to the table, pulled out a chair, and sat down next to him.

John had enormous recuperative powers, and however much he drank at Bread Loaf, he took his teaching seriously. To all his students, and to me that day, he paid meticulous attention. I didn't know it then, but he was famous at the conference for reading anything and everything students were brave enough to press on him. If a student had a novel, the stated limit of pages one could give a faculty member was thirty. John routinely asked to read the entire manuscript. He even read the work-in-progress of his staff assistants, just out of interest. He seemed to get the sense of a page in an instant, and he remembered everything.

That day in the barn I found him focused, intent, sober. He smelled faintly of pipe tobacco, his hands were steady, his eyes were clear, his hair was combed. He wore simple khaki trousers, the kind my dad wore around our summer place, and a blue work shirt.

There's an intimacy between teacher and student, and especially between teachers and novice writing students. Quite often, the beginning writer reveals much more than he or she realizes in the choice of topic, the style of presentation, the diction. I only realized this later when I taught writing at the college level. The soul, laid bare, is vulnerable. The student who is hurt, withdraws, drops the class, quits writing. The student who is not hurt is relieved, exalted, exhilarated.

This was my situation during that first conference with John. I'd gotten as far as I had on beginner's luck alone; I had no concept of how success was typically achieved as a fiction writer in the United States at that time—that one entered a graduate program, found a mentor, sent out stories to small-press literary magazines, eventually accumulated enough published stories for a collection, and followed that with a novel. I had no idea there was a method. I was following a haphazard hit-or-miss process; I was an innocent.

The manuscripts John was reading were both fiction and nonfiction. They included short stories and a long biographical narrative. John dismissed the latter—"You have no trouble with this kind of writing"—and concentrated on my fiction.

I got much more than I had bargained for from my brief conference. "You're the most capable of real art of anyone I've seen here. Your imagination is wonderful. You're a natural. What you do, you do spectacularly well. But these aren't stories." The words rang in my ears. John pointed out long stretches of prose where he had made no comments. "I don't do that for everyone." He pushed at his hair as he spoke, leaning forward, occasionally swiping at his upper lip, gesturing with his fingers curled in a loosely closed fist.

The work I showed John had been ripped apart by the writers' group I had joined in Cambridge, but my application to the Massachusetts Council on the Arts had been granted: I was one of ten winners, statewide, of a $3,500 fellowship. A member of the writers' group, which I had quit, telephoned me after the grant winners' names were announced. "Is this Susan Thornton?"

"Yes." I got ready to enjoy myself.

Now the voice turned suspicious. "Is this the *same* Susan Thornton who won the grant?"

"Yes."

"Did you submit the stories we looked at in group?"

"Yes." My pleasure was mounting to a delicious high.

"Did you make any of the changes we recommended?"

"Not a word."

One story describes a high school boy who is taunted by his classmates into stealing the bra of an attractive girl. He breaks into her home and discovers not an ordinary suburban tract house but an unknowable mythological territory. Another describes the anguish and confusion of a young woman who reluctantly begins to correspond with an inmate at a federal penitentiary and then goes to visit him. A third describes a high school girl who fends off a rapist by biting through the knuckle of his index finger. John queried me on that one. "I was trying to see how much I could gross out the reader," I replied.

"Well, we can all do that," he answered, dismissive. I realized, awed, that the plural "we" meant I was being initiated into an elite group as a writer.

Mostly he saw my heart in that work, the heart I was too shy to show in person, the heart I was only brave enough to put on paper in the solitude of my writing space. I was quite a lot braver in print than I was face-to-face.

He urged me to come to Binghamton to study with him at SUNY, the State University of New York. I said I had thought about going to Iowa to the Writers' Workshop. This was not really true. Mostly I thought, when I thought at all, about Cambridge and about Jack.

John frowned. "You wouldn't get in."

I looked at him, startled.

"You don't know how a story is written. You have to follow the rules. Besides, what you're doing is pop art. There's no room for what you're doing. They don't go for originality. I went to Iowa and didn't learn anything. I hid in Medievalism and wrote exercises." He paused.

"Now, *my* writing program is the best in the country. It's the most selective. We've got an amazing faculty: Dave Smith and my wife, Liz Rosenberg. It's the best."

I still didn't understand what he meant by saying that what I had written weren't stories. He explained. "Your character has a mind. You shouldn't take his mind away from him by putting him in a trance. Let him use his cunning to get in or out. Then the reader will say, Fine, he did it, or, Too bad, he tried."

He gave me more information than I could absorb, reciting his dictum over and over, "The character has to have a will, to pursue something, to overcome obstacles or be crushed by them." I vaguely understood that I hadn't done that. He pointed out that in each piece I'd written what he called a victim story, a story in which events happen *to* a character and he or she does not act effectively. He said the symbolism I used in one story was too obvious; he criticized the opening of another, saying, "You're better than this hook you use." He advised, "Take a course in fiction analysis from someone good, who can show you, for example, how Joyce works." He added, "Some of these stories are portraits; there's no action." I listened until my ears ached, trying to take it all in.

Another student was waiting, leaning forward in his chair and glancing at us. John gathered the sheaf of pages in his hands, tapped them on the table to even them out, and handed them to me. "Thank you," I said. He nodded. I got up from my chair and the other student stood too. John looked over at him and then reached to his left for another packet of stories. I clutched my pages to my chest and hurried to my dorm room, where I took out my notebook and, starting at the back, wrote down every sentence I remembered John saying during our conference. I could hardly believe his assertions and had no idea what my next move should be, personally or professionally. How serious was I about this writing? If I was that good, what should I do about it? Should I make a gamble and go to graduate school? I'd already been to graduate school and it was no fun at all, not like college.

I had no desire whatever to move to Binghamton, which I regarded as a moribund, isolated, upstate New York town with little to recommend it. I'd escaped what I saw as the narrow, provincial world of Rochester long ago. In Cambridge my circle of friends and acquaintances included leaders in the black community, members of the Social Register, an heir to the Morgan fortune, real estate developers who were rebuilding the Boston waterfront, writers for *The Boston Globe*, the first violist of the symphony, poets, fiction writers, computer programmers, saxophone players, college friends living *la vie bohème* in the industrial slums of Somerville—a host of interesting people. The cities of Boston and Cambridge were vital, exciting, beautiful to me. Why would I leave all that behind for the drudgery of graduate school in a small town in upstate New York where I didn't know anyone? Admittedly, John Gardner was an exciting teacher. But trade the life I had for the opportunity to sit in a classroom once a week with him? Even if it could lead to a published book, a concept I liked, in the abstract, it seemed a sorry exchange. Besides, there was Jack, whom I wanted to marry. I wasn't interested.

I put aside the idea of changing my life and concentrated on the bookstore and the evenings and late nights at Treman.

I roomed upstairs from Blue Argo, and she and I became best of pals. When I was cold I borrowed her sweaters; when I'd warmed up I forgot to return them. She was the hostess at Treman and used her Georgia drawl, her sparkling dark eyes, and her broad smile to advantage. We quickly discovered an affinity for gossip and began what we called "Rumor Control," a running tally of connections we observed among conference staff and students. She too had a boyfriend off campus, so we were the perfect reporters for other people's romantic failings.

As I had the year before, I attended lectures, took notes, shared jokes at Treman—and whenever John walked through a door, I knew immediately where he stood in the room.

4

"But How Can Someone Be Scared of Me?"

Many nights John and I talked together at Treman, sometimes just the two of us, sometimes in a larger group. Often we all stayed up until two, three, even dawn. John and I observed each other, began to get to know each other. He knew his reputation and accomplishments put people off; people were shy to approach him.

Ron Powers, who had won the Pulitzer Prize for his books about television news and the popular media, sought me out one morning. Ron was tall, with an easy smile and a salt-and-pepper beard. His résumé was crowded with accomplishments, but at least one writer at Bread Loaf threw him off guard. "I went over to say hello to John Gardner," he confided. "As soon as I shook his hand and he looked at me, I lost it."

"That's easy to do," I told him. I meant to be reassuring, because I was touched Ron would confide in me, but I was lying. I was finding that I was not intimidated by John but, instead, interested in him and comfortable in his presence.

How and why did I get over my shyness of the previous summer? I was still as far as ever from my ultimate goal of publishing a novel. One reason was that I didn't take it all quite so seriously as everyone else did. I had ambitions as a writer, but I'd done and seen other things in my life. My work at the *Bay State Banner*, New England's only black newsweekly, had been an invaluable experience. My work in Roxbury, the "inner city," the "ghetto" area of Boston, had coincided with the worst of the school busing crisis of the mid-1970s, when federal courts had ordered the desegregation of Boston's public schools. Residents of South Boston protested and stoned the buses of frightened black children that appeared in their streets; residents of Roxbury responded by burning their own neighborhoods and occasionally stoning white motorists.

One workday morning the neighborhood of our offices was closed off by the police. A colleague picked me up in her station wagon. We drove along Massachusetts Avenue, then turned onto Washington, where we had to stop at a yellow police barricade. My colleague rolled down her window to speak to the uniformed policeman in riot gear. "We work at the *Banner*." He frowned at us, two white women in a car, but moved the barricade and waved us on.

Melvin Miller, the publisher, had told me when I interviewed for the job, "I wouldn't put a white woman on the streets of Roxbury unless she had a pistol permit or a black belt in karate." I had wanted a reporter's job but, hearing this, settled for a position in the office as editorial assistant. It was by far the better choice. My task was comparable to that of managing editor. I initiated and wrote a series on how Boston's taxes affected the inner city; I began a correspondence with a writer in North Carolina who contributed a series on school desegregation in her town; I edited the work of prisoners, music critics, and local churchwomen; I began to see beyond the vacant buildings and littered streets to the richness of the community around me. During my two years at the *Banner*, we won an award from the New England Press Association for general excellence.

Once our freelance photographer brought in a photo of a dead man in the street. A shootout between police and a would-be robber at the local bank around the corner from the office had had this fatal result. In the photograph I held in my hands the dead man lay face down, his blood flowing into the gutter. I looked at the photo and knew my editor would not publish it. People assume that journalists always go for the sensational; however, the *Bay State Banner* was a community weekly. Our editorial policy was to emphasize the positive and steer clear of the inevitable crime and violence, leaving coverage of those events to the city dailies. The photographer protested my decision. What did a white girl know about black journalism? I showed the photo to Mel Miller. He glanced at it, grimaced, and cast it aside. "We're not printing that."

On another occasion my task had been to attend a Roxbury town meeting, where Governor Michael Dukakis was to speak, and to interview the governor afterward. On that stifling summer night I was the only white person in the crowded auditorium. The lady next to me fanned herself with her program; the backs of my legs stuck to the leatherette of the folding chair. I'd done my homework and had a series of elaborate questions for the governor. Mostly I was interested in the adverse effect of city and state tax codes on Roxbury. I wanted to get the governor's opinion of what might be done at the state level to alleviate this. When the talk was over, the governor's aides hustled him backstage where I was to meet with him. I gathered my notes and my courtesy and went for the interview. After complimenting Governor Dukakis on the speech and asking a few preliminary questions, I got to the meat of my interest: the tax codes. The governor didn't answer my question but reiterated points I'd already made. Did I know more about the issue than he did? I concluded the interview—while the freelance photographer I'd assigned was still clicking his shutter in the governor's face as if he were a paparazzo stalking an elusive international star—and went out to telephone for a cab. As the stifled auditorium emptied, mine was the only white face; a tall, slender dark man strode directly across the room to me: "Did you call a cab?"

The famous and the infamous trooped through our offices at 25

Ruggles Street in Roxbury. Muhammad Ali came to hold court one hot summer afternoon; I was struck by the cherubic innocence of his unmarked face, the gentle courtesy of his manner. A colleague met and interviewed other figures of art and legend: Martha Reeves, Smokey Robinson. I asked her, "Don't celebrities make you nervous?"

"Mean people make me nervous," she answered.

"But how can someone be scared of me?" John remarked, rocked back on his heels, drink in one hand, pipe in the other. "How can you be scared of a man with a potbelly?" He put down the glass and patted his stomach familiarly.

What I noticed was his kindness, his interest, his wit. He saw the world in terms of story, as I did, and often he encapsulated people's lives for me. "He was saved from alcoholism by his wife," he remarked of one friend. Or, of another, "She's a woman who lives alone and belongs to everyone." He would sketch a life in one or two brief sentences, reducing all to story, his governing metaphor.

He used his vast intelligence, his immense learning, and his capacious knowledge with a sense of fun that intrigued me. Ideas were a game to him; argument was like tennis, or a noncontact boxing match between martial arts students. The point was the exercise, not to hurt, not to win or to lose. He had high standards and would not suffer fools, but I never saw him use his intelligence to put someone down. By his presence and contributions he lifted an argument above the banal and into a realm where ideas took on substance, weight, were seen as the mysteriously powerful motivators they are, to mold people's behavior and thereby shape their lives. He voiced outrageous opinions, as if lobbing a hand grenade into an overdecorated parlor, then stood off, rocked back on his heels, elbow close to his chest, pipe clamped in his stubby yellow teeth, waiting, with a street urchin's grin, for the reaction. Then when the explosion came, with his listeners red in the face, sometimes shouting, waving their fists, spittle flying from their lips, he leaned forward, calm, eyes bright, with yet another flamboyant opinion.

At Treman after an evening reading he expounded a theory for Ambrose Clancy. Ambrose, at the conference as a fellow, had the soft manner and easy, fluent speech of the poetic Irish at their best. His novel, *Blind Pilot*, describes "the Troubles," the Irish rebellion against British authority.

"The easiest way to understand the Irish and the Welsh is to see their similarities to the American Indian and the American Black," John began, tamping new tobacco into his lit pipe with his index finger, already sooty. His fingers, I had noticed, were none too clean.

"We Welsh are the Blacks, enslaved by the English, put to work in their satanic coal mines, treated like beasts of burden. What do we do? We curse, yes; we hate, yes; but we also sing!" John tipped his face to the side and screwed up his mouth into a crazy grin, delight lighting his pale blue eyes.

"The most musical people on earth are the Welsh, outside American blacks, of course, and, like them, the Welsh stay united and create beauty out of slavery."

"Now John," Ambrose demurred, stroking his neatly trimmed brown beard with his stubby fingers. John didn't let him get a word in. He held up his pipe stem for emphasis. "Now the Irish are the Indians, living out on the frontiers of Britain, considered by the English as wild, primitive, violent." He spread his fingers and looked through them, an outlaw peering through underbrush. "Savages, in fact. When the sun sets in Ireland, the Englishman is afraid." He hunched his shoulders and looked comically from side to side, acting it out. "The night belongs to the natives; they'll come and get you, slit your throat, burn your house down."

Sensing argument in his listeners, who were clustered around, intent, waiting to pounce on any lapse in this fantastic argument, which seemed constructed purely of language and theatrics, John began to talk faster. "Have you ever heard of the eighteenth-century guerrilla organizations, the White Boys, the Peep of Dawn boys? That's what they did, struck at night, like good Apaches or Sioux. The Irish, like the Indians, never surrendered. Never!" He threw his head back, eyes wide. "Never gave an inch against a vastly more powerful enemy. They were slaughtered, the victims of genocide. Like the potato famine, right? Genocide, pure and simple. But the Irish were lucky. They had America to flee to. The great awful irony is the Indians didn't have America as a refuge."

"And the Welsh?" asked Ambrose, skeptical, trying to bring this vast billowing sail of a conversation back under control.

"The Welsh?" John applied a lit match to his pipe bowl and, puffing rapidly, sent up a cloud of fragrant smoke and then batted it away from his face with a half-curled hand. "Peasants. They went to ground. Acted mad or stupid. Joined up another choir, pretended they only liked to sing." He opened his hands again, the trickster, the magician who had just pulled a full-grown chamois out of a hat, the wizard of words and late-night arguments.

"Irish as Indians." Ambrose was still unconvinced. "I just don't buy that, John."

John picked up his drink and took a sip, his expression boyish, cocky. He shrugged and changed the subject. "Relative of mine left his valley in Wales—dark, dismal place, right? Just like Susquehanna, where I live now. That's why I like it. Great gloomy dark hills. The Endless Mountains of Pennsylvania. Mysterious place." He took another sip of his drink. "This relative sent money back to Wales to get his brother over. Dribs and drabs—right?—dribs and drabs. With each drib and drab he wrote long, poetic letters, exaggerating how well he was doing in Remsen and how wonderful it was."

"Remsen?" asked Bob Houston. Bob Houston wore a pencil-thin mustache and a leather vest. His work included thrillers, like *Monday, Tuesday, Wednesday*, and a fine serious novel of corruption and greed on an international scale, *The Nation Thief*.

"Small town near Utica, New York," John answered. "Nothing there now, really; once the home of many many Welshmen. But exaggerate might not be the word. The brother finally had enough money for passage to New York. He arrives in New York Harbor, looks around at the spires and towers and looming buildings, the bustling streets and commerce of Manhattan, and turns to his companion and says with awe and wonder in his voice—" John waited to be sure all the members of the circle were listening hard—"and says, 'Glory be to God, if this is New York, what must Remsen be?' "

David Martin asked John about his interest in the supernatural, the magic that ran all through his work. Did he believe in such things?

"Absolutely not," John asserted. "What do you take me for? But I'll tell you a story. I was living out in the country once, in Illinois, on a farm, a beautiful place of hills and streams. We had horses. One late night, plagued by insomnia, I went out, saddled my horse, and took off for a ride. The only other person in the house was my daughter, Lucy, about eleven. She woke from a nightmare, a dream of me, thrown from a horse, lying injured late at night on hillside near a creek on our property."

Blue Argo, who was listening intently, shivered inside her belted cardigan sweater. A faint dawn light was just beginning to turn the windows silvery. We were all tired from standing up all night, but no one was going to fade out while John was talking like this in the kitchen.

John continued. "Lucy ran to my room to find me gone. Checked the stable and found the horse gone too. In a panic, she telephoned a neighbor, who was the county sheriff as well, and told him I'd been thrown from a horse and described the place." John pushed a lock of hair back behind his ear, leaving a black smudge of soot on his temple.

"He calmed her down, said he'd take a look. Dragged himself out of bed, got dressed, got in his truck to drive over. Now, he had a spotlight on the side of the truck, and he parked just at the edge of the creek and ran his spotlight up and down the hillside." John opened his fingers and fanned his hands back and forth in the air, an imaginary spotlight. "Nothing. He was ready to go back

41

home when I came riding over the crest of the hill. The spotlight spooked my horse and he threw me." He pointed with his pipe stem. "It was the *exact place* of my daughter's dream."

On another evening, talk became more literary. There was always much discussion of the novel of ideas versus the novel of action. John, of course, always argued for the novel of ideas. Now talk turned to basic novel structure.

"There are only two openings for a novel," John asserted. "A stranger comes to town, and a person goes on a trip. Some disruption of order. That's all it is."

Blue Argo spoke up. "*Moby Dick.*"

"Ishmael goes on a trip," he answered.

Blue squinted, tried again. "*David Copperfield.*"

"A stranger comes to town. I am born."

"Virginia Woolf doesn't follow that pattern," someone objected.

"That's why she's boring," he retorted. Then he was surprised by the hurt he had engendered. For him it was just a game.

I watched as time after time people approached him with some self-deprecating remark, usually apologetic—they didn't want to bother him, they had forgotten to call. His standard answer was, "No harm, no harm," a comment meant to reassure, spoken around the pipe stem clenched in his teeth, as he looked down at the floor or, suddenly, up from under his eyebrows with an intent, penetrating glance. For he was shy too, for all his ebullience, the lengthy monologues, the hugs he bestowed on friends.

As well as leading conversations at Treman, John was the subject of conversation as well. "I get a sad feeling from Gardner," Ambrose observed to me.

"Life is sad," I answered.

Ambrose began comically to pat his pockets—"Where's my pencil, where's my pencil?"—as I laughed.

While I observed John in public and in private, in the small rooms at Treman, I noticed how his bluster and wit insulated him, how he alternated between being open and closed, expansive and private as an oyster. That summer he constantly wore a yellowish-green paisley sports jacket. "I got this in San Francisco in the sixties," he claimed. "I have another one in pink." The dress code at Bread Loaf was almost aggressively casual: jeans, running shorts, sneakers in daylight hours, worn belligerently as if to point out that writers needn't be sedentary and fat but could be fit and sexy if only they jogged as hard as they wrote. John would have none of that.

For evening cocktail parties women wore light summer dresses, men a jacket and tie. John showed up in that ridiculous loud paisley jacket, day or night; at once he stood out and was invisible. People saw the jacket instead of the man; I began to realize it was a disguise, protective coloration, a mask.

One night at Treman I observed the following exchange: "What do you think you're doing?" Stanley Elkin asked, as John casually helped himself to a cigarette from the pack in Stanley's breast pocket. Stanley was seated, John standing over him. Because of his MS, Stanley walked with a cane, had an unsteady, lurching gait, and once he fell into an armchair, he stayed there. He and John were old friends; one account had it that Stanley had introduced John to his literary agents, Georges and Anne Borchardt.

"It's easy to steal from you, Stanley, 'cause you're a cripple."

Stanley shook his head.

The cigarette was a low-tar brand. John lit it up, inhaled, and then said to Stanley, "God, this is awful. What are you, a health nut? You want to live forever?"

"Just until next month would be fine," Stanley answered with some asperity.

I overheard Stanley talking to someone about one of John's books, *The Sunlight Dialogues*. "I have this student who absolutely loves that book." Stanley rolled his eyes. "Loves it, can't get enough of it. I said to him, 'Isn't it kind of slow?' The student said, 'Yeah, well, wait till you get to page 235. Just wait till you get to that page and then find out what comes after it. You'll love it. It gets really exciting.' So," Stanley continued, "I went home and I read and I read and I read until I got to page 235, and then I turned the page, and you know what comes after page 235?" His listeners leaned into him in a tight little circle. Stanley waited till he had everyone's attention. "Page 236!" he crowed, triumphant.

Bread Loaf has been a bitchy competitive place for as long as it has existed. Robert Frost once disrupted a reading by his rival, Archibald MacLeish, in the Little Theatre, by secretively emptying his pockets of crumpled paper and dried leaves, mounding them onto the floor by his feet, setting fire to them with a match, and then fanning the smoke and shouting, "Fire, fire!"

One night as John left Treman, he patted Stanley on the shoulder. "Be well," he said.

Stanley looked up. "You should have told me that thirty years ago. I'd have taken your advice."

That summer, 1980, John's first wife, Joan Gardner, hired a private plane to fly over the campus and drop leaflets she had printed. "Author of *On Moral Fiction* is immoral," she wrote. "A fraud who is late with his alimony, neglects his children." She asked the pilot to drop these leaflets on the center of campus at lunchtime, when all the contributors would be out and about. From the air the fields, green hills, and yellow buildings looked alike to the confused pilot; he dropped the bundle of papers on the wrong meadow. No one saw them except Nancy Willard's young son and Stanley's son and daughter. The youngsters gathered up the leaflets and presented them to the conference staff, who quietly burned them all. No one else knew anything about it; no one even told John. It's a measure of the affection and respect he inspired that the incident stayed secret. Bread Loaf was a safe place for him; the staff knew that and wanted to keep it that way. Also, no one wanted to believe Joan.

John and Joan were second cousins, childhood friends. They had been married for twenty-three years. In August of 1980 he had been separated from Joan for five years and divorced for six months. In his cups, to a group at Treman, I overheard him say, "My ex-wife, whom I still hate very much." I wrote in my journal, *They are still very involved with each other.*

Alcohol was a large part of the ambiance at Bread Loaf in those years. It added a sheen to the excitement of being "up on the mountain" surrounded by the famous and the hungry. Traditional to the conference was the first outdoor cocktail party, where the faculty—those men and women whom one has read on the page, pored over in bookstores, studied in libraries—are suddenly there in person, drink in hand, on the other side of the lawn. If you are brave enough you can accost them, ask for an autograph, or, for the exceptionally brave, press a manuscript into their hands. I always felt that Bob Pack knew what he was doing. He had a campus full of eager young writers, introverts all, in a claustrophobic, isolated setting, and the way to get them relaxed was to get them a little drunk and let them mingle with their heroes, not-so-eager older writers, introverts all, in a claustrophobic, isolated setting.

To understand Bread Loaf in the early 1980s, imagine a remote summer camp of keyed-up adolescents with adult wants and add a patina of liquor. Breathe over it all the aphrodisiac of fame and the throat-closing desire for success, a dash or two of one-upmanship, the sense that "This is the chance of a lifetime," and you won't be far wrong.

For the staff there was the daily troop across the lawn at noon-time for Bloody Marys, or Virgin Marys, and a cocktail hour with open bar that began at five and ran until supper.

I learned to fix my own drinks after I asked John to fix me a gin and tonic—he returned, polite, courtly, courteous as always, from the kitchen and handed me a glass. I took one sip and was overwhelmed by the taste of gin. "This is awful," I said. "You made this like a martini."

He shrugged. "I made it like I drink them."

There was a challenge, I suppose: could I drink like the famous? I poured the drink out and made one fresh.

Treman was a bottle club. For those who wanted a drink after the readings, Ben Reynolds, the bartender, made runs to the Middlebury liquor store. If you wanted a bottle, he got one for you, marked it with your name, and locked it in the closet. There were nights at the conference where the evening began with John holding a full bottle of liquor marked with his name—the liquor closet at Treman was full of bottles marked with well-known names in American letters—and the same evening might see John later, the first bottle empty, starting on another, full but marked with an unsteadier hand.

5

———

"What a Wonderful Lover He Would Make, but No Kind of Husband"

In my notebook that summer I wrote a comment John made in his lecture. He reminded his audience: *The people you write for aren't professors. They're people who go to Chicago on the plane.* A second, more surprising remark: *You are made in the image of God. Nothing can hurt God.* I have never, before or since, heard a lecturer in a secular setting say such an astonishing thing. Part of John's attraction for me was that he would say, and believe, these things, which I also believed.

John had wit, too; when Ron Hansen knocked on John's door to tell him the staff picture was being taken, John said, "That's all right, my shades are drawn." Later he asked me, "What do they do with those pictures anyway, use them for calendars?"

On the morning of August 16, my journal notes: *At Treman till 2:30. John Gardner was telling a story about going to Florida on a reading. He said the people who organized the reading knew his history, that when he went to a college to do a reading he got drunk and slept with people, so they assigned him a chaperone, a beautiful woman. He got drunk and later that night, he said, "I woke up inside her." He leaned his shoulder into mine as he said this, and I moved away. I couldn't understand; this doesn't fit with*

47

my image of him. It doesn't reflect well at all. I recorded and quickly forgot this insight. I didn't want to think that this man I admired so much, this teacher who thought so highly of my writing, was promiscuous. It seemed incomprehensible. Later I realized that this had been a clumsy pass, and I was repelled.

I more easily remembered another comment, one I found flattering: "You don't know shit from shinola about writing fiction but you're a natural talent."

I reveled in his company, in the talk. Writing is a lonely life; many writers feel isolated, different. To be with a group of other writers that accepts you is affirming, enriching; I began to crave it. I didn't know it yet, but the affection and acceptance I found at Bread Loaf was something I wasn't getting from Jack.

I paced myself; every other drink I took was ice water. I took naps in order to stay up all night. John's company was fascinating and I didn't want to miss a minute. During the day I noticed other people were jealous. Someone would stand next to me at the salad bar and lean in close. "I saw you talking with John Gardner." A raised eyebrow, a smile. "You're lucky." One night I sat next to Patty Pack at dinner. After every remark I made, no matter how banal, she leaned forward to the table and announced, "Susan says . . ." I was quite obviously moving up the hierarchy because John had befriended me. I shrugged all this off. I enjoyed being part of the inner circle, but I didn't see any way that this would affect my everyday life. I thought of Bread Loaf as a twelve-day cocktail party, a place to have fun. I enjoyed getting to know John and thought it would just be a once-a-year thing. John was easy to talk to, very approachable. He was down to earth, direct. If people wanted to talk with him, why didn't they? I totally forgot my unease of the summer before and simply adopted him as a friend.

In the meantime I was noticing that Liz spent her evenings alone in the room in Maple while John held forth at Treman. I was flattered, intrigued, didn't want the evenings to end. I wondered what it was like for Liz; surely she felt left out? One night he mentioned that she had the flu; he left her alone in the room, and I heard him telling Hilma Wolitzer, "I left a note on her pillow: 'The phantom loves you.' " That he shared such details of his life with listeners at Bread Loaf was characteristic; he always operated outside conventional boundaries. Even in my infatuation I thought if Liz had the flu he had no business hanging around so long at Treman. I wrote in my journal: *What a wonderful lover he would make, but no kind of husband.*

In hindsight I can see that he was beginning to pursue me; at the time, I didn't take it seriously. I was always emotionally dishonest. I didn't know how to feel my feelings or to predict how other people might act in response to my behavior. I flirted with John but told myself he wouldn't respond. That he might didn't fit into my plan for my life, so I just told myself it wouldn't happen. I was attracted to John, but I didn't wish to act. I noted my infatuation in my journal and deliberately held back. The path seemed too perilous; I was too vulnerable. This man could be my teacher, could advise me about writing; I didn't want to jeopardize that for what promised only to be a one-night stand. The danger of Bread Loaf is the cruise-ship feeling. Everyone knows it will be over soon, and there is an atmosphere of liberty and license in the air.

My parents came to Bread Loaf to visit me and to hear John's reading. They stayed at an inn not far from campus. The night before John's reading, he was joking with David Martin. "How about I ride my motorcycle into the auditorium? What do you think?"

"What do I think? I think that would be great, John, just great." David was a serious literary artist who affected the persona of hoodlum; the jacket photo of his first novel showed him in a torn T-shirt with a cigarette dangling from his lip. Now he seemed to be encouraging John to reenact a scene from *The Wild One.*

I pictured it clearly—the noise of the machine reverberating in the echoing wooden space of the theater, the smell of the exhaust, John dismounting and removing his helmet with the nonchalance of an outlaw—and almost believed it would happen.

John announced to the listening circle that he intended to read a story about a motorcycle gang who stole a Labrador retriever so it could be killed, cooked, and eaten. He had indeed written such a story and published it as the title piece of the collection *The Art of Living.* "You can't do that!" I exclaimed. "My mother, who is one of your biggest fans, your biggest fan in the whole *world,* who loves *all* your books, my mother is driving up here all the way from Rochester, New York, to hear you read. And she *loves* dogs. She *adores* them. She will be so torn up, so destroyed if you read that story. You just can't do that!" He didn't say anything, just rocked back on his heels, in his soft, worn, tassel loafers, watching me with those hooded ice-blue eyes.

The next night, the night of his reading, I waited by the door in a fit of nerves. I'd saved front-row seats for my parents, and they were late. The hosts at the Chipman Inn in Ripton served an elaborate dinner as part of the package deal; I'd warned my mother not to stay for dessert; I knew that, ever careful of the niceties, she would be unable to leave the table until the last politesse had been exchanged. Five minutes of eight, two minutes of eight. The theater long since filled, the audience hushed. John stood back from the podium, by the stage, his manuscript folder in his hand, the spotlight gleaming on his freshly shampooed hair. Eight o'clock came and went. I got up from my jealously guarded seats, now the only vacant seats in the theater, and stood by the door. Five past eight. With sudden resolve he strode to the podium, and I saw my mother and father coming up the path in the dusk. "Quick, quickly." I grabbed Mother's hand, and she and my father and I slipped into our seats just as John opened the folder on the podium.

Once he started I sat in terrible anticipation. He began to read in his rich tenor voice, with just the hint of the Western New York pronunciations still lilting at the edges of his diction. He read:

Forty-five years ago, when Remsen, New York, was called "Jack" and nearly all the people who lived there were Welsh, my uncle, or, rather, my maternal great-uncle, E. L. Hughes, ran the feed-mill.

When is he going to get to the part about the dog? I wondered. I waited to see what would happen, what my mother would do. The story limns a *Gymanfa Ganu*, a Welsh hymn sing, goes on to tell of a suicide and a wake, and makes a powerful statement about faith, redemption, and the power of love and art. At last I relaxed. There wasn't going to be any dog murder. Mother sat transfixed, her face rapt, hanging on every word, not knowing her narrow escape. John had changed his plan and read the story "Come On Back."

My parents stood in the receiving line after the reading. I introduced them to John and each shook his hand. Later, John said to me, "Your father is so shy." I was touched by his sensitivity. He knew my father's heart only by shaking his hand. I asked Mother what she thought. "Those eyes," she said. "They look right through you." I reported this to John, who laughed. "Not in a scary way, I hope."

I saw my parents back over to the Chipman Inn and settled in at Treman. By early morning, the crowd had dwindled down to John and me, Ambrose, and Bob Reiss. Bob had a narrow, rangy frame, a mop of unruly dark hair, and an infectious high-pitched laugh.

John was drunk, tired. It had been a long night of drinking and talking; we were none too sober, all of us; as we walked, Ambrose hung back at first in case John fell. "You all right, John?"

John stumbled down the road next to me. "I really like your parents," he said, with emphasis. "And I really love you." I looked at him sideways. What could I believe? It was four in the morning. He'd been drinking all night.

And I really love you. The words echoed in my mind.

Earlier that week he had noticed my polished, manicured nails and my emerald ring, purchased with the first money I had made as a writer, when I sold an essay to *Skiing* magazine. John looked critically at my hand. "These fingers," he mused. "I just don't get it. You're a farm girl at heart."

In his fantasy I may have been a farm girl, and later I tried to become one for his sake, but I felt he had misread me. I was not a farm girl. And now he said he loved me. I wrote to him later, *I felt like you were looking at someone over my shoulder.*

We ended up sitting by the small pond where John Irving's two sons went swimming during the day. Eventually Ambrose and Bob took the hint I was too dense to see and wandered off to leave us alone. John leaned into my shoulder. "I'll tell your fortune," he said.

I leaned away. "I knew an East Indian once who said he always used that ploy so he could get to hold a girl's hand," I said, teasing, wanting to put distance between us. Here was the pass he must have thought I had been angling for. That I resisted probably puzzled and intrigued him. I, on the other hand, even though I had flirted with him, had not predicted this would occur and reacted as I felt in the moment, with disinterest.

"I don't need that," he said, and leaned in closer and kissed my cheek. I was still unmoved. He looked at the backs of his hands, and I looked also. The pale skin was freckled. "Age spots," he said sadly. We sat by the edge of the pond for quite a while. At last he importuned me to lie down. He asked if I would make love with him, but I said no, and he listened. I let him hug me, but I didn't respond or encourage his advances. I was determined to avoid an erotic encounter. For one thing, the sun was coming up. Anyone from the conference would instantly recognize John, even if they didn't know me. Did I want any passerby to see us in this unsheltered spot making love? I was not interested in a quickie in the grass that would leave me embarrassed, ill at ease, just another conquest.

After a while I suggested that we go; he got up, walking as if discouraged and looking down.

Much later he wrote to me about this incident.

> I remember lying with you beside the pool/pond/swimming hole after all our friends—real friends—had discreetly [sic] moved off. What I wanted to say was, "Please, please, please, Susan, make love to me or I'll die of the terminal shakes!" but what I said was, "I want you to know I love you, Susan. But I am a moral, responsible person," to which you responded, like ox-eyed Hera, "Me too." Jesus Christ how I loved you for that! You don't know what it's like to be a famous personage. I get letters all the time from women who don't know me (I told you this, I think) who want to have a baby by me, et cetera—no complications, just good genes. I knew, by the time we laid down together by that pond or whatever, that you were my real friend and you liked me a lot. I guess I knew that if I wanted you to, you would make love with me. I guess I wanted to be sure you wouldn't be making love simply to the Great Man, or making love out of pity, so I told you what I felt and still feel (obviously) that I love you—I don't know if I mentioned that I love you terribly, starvingly, so that I can hardly get my breath. And you did exactly what was right—for my needs anyway: you showed by every gesture and touch that you were willing to be just my dear friend, if that was what I wanted.

The next day Ron Hansen leaned into my shoulder, conspiratorial. "I've heard whispering about you."

I waited.

"Mary Morris saw you kissing John Gardner."

I thought it over. I had seen her walking by when John was hugging me. I decided to brazen it out. "She's out of her mind."

John didn't make another pass that summer, but continued in his extravagant praise of my work, rocking back on his heels at Treman, telling a visiting writer from *Time* magazine that I was the brightest talent he'd seen since reading *Going After Cacciato* in manuscript. The visiting writer leaned forward, brightened his look, asked my name. I held back, my drink in my hand, against my chest.

Before the end of the conference, John urged me again to come to Binghamton to enroll in the university and take his graduate seminar on fiction writing. I noted in my journal his comment: *Two-thirds of his students are publishing.* Other writers couldn't understand my reluctance. "The man's taken a shine to you," Bob Reiss urged. "You're the favorite's favorite. You should go for it." I shook my head; I couldn't leave Cambridge and had no interest in Binghamton, even if two-thirds of John's students *were* publishing.

I have a photograph taken at this writers' conference. It shows a group of five people: Joyce Renwick, myself, John, Betsy Sachs, and Blue Argo. Joyce Renwick, the staff nurse, had known John for some time and had published an interview with him in a limited edition with the *New London Press*. In the photo she leans her blond head forward and smiles. John is at the center of this group of women. He has a drink in one hand and his pipe in the other; we are all smiling, shoulder to shoulder, posing for the camera on the lawn at an afternoon cocktail party. When I got home I had the photo blown up and framed the central image—John and me—and hung it on the wall in my bedroom. It stayed there for the entire year, from August 1980 to August 1981—an image of a future I didn't even know I wanted.

6

"A Lot of Confusion":
Visiting Susquehanna, Fall 1980

While I would not commit to changing my life and moving to Binghamton to study, as John urged me to do, I agreed to stay in touch with him, to visit and bring stories I was working on. It didn't occur to me that John might be in love with me and using this arrangement as a way to further his pursuit; I took it at face value, as an offer to encourage my work. I was pleased that he invited me to his house, and I was curious to see it and to find out a little about his life in Binghamton. I figured I could have it both ways; I could stay in Cambridge, where I was in love with Jack and genuinely happy, and still have the opportunity to work with John.

To have individual tutorials with a teacher like John Gardner seemed the icing on the cake of a perfect life. I still hungered for advice on my writing, and other writers weren't as generous with their time. I had received a rebuff earlier that year from Tim O'Brien when I ran into him at the Wordsworth Bookstore in Harvard Square. I watched as Tim rearranged the bookshelves, turning his books so the covers faced out, edging aside the books next to them. "Could you read some work for me?" I asked.

Tim shook his head. "This is a lonely business."

John and I set a date for October; I rented a car and broke my trip in Albany, staying overnight with Betsy Sachs. All evening I was keyed up; tomorrow I would see John. I was filled with happy anticipation; I wanted to reconnect with the energy and magic I had felt at Bread Loaf. The next morning I drove two and a half hours to Binghamton. I found the library tower at the State University; then I couldn't find his office. I collared a student at the main entrance of the library and demanded that he help me find John Gardner; I was surprised that he didn't know where this famous and wonderful writer was. The student was a polite young man and guided me through a labyrinth of basement corridors until suddenly a door opened and there John stood. I stepped into the office and surprised myself by saying, "There's the man I want!" and grabbed him in a big hug. The student was forgotten; he tactfully faded away.

I was astonished to find John in a small cluttered office with a window opening directly onto a parking lot and no amenities—no rug, no easy chair, no oak bookcases—just a linoleum floor and a metal desk, two or three tin throwaway ashtrays, institutional metal bookshelves, and dead flies littering the windowsill.

John hugged me back and hustled me off to the student bookstore, where he cashed a check and said we would go to lunch. That meant I had to drive; when he opened the car door and sat in the passenger seat I was faint with terror. The interior space of a car is private, enclosed, intimate; when he sat in the passenger seat, a door of possibility opened in my mind.

He directed me across a river and into a traffic circle. Traffic was fast and random. Jumping into that circle looked more like playing chicken than driving.

I drew in my breath. "I don't want to do this." I was upset to be on a roadway where I felt uncomfortable, but now there was no way out.

He chuckled over his pipe stem. "They're coming to get you."

He chose an unpretentious diner that looked at first glance like any upstate greasy spoon, but it was clean and neat and served wonderful Middle Eastern meals; I was pleased and surprised by his choice.

John was clearly delighted to see me, sitting across from me, smiling, catching a lock of his silver-white hair between his first and second finger and smoothing it behind his ear. We talked about writers, books we'd been reading; I told him about staying with Betsy; he smiled some more, put his elbows on the table, interlaced his fingers, and rested his chin comfortably on the cradle they made, listening attentively to my every word. He was acting a lot like a seventeen-year-old on a date.

After lunch we returned to the university. At his desk we went carefully over my story. He approved most of my changes and I was pleased by his suggestions; I felt I was progressing with my work. When we were done, he said he'd get on the motorcycle and lead me out to his house in Susquehanna. He had traded in the Honda I remembered from the magazine photograph in 1979; he now drove a Harley-Davidson. As we headed south through the city, he stopped ahead of me at a traffic light. As he put his feet down, in his tassel loafers, to balance the bike, I looked at his legs. It suddenly occurred to me that he was a sexual being; I hadn't had that thought about him before. I never looked at him the same again; that was the moment I fell off the ledge of longing and into love.

We ended up driving on a four-lane highway. John went fast and I was scared he would lose me; I had no idea where we were going and Susquehanna seemed miles off the beaten path. He had told me he didn't have a clear image in the mirrors on his motor-cycle—one was loose—and he wasn't always sure if I was behind him. How could I find his house—I didn't even know the address—if I couldn't keep up with him? My hands were slick on the steering wheel. As I followed something flew off the motorcycle. It was the top of one of the luggage carriers that rode on either side of the rear wheel. If I pulled over and picked it up I would have it, what-ever it was, but I would lose him. I felt guilty and nervous. Later we pulled off onto a secondary road. He turned his head, noticed the missing top, slowed the bike, and pulled off the road. I pulled off onto the shoulder. He asked if I had seen the top of the luggage carrier fly off. "Yes," I said, "on the big road." I had not noticed the route number. He nodded and I felt at fault, but didn't say any more. I followed him down the two-lane road until we got to the bridge leading across the Susquehanna River and into town.

Susquehanna had been a railroad town, the hub for northeast rail travel, a center for all travelers to New York, Buffalo, Cleveland, and Chicago. Passengers who arrived by rail saw first a grand old railroad hotel, European in flavor, and found a main street crowded with hotels, three vaudeville houses, and many active businesses. The economic center of the town was the "shops," built between 1861 and 1864, a locomotive works that could build thirty-six engines at a time and was the largest manufacturing building in the world until 1877, when the Thyssen steel mill was built in Germany. This cathedral of the industrial age was 1,200 feet long, 120 feet high at its highest point, and covered the equivalent of four city blocks.

Susquehanna's population reached 8,000 in 1930, when there were 3,000 railroad employees, not all of whom lived in town. By the time I first saw Susquehanna in 1980, rail travel had ceased, the locomotive shops had been abandoned, and population had shrunk to 3,000 folk. The only industry was a dingy lingerie factory; the road into town went across an iron bridge, down into a dark, narrow culvert that flooded every spring, and up into Main Street. Nothing was left of the theaters and vaudeville houses. Instead, ramshackle three- and four-story brick buildings crowded against each other and housed dingy department, drug, and hardware stores. To my left as I entered town lay a blackened rectangle of earth and the ruined foundation of what had been the only chain grocery store.

I followed John up a hill so steep it seemed nearly vertical and past a church that clung to the side of the hill; the streets and lanes off to my right veered up ever steeper hills. I'm in Appalachia, I thought. Why does he live out here?

John's house sat on a small hill overlooking the road; I followed him up the drive and parked at the back. We came in through the back door into the square yellow kitchen with a wall oven. Mail was strewed over the counter; on the doorjamb next to the phone, names and telephone numbers were scrawled; a Dutch door led into a cavernous living room with a cast-iron Franklin stove at one end and green wall-to-wall carpeting. The windows looked out onto sugar maples in the front yard and the wooded hills beyond.

Liz had a small beagle named Esmé. It jumped all over me and I made much of it, glad for a distraction. Liz came in, wearing a long skirt and a light tan jacket, carrying an armload of dry cleaning, with her purse, a colorful woven bag, slung over her opposite shoulder. She nodded at me, said hello, and smiled. *Please let her be nice to me*, I remember thinking. *Please let her be nice.* John and Liz were polite with each other—I sensed a distance between them.

We talked about their life at the university; I hadn't known that Liz was an assistant professor in the English department. She mentioned that she and John had given a reading together for the students in Creative Writing. "Oh?" I said. "What did you read?" I had the vague idea that perhaps she read something of John's, but that seemed an odd sort of presentation.

John flashed me a hurt look, and I realized my faux pas as Liz said, "Of course I read my own work."

"Liz is a wonderful poet," John said. "Much better than me."

I bit my lip, glad that Liz had chosen to be gracious, and not to flatten me with a more acerbic answer. I'd been intimidated by her confidence and verbal quickness at Bread Loaf and now realized I'd made a serious error here in her house.

Liz was making a sweet potato casserole for supper—John and I stood in the kitchen sampling this dish as she peeled the cooked sweet potatoes and put them in a decorative casserole dish with lots of spices and an incredible amount of butter. I felt like a child snitching food in my mother's kitchen; looking at John, I imagined he felt the same. At one point I mentioned someone having "terrible teeth."

"Watch yourself," he said and looked at me sideways, mock fierce, showing his own stubby yellowed teeth. We were waiting for John's parents and his Aunt Lucy Preston; they were coming in from Batavia for a celebration of John's work. A professor of theater at the university, John Bielenberg, had adapted John's novel *The Sunlight Dialogues* for the stage; it was to premiere that night at the university.

John Senior, Lucy, and Priscilla arrived, very late. They complained of traffic and construction on the highway and asked "Were you worried?" "Yes," John said, and then laughed, to take the edge off it. John Senior was tall, handsome, and moved with assurance. John introduced me, and his father shook my hand warmly and said, "Nice to see you again," in a mellow, vibrant voice. I found this encounter a little odd. He couldn't remember me—we had never met—and was almost flirtatious. John's Aunt Lucy had the high cheekbones and confident glance of a woman with classic beauty. She wore her abundant snow-white hair in the upswept style of a Gibson girl. Priscilla, John's mother, was short and squat, her once-pretty face now squeezed out of shape as if by a vise of time and life experience.

I wasn't sure what to do. John and I had only agreed to the fiction conference. Now it appeared a big evening was planned. Surely I could stay for it, but where would I sleep? He hadn't said anything about my staying over or, if he had, the idea made me uncomfortable. And, knowing I was coming to Binghamton, I had told my mother I would drive on up to Rochester, and she was expecting me. I felt very uncertain. If I went to the play, I would have to call Mom and say I wasn't coming; after the play I would be much too tired to drive all the way to my parents'. At last I decided to leave, made my good-byes, left in the middle of all the hustle and bustle, and drove up to Rochester, another four hours north. Late that night I sat at the dining room table, writing John a letter. "Who are you writing to, Sue?" my mother asked. The letter went on for pages and pages. Abashed by my own interest and intensity, I did not mail it.

Later John wrote to me about this visit:

> When you came to Binghamton, I felt crazy: I could have driven you anywhere on the motorcycle—we have wonderful romantic secret lakes. Admit it, I was a prince! And then all those letters I wrote to you that I never sent—all extremely polite propositions. I went to visit my friend Duncan Luke in Boston and talked about you, and he said, "Look, you're really boring about this. Why don't you just call her?" But I didn't. I was a Good Person. Duncan was of course deeply disgusted. I wasn't fun.

With one part of my mind, I was still denying that he might be pursuing me and pretended only that he wanted to read my work. With another part of my mind I was eager to see him. We arranged a second visit in November; it didn't go well. I was working on a draft of a story called "The Have-a-Heart Trap." In this story a white boy from the suburbs of Boston is lost in Roxbury; he meets an old black man who turns out to be a wizard and a shape-shifter. John liked the way it melded ordinary reality and the fantastic.

I telephoned John to make an appointment, we set a date, and I arranged to rent a car and drive out to Susquehanna. He said to come directly to the house. I had called during the week before and spoken to Liz; she said John was out of town. I thought about calling just before I left to reconfirm but decided not to. I went to a party in Boston the night before I was to leave, thinking all the time, Tomorrow I will see John Gardner. It was like a bright gem I held close in my bosom.

I got up early and made the drive across Massachusetts to the southern tier of New York. It took me seven hours; when I got to Windsor, New York, off Route 17, I was tense and tired. At a pay phone on the street I telephoned John's number.

John had forgotten the appointment. He said it was lucky I had caught him; he was on his way to do some Christmas shopping but I should come to the house anyway. I followed his directions through the winding roads. As I pulled up, Liz was coming out into the yard with a trowel and a basket of spring bulbs. She was wearing dark slacks and had her hair tied back with a scarf.

"John's in the house," she said. "He's taking a bath."

Taking a bath? I thought to myself. It was four o'clock in the afternoon. I let myself in through the front door and John came rushing from the downstairs bathroom, dressed in slacks and an open-collared white shirt; his skin was damp and pink. We hugged and he hustled me into the living room. We sat on the couch, hunched over the low glass-topped coffee table on which I placed the draft I had been working on. I was hungry. John didn't offer me anything to eat or drink, didn't make any small talk, didn't even ask me how was the drive, simply looked at the manuscript. I had come to expect this fierce concentration, this focus on writing and story, and was not surprised. I looked over his shoulder, went into the kitchen, and found a box of matzos in the cupboard. I took out two crackers and brought the box into the living room. He exhaled smoke and pored over my pages as I munched on the matzos with a dry mouth and looked around the room. At last he gathered the pages in a sheaf, tapped them on the table, and said, "A lot of confusion in this story."

It was too much for me. The long drive, the forgotten appointment, the matzos, and not even a cup of tea; my eyes filled with tears. He turned, looked directly at me, and touched my shoulder. Suddenly I felt better. I was still a good person, he still liked me, even if my work was faulty. Later I realized I came to rely on this quality; he paid close attention to me and my feelings and knew the right gesture to get me through a difficult moment. I felt we were in tune with each other in a special way that excluded anyone else; I felt this even sitting on a couch in his and Liz's living room.

Point by point he showed me where the story went off track, where I'd brought in extraneous detail, where incidents were repeated. Liz came back in and went upstairs to change; they were planning to go out for dinner. John asked me if I knew whom he was having dinner with, someone named Quackenbush. The question made no sense to me. How would I know one of his friends in Pennsylvania? I would have been happy to go along with him to dinner, but he quite pointedly didn't invite me. I was irrational to expect it; he and Liz had been invited by one of their friends. This wasn't like Bread Loaf where I was part of the group; this was his real life and I wasn't a part of it, though I realized I wanted to be. Liz came down, wearing a dressy blouse and a long slim skirt that flared around her ankles. She looked in at us, smiled, and went out again to the adjoining hall. "Jonathan?" she called to him. I had never heard anyone call him that; we both looked around. I was so intent on him that Liz's voice was an interruption.

I felt I had no choice. I had to leave, but I didn't want to. In October we had had time to talk, to have a meal together. Now I realized I would have no special time with him alone. He read my work as promised, but I wanted more. I felt I had been shoehorned into a busy day. I had driven a long way for nearly nothing. I was angry, disappointed, and confused by my emotions.

Ever polite, I hid my feelings, said a cordial good-bye, and got in my car. As I drove away, John and Liz stood in the doorway of the house. John was looking after me.

From Windsor, I telephoned Sue Watkins. I really didn't want to drive all the way back to Boston and was happy to hear Sue's voice when she answered the phone.

She was at her parents' place outside Elmira. I left Windsor and drove two hours to the house. I had met Sue in 1978 in the town of Dundee, New York, where my parents had their summer home. Sue was a newspaper editor and a novelist; we took to each other immediately and spent hours discussing books and writing. Now we sat at her parents' kitchen table, and I sipped from a glass of scotch. Sue leaned back, her open, pretty face framed by wild curly red-brown hair. "So John Gardner shit all over your story," she said. I nodded as if that was pretty much my view also. There was more happening in my heart than I could look at clearly myself, let alone talk about with a friend.

At home in Cambridge I told Jack, "He forgot the appoint-ment." It seemed safer to offer only the bare bones of what had happened. I didn't want to mention all my confusing feelings.

He shook his head. "That's why it's a good idea to confirm these things in advance."

I was just as glad I hadn't called: what if John had said "Don't come"?

I had not been honest with Jack about my feelings for John, as I had not been honest or clear with myself. I was beginning to think of John more as a man whom I desired than only a teacher for my work, but, as usual, I did not fully acknowledge these feelings to myself, nor did I share them with Jack.

I told my mother.

"His wife just didn't give him the message," she said.

After that I decided to let it go. I wrote to John once, a careful, polite letter; he didn't answer. I felt too awkward to call and sug-gest another conference. Instead, I stayed in Cambridge and con-tinued to write. I concentrated my energies on Jack. We had a magical trip to Switzerland in February of 1981, where we stayed with his friends in their condominium at Gstaad. The four of us got along famously, the skiing was divine, with bright sun and a blue sky every day and the joys of the immense mountain—I re-turned to Cambridge exhilarated.

But that photo of me and John still hung in the bedroom at my apartment. I made plans to go back to Bread Loaf for the confer-ence of 1981; this time I would manage the bookstore. In May I found a card in a Cambridge bookstore that showed a broad-shouldered man, his long white hair blown by the wind, standing by his motorcycle with his back to the viewer.

I showed the card to Arlene Walsh. "Should I send this to John Gardner?" Since we had met on the bus going up to the conference in 1979, Arlene and I had become friends and confidantes. She read and praised my poems and short fiction; now she encouraged me in a new direction. "You *must* send that to Gardner. It's a *won-derful* card."

I wrote a simple message and signed it "Love." There was no response. I decided that John was not interested in me. He was a married man, after all.

On a mountaintop in Switzerland would have been a magic moment for Jack to propose, and I would have accepted, but he didn't. Jack still looked to me like the perfect partner. I imagined that through wishful thinking I could make him become the attentive, thoughtful lover I desired. My thoughts were confused and my behavior contradictory. I wasn't honest with him, but I thought I wanted him to be honest with me. We had difficulty communicating our feelings to each other, yet I felt comfortable with that difficulty.

He had smoothness and charm but was cool and distant. Some Saturday nights he would neglect to call but then would know all about the most recent lyric opera performance. I knew he saw other women; I suspected he slept with them. I pressed him for more emotional involvement; he withdrew. In July he went off to Salzburg, Austria, to an international conference of economic theorists, and I wrote him a letter in which I asked him what our future would be. He wrote back that he cared for me, I had helped him through a difficult time, he hoped still to spend time with me, but there would be no marriage; he wasn't ready.

I was bitterly disappointed and denied the reality he presented. The rational thing would be to break off the relationship; however, I did not. I'd been so lonely before; surely I could turn him around.

I poured out my distress to Arlene. "We'll go see David," she announced. "Oh, Arlene," I protested. David was a fortune-teller who had an office in a seedy downtown Boston neighborhood; Arlene put great store in his psychic abilities. Despite my protests I went and waited, leaning over a cloth-covered table in his cramped apartment, as he scrutinized tea leaves. He wouldn't look at me. "Marriage, if at all, will be delayed."

I knew he had to be wrong; Jack *looked* so perfect. I was now thirty-one years old. I wanted to marry, to have a family, to have a man in my life who loved me. My single life in Cambridge had once offered freedom and fun; now it seemed confining and sterile, a dead end, a trap. I could not have said it out loud, but I was frightened about my future.

7

"You Have a Responsibility to That Eighty-Year-Old Lady": Bread Loaf Writers' Conference, 1981

By the summer of 1981 I had acquired a used Volkswagen station wagon and drove up to Bread Loaf from Cambridge, arriving the day before the conference started, as did all the other staff. I spent the afternoon in the bookstore, unpacking boxes and arranging the shelves, and finished just in time for the introductory party in the barn. I strolled in and immediately saw John, with a drink in one hand and his pipe in the other, standing in front of the fireplace with a group of people. John looked different; his white hair no longer hung to his shoulders but was cut short, like a 1950s teenager, a middle-aged James Dean. He'd lost weight and looked trim and attractive, wearing casual slacks, tassel loafers, and a corduroy sport coat in a kind of golden yellow color. I stopped to get a drink and then walked over to the fireplace. John watched me enter the circle of people. I had time to notice the intent look in his eyes before he darted forward and kissed me on the throat. His mouth was hot and wet. There was a moment of shocked silence.

"Well!" said Blue. "*I'd* like one of *those*."

I retreated from my confusion by taking a sip from the drink in my hand. We had not communicated since the previous November, but here was no ordinary kiss. I wasn't sure what to do, so I did nothing; I acted as though he had merely nodded hello. We talked for a while. He was alone; conversation revealed that Liz had stayed in Pennsylvania. After a while I excused myself and went off to bed. I had a single room that summer at the top of the stairs in Cherry Cottage. John didn't say good night or follow me out. I went to bed and fell asleep. Sometime later, about two in the morning, I heard Blue's voice. "Oh, Susan won't mind." She was on the porch downstairs; I came instantly awake.

I heard heavy footsteps on the stairs and then John's voice in the hall, as he opened one door after another. "Oh, excuse me, sorry, go back to sleep." Then the door of my room opened and there he stood, blocking the light from the hall. His shoulders were very square. I sat up in bed and pulled the covers to my chin.

He saw that I was awake and said he'd wait for me on the porch. After he left I got out of bed and put my clothes on. I went down to the front porch and sat on one of the wicker chairs. John sat on the porch floor at my feet, leaning against the support of the stair railing. He waited for Blue to leave and then began to talk. He talked fast, gesturing with his hands, keeping a distance from me, and I could hardly believe what I was hearing. "I think you and I ought to become lovers," he began.

The blood pounded in my ears. I stalled for time. "Why didn't you write to me?" The unhappiness I had felt in November came immediately to my mind. I was also annoyed that he had not answered my letter and my card.

He shook his head. "I wrote you a thousand letters and threw them all away. They all said *Be my lover*."

My breath quickened and my heart began to race. Then I thought, I better throw some cold water on all this. "What about Liz?"

"She'll find somebody else."

The baldness of that statement and what it implied took my breath away. His words seemed tantamount to a marriage proposal. What surprised me most was that I was ready—indeed, maybe I had been waiting—for just such a proposal. At the same time I doubted anything would be that simple. I knew I was in love with him and I was going to say yes, but I didn't know what that might mean. My heart was beating fast. He kept talking.

"You're going to have to make love with me sooner or later. Someday you're going to be an eighty-year-old lady with nothing but memories. You have a responsibility to that eighty-year-old lady."

This line worked because he was echoing my own thoughts. "Where are you staying?" I asked him.

He told me his room number in Maple.

"I'll meet you over there in a few minutes."

His face changed, and he stood up to move toward me. I stood too. As I did so I heard footsteps on the gravel path next to the cottage and heard voices; I turned and saw two staff members strolling by. One waved, and I waved back. John nodded and stepped off the porch.

I went up to my room and thought about what I was doing. I thought about Jack, who didn't want to marry me. I thought about my attraction to John, which was very real. He had been charismatic before; now he was passionate, and passionate about me. I thought about the isolated cruise-ship atmosphere of the conference, how it was a bubble of twelve days that seemed removed from ordinary life. I thought about married men who made promises but never left their wives.

At last I stopped thinking and started across the dark campus in the direction of Maple Cottage. Without looking up, I walked into the first large yellow dormitory I came to and up the broad uncarpeted stair. My footsteps echoed, and I prayed that I wouldn't see anyone. Then I began to breathe faster. The second-floor corridor didn't look right: why couldn't I find his room? Where was he? This was taking way too much time. What if I ran into someone else from the faculty, John Irving, for example, or Tim O'Brien; I would see the smirk, the knowing look, and realize I would be the subject of gossip, the butt of jokes, among the drinkers at Treman. I walked around the second floor hardly breathing, looking for a room that wasn't there. Then I started to think. I must have walked into Birch Cottage and not into Maple. The yellow frame buildings at Bread Loaf look alike, and I'd overheard comments the previous summer at Treman from embarrassed writers who had done the same thing.

I went down the stairs, into the next building, and again went up the stairs. My heart was loud in my own ears. John's door on the second floor was open; he was standing at his desk, reading a manuscript. I appeared in the doorway, and he strode across the room with open arms. "Welcome, welcome." We held each other in a tight embrace. I was breathing hard. I was nervous, so I began to talk rapidly and told him about walking into the wrong building. "I know." He smiled. "I did the same thing." Immediately I felt that everything was going to be all right.

His room had twin beds, as had mine the first year, but these were nicer, with turned and polished maple bedsteads. On the table next to the window were his typewriter, a pile of manuscript, tobacco tins, his pipe, some pencils.

We lay down together on one of the single beds. He looked into my eyes. "What do you want to have happen?" he asked me.

"I don't know," I replied. "I don't know." I had so many thoughts and feelings I couldn't voice any of them. I was tense; I anticipated an initial awkwardness, getting out of our clothes, and didn't know how that would be. I also felt apprehensive. What if he were selfish, inexpert, an inconsiderate lover?

"What a joy to hold you in my arms," he said. "I was going to write you a poem; I didn't know what to do." As he spoke, his words and his tone and his close hug reassured me and I began to relax.

His words made me glad; when he said he'd written several letters that he hadn't sent, I knew he was in love with me. He kissed me, and I kissed him back. His mouth tasted of gin, a sweet taste, like perfume; the scent of his tobacco seemed to cling to his worn blue work shirt, to the scratchy skin of his face.

Getting out of our clothes wasn't as awkward as I'd feared. He asked if I was protected against pregnancy. I nodded. We left the light on. In our lovemaking he was tentative, exploratory. He pulled me on top of him and let me take the lead. As he embraced me, he said, "This is heaven. How heavenly to hold you in my arms."

I remember the room as filled with light.

Afterward I felt like crying. In my journal I find, *What a relief after twelve months of erotic tension.* Now I acknowledged to myself openly what was covert before: I had wanted him. I had liked him as a writer, as a teacher, as a person. Now I loved him. I was relieved to find that he approached lovemaking with the same generosity and exuberance of spirit that characterized his entire being. In that first encounter, I committed to him—and he was unavailable. My heart was full and breaking at the same time. I wanted badly to marry him, to make him mine, and I couldn't; he was married already. He had tied himself legally to Liz. I could hardly sort out my feelings and didn't want to burst into tears in his arms; to distract myself I began to talk.

I asked him about his haircut. "You look about fifteen," I said.

He smiled. "I got it cut because I had a part in a play. I went to the worst barber in Susquehanna County and asked for a short haircut and then fell asleep in the chair on purpose."

"What about that card I sent you? With the man by the motorcycle? Did you get that?"

He nodded. "I'd seen it before."

"What made you think you could come on to me like you just did?"

He tightened his grip around my torso, his square hand kneading the flesh at my waist. He grinned. "You signed it *love.*"

We talked a lot. It was like being with him at Treman, only better, because we were alone, we were now lovers, we were talking in bed in that intimacy brought by nakedness, by embracing.

I told him about all the parts of his work I'd liked. I started with his story *Vlemk the Box-Painter*, which I had purchased in a lavishly illustrated edition published by the Lord John Press. "I wrote that in two days and two nights on no sleep," he said. "I had seen a painting in a secondhand bookstore that gave me the idea for the story. After I wrote it, I went back to the bookstore and looked again at the painting, and it was by Vlemk. I hadn't known that before." He widened his eyes, mock scared. "Spooky," he said, and grinned so that I saw the gap in his mouth behind the eyetooth.

I asked about his collection *The Art of Living*. "I was given the title for the story and asked to write it by a convention of hollow-eyed Jungians with uncombed hair." As before, I was delighted by his directness, his sense of humor, his odd statements.

I was pleased to have new insight into his work, to see more clearly how his mind operated. The huge pile of paper on his desk, 1,100 typed pages, was a nearly final draft of *Mickelsson's Ghosts*. "It's a ghost story that becomes a tragedy," he said. "It parallels my other book, *Shadows*, which is a detective story that's a comedy. That one's gonna end with the alcoholic detective running through a rock fall, stones falling out of the sky." Here John mimed a man running, holding his hands over his head, comically glancing at the sky. "Like the universe is tricking him. I've seen such a thing," he asserted, "in California."

He also told me he was working on a translation of the Gilgamesh epic, the first epic poem, different from the Judeo-Christian tradition. "In the Gilgamesh story, man is not thrown out of the garden; instead, the leader of the tribe has to build a brick wall. See, he kills, abuses his own men to build the wall to keep the enemies out. Each year they come to steal, because the people plant corn to eat. Gilgamesh enslaves his own people to build a wall: that's the sin.

"Talking and fucking are the same," he observed. "We talk better in bed." I found this outrageous statement perfectly believable and wrote in my journal: *Felt so happy to be with him, and the sex just gave us a chance to get comfortable with each other so we could talk. Didn't know where the betrayal, if any, lay. Could understand that Jack could do that with other girls, and it wouldn't touch me. For a minute only.*

He touched my hipbone, and said, "Ilium."

"What?"

"It's the name of that bone."

"What are you thinking about?" I asked.

"Buckwheat."

"Buckwheat? Why buckwheat?"

"I don't know. The name of your bone I was touching is the ilium, and that made me think about Helen of Troy, which made me think of buckwheat. When I was a little boy growing up on the farm, we were poor and ate a lot of buckwheat."

Then he told me about Gilbert. Gilbert was the younger brother who had died in the accident John described in his story "Redemption." I had been correct when I read that story in the Cambridge Public Library and knew in my heart that it was John's life, disguised as fiction.

Certain details in the story had been changed from life. The accident happened as John was driving a tractor dragging a cultipacker, a heavy farming implement. John was eleven, rather than twelve, as he stated in his story. John's sister, Sandy, was on his lap. Gilbert was riding on the connector between the tractor and the cultipacker. In the story "Redemption," John implies that this accident happened in the fields behind the house, but instead it happened on the macadam road just in front of his parents' house; the children had been bringing this equipment home from another farm. The tractor ran out of gas, and gave a little jerk as they came down the hill in front of the house. Gilbert fell off, landed on the road in front of the cultipacker, and was crushed to death.

"I looked back and saw the cultipacker at his hips," John told me. "Then I looked again, and it was at his head."

The day Gilbert died was April 4, 1945. It was the Wednesday after Easter, and probably a school holiday. It was unseasonably warm. Many years later, Priscilla, John's mother, told Liz Rosenberg her memories about the day in an interview Liz published in *MSS* magazine. Priscilla said that when the boys left she had not seen any danger. The family rule was that the children could not ride on the tractor with another youngster driving. When John left, he was towing a flat wagon that rode close to the ground. If Gilbert and Sandy rode on the wagon, they would be perfectly safe; Priscilla gave her consent when Gilbert came running in and asked if he could go with his older brother. Priscilla said one memory haunted her: she did not ask them how they were coming back. The plan was for the children to drop off the wagon at another farm, and bring the cultipacker back home.

Farmers use a cultipacker in the springtime to break up clods of earth and drive stones deeper into the ground before planting. The implement consists of two long rollers, one behind the other, each made up of parallel knobbed wheels. The wheels of the first roller are spaced widely apart to break up the earth; the wheels of the second roller are placed more closely together to continue this process. A cultipacker weighs between one and two tons.

John drove the tractor out onto the macadam road in front of the house, with the big wagon hitched on the back, and Gil and Sandy rode in the wagon. At their uncle's farm they unhitched the wagon, hitched on the cultipacker, and started off for home. Here is where the danger began, for there was no place for Gil or Sandy to ride. Sandy sat on John's lap, as he drove the tractor, and Gilbert rode on the crossbar behind John where John couldn't see him. Priscilla remembered Gilbert didn't have anything to hold onto. In front of the Gardner's house, the tractor ran out of gas coming down the knoll, and as it did, it jerked. Gilbert fell off and down in front of the cultipacker, which rolled over him. A neighbor came, picked Gilbert up, and brought the children to their home. Priscilla remembered: "And Bud came running into the house, crying, I've killed Gilbert! I've killed Gilbert! And I said, You have not! Don't say such a thing."

All his life John blamed himself for this accident. He should have been able to put on the brakes; he should have been able to stop. That he continued to drive meant he had killed his brother.

Some adult must have supervised this arrangement, must have given implied consent to the way the children rode back to the Gardner farm. Why did no grown-up suggest to John that Gil and Sandy walk back instead of ride with him? Though John always took sole responsibility for this accident, it seems to me the responsibility was not totally his.

John never worked out this situation as one of shared guilt. He always blamed himself that he didn't put on the brakes, and instead continued to drive. Yet the accident happened as the tractor ran out of gas and they were coming down a hill. Even if he had braked the tractor, he couldn't have braked the rolling cultipacker.

The neighbor took the family to the hospital and Priscilla held Gilbert in her arms, not knowing if he was alive or dead. When they got to the hospital, a nurse, a friend of Lucy's, met them, and knew right away the child was dead, but couldn't bear to tell Priscilla.

John Senior had been away from the farm that day. When he came home the first thing John Senior saw was his five-year-old daughter, covered with her brother's blood. He rushed to the hospital. When he was told about the accident he sat silent, while, Priscilla remembered, "Bud was sobbing so. . . ." Priscilla glanced at John Senior, who put his arms around John to comfort him and told him that he couldn't have helped what happened.

Priscilla maintained that she and her husband didn't find out until years later how their oldest son blamed himself. When they did, John Senior wrote John a letter. He told him of an incident the previous summer, 1944, when Gilbert was five. John Senior had been mowing hay. Gilbert was riding on the hay rake behind the tractor. John Senior noticed Gilbert was getting sleepy, and told him when he got to the end of the row, he would lay him down for a nap. John Senior continued to drive the tractor, and when he got to the end of the row Gilbert had fallen off the hay rake, and had been rolled along the ground with the loose hay, not hurt at all. John Senior wrote to his son that Gilbert might have been killed that day.

To share the story of Gilbert with me the night we became physically intimate was clearly important for John: to tell me face-to-face what he had told the world, cloaked by the guise of writing fiction, in his published story. To tell me with his voice, to see what I would say in the moment, was significant to him.

"I love you because you forgive me," he said.

What else could I do? The tragedy was so enormous. I did indeed forgive him, insofar as I could. However, I feel he was not able to forgive himself; and his guilt over Gilbert, his guilt over his failed marriages, his guilt over so many other things drove him so that his life itself was compromised.

We slept apart, in the twin beds. In the morning he told me a dream. "I woke up from a beautiful dream and I thought I was still dreaming; I couldn't tell which was the dream and which was the reality. I saw you in your bed and me in my bed and your bed was banked with flowers and flower boxes. Just overflowing with flowers."

That morning as we hugged, he said, "What a good idea!" I understood that he meant that we had made love, had passed the night together. I shook my head. "No, it's a bad idea." I think we both felt relief that we had acted on our feelings, but I saw a difficult passage ahead. As he hugged me, I reconsidered. "A bad idea that's a good idea," I conceded.

He turned away and began to look at his manuscript. I took the hint and started for the door. Then John said, "I won't walk out with you, for Liz's sake." His words pierced my heart. Here was evidence that I was *less than*. I had no right to be there; I was not his wife but rather an illicit partner, who had to remain hidden, clandestine. He didn't want people to see us together. The pain cut so deep I couldn't let myself feel it directly and, instead, focused on a surface annoyance. I had not planned to make a public issue of our new relationship. Couldn't he see that? Didn't he know I would be discreet? It seemed imperative not to hurt Liz. I shut my mind to the fact that my actions would ultimately hurt her a great deal. In addition, as far as possible, I wanted to protect my own privacy. Having started as a joke, with Blue, our gossip mill called "Rumor Control," I knew only too well how quickly news of a new pairing circulated around the conference. I slipped quietly out of the building and went back over to Cherry cottage to my room to change.

Later, at ten o'clock, I sat in the second row of seats in the Little Theatre for John's lecture on fiction technique, and as I always did at every lecture, I took notes.

He quoted Aristotle—"You can't tell what a person's life is like until you know how they die"—then commented:

Note Marquez in *One Hundred Years of Solitude*. He introduces characters and tells us their death right away.

Writing is a high way of thinking, a lab test. Don't bushwhack the reader with withheld information. There's an ancient contract between the teller and the reader. If there's a victim, there's no suspense. Don't tell a victim story.

Don't be a grown-up. Stick to the foolish work of making real art.

Start with character, not situation. Plot exists so the character can discover and reveal what the character is and is like. Theme exists so the character can be somebody. The central character wants something. He goes after it despite opposition, including his own doubts, and arrives at win, lose, or draw.

There can be no great art without a certain strangeness, one moment when the reader's hair stands on end.

To be a great writer you should write at the most childlike level. Tell your most favorite story. Two story possibilities: a character goes on a journey, a stranger comes to town. Fiction is always about change in circumstance. When you change patterns, you have to examine your patterns. You need to have a character who wants something; a character actively pursues.

Fiction is a way of getting the id out of the mirror. You can get deeply in touch with the unconscious. The fairy-tale form is like a cup. You fill it with your wine.

Write this: The bear who knocks on the door and says: "Can I marry your daughter?"

Now, to stand outside the theater and wait for John to emerge from the crowd of students and admirers was a precarious, erotically charged experience. I was filled with suspense. What would he do or say? I loved him now, and he could hurt me. What if he were cool, distant? If he brushed me off at that moment, turned me back into another student, I would have been crushed. I waited at the fringes of the group. It had only been a few hours since we had been together; I felt my heart lay in the balance. He saw me waiting, smiled, and gestured for me to stay, and I started breathing again. He came over to stand by me. "That was a great lecture," I told him.

"Was it?" He didn't seem interested in the lecture or what I thought of it. He was looking into my face.

"I have to go do the bookstore now," I said. Gravel crunched under my feet and I was aware of other students, admirers, fans, several holding copies of John's books, standing aside, waiting for John to turn to them.

"OK. See you later for lunch." He smiled and turned to the student waiting at his elbow, holding out a book for him to autograph.

"Mr. Gardner, could you . . . ?"

"Certainly," I heard him say. "Who would you like me to make this out to?"

We had had a casual exchange, but I knew from the look on his face, a warm, special look, and from the way he watched me, that I was important to him; it wasn't just a one-night stand. I was greatly relieved, for this had been a deep-rooted fear, that the famous author would simply use and discard me. Throughout our developing relationship, I always had more invested than I thought I did. My heart yearned toward him while my mind stood back and scolded, "No, this will never work. It's way too risky. Don't even think about it."

I wandered back to the bookstore and my duties there in a daze. Now I had a few moments to myself, on that August morning, and my entire surroundings were charged and special. The sunlight refracted brilliantly off the yellow paint of the inn and the green trim of its windows; the gravel crunched under my feet; a little breeze carried to me the smell of new-mown grass over by the tennis court. I heard the distant motor of the lawn mower; it seemed to come from very far away, cushioned from me somehow, as if I were in an exalted state. I felt I had entered a new world of possibility, where every atom, every micron, was vibrant and mysterious. I was not only somehow more intensely alive, I was safe as well, in a way I never had been before.

John seemed to see and to love a larger part of myself, a part that now seemed possible to achieve, as long as he loved me. It was partly this sense, that he saw possibilities in me that I didn't, that drew me so magnetically. His love seemed to offer me an enhanced life, which only his love would help me fulfill.

As well as talking and telling me how he felt, sharing his thoughts and feelings, John listened. How I loved him for that! A man who would talk, a man who would listen—he was irresistible. I'd never had anyone listen to me with such careful attention. He loved me enough to keep still; he sought out my thoughts, my feelings, my opinions. Other connections paled in comparison; other men friends, including Jack, even my father, whom I loved dearly, only lectured or harangued, showing off their knowledge and outlook. Here was someone with immense learning, multiple accomplishments, who was like a sponge for everything I told him. My sense was that John offered me, in those days at Bread Loaf and throughout our relationship, a powerful, unconditional love: fierce, uncompromising, total love. I felt I had come home, had found the soulmate I had yearned for. This was an overwhelming feeling; I was suffused with happiness and relief.

For the rest of that day I ran the bookstore and he read student manuscripts, talked with writers in the barn, and worked on finishing the draft of *Mickelsson's Ghosts*.

At the salad table that evening I stood next to Mary Morris, and together we bemoaned the lack of interesting gossip. "It's so tame this year. No scandals," I remarked with authority. As I spoke I looked across the room and saw John, and my hands began to shake. Mary, busy manipulating the salad tongs, didn't notice.

After that evening's reading, John and I talked at Treman as before, and the atmosphere, once intense, suddenly became charged with the love I was feeling and my sense that it had to stay secret.

Around midnight, someone asked me if I wanted another drink. John overheard. "She's leaving," he said, and looked directly at me. I felt cold all over and began to shake. I put down my glass, got my jacket, and left. He followed, reached for my hand, and we went to my room.

That night was different. We had become lovers; now we could explore new territory. Holding me in my narrow single bed, he looked into my eyes and told me over and over how he loved me. "It really delights me that you're such a good writer. Of course, I'd love you even if you weren't."

"I love you too," I told him. I felt loved, approved, accepted, in a way I never had before. I had always had a passionate nature but had discovered to my sorrow that quite often my partners, especially Jack, seemed alarmed or frightened by depth of feeling. I had felt isolated, shamed. John wasn't like that. I found a partner whose passion matched my own. Later he wrote to me, *In finding you I found someone I can love with unbounded sexuality and spirit; I mean soul.* We each imagined the other was the source of our sensual freedom, but this spark sprang out of the meeting of our personalities and the affection we already knew. The magnetism was almost mystical. I wrote later in my journal, *I couldn't tell which was his body and which was my body.* As we became more comfortable with each other and as our physical connection deepened, I began to lose myself in a crescendo of joy I had never experienced before. I realized I was prepared to give up a great deal, to walk down almost any road, in order to keep this man in my life.

Liz was still in Pennsylvania, and on Friday, the end of the first week of the conference, John had to go back to Susquehanna. The Laurel Street Theatre had scheduled its production of *Meet Me in St. Louis* to coincide with the first weekend of the Writers' Conference. John had arranged the music, rescoring it in high camp style, and had a singing role in the production.

In my elderly Volkswagen, I drove him down to the Middlebury airport, where Gene Biesecker from Susquehanna waited, pacing by his plane, as we pulled onto the grassy airstrip. Gene was tall, lean; his uncombed yellow-blond hair stood up on his head. He wasn't pleased. "John, you're late." John nodded, hugged me good-bye, and climbed into the plane. Who was this Gene Biesecker, who treated John with none of the deference he received from conference staff and faculty?

I drove back up the mountain to the Bread Loaf campus and lay down in my room for a nap. At seven P.M. my assistant in the bookstore came rushing in to find me: she couldn't start the cash register. I got up and went to the store with her. She'd neglected to turn on the light; the electricity for the register came on the same cord. To the assembled group waiting with purchases, cash, and checkbooks, Suzanne announced, "I had to get her out of bed." One remarked, looking sideways and sly shy: "Was he mad?" I felt confident enough that no one knew of my connection to John that I took this remark as teasing. Besides, if they really knew John's schedule, they would know he and I had been in a car on the way to the airport and he was no longer present at the conference. I decided to play along. "Oh, yes," I replied. "He was ripping."

*   *   *

John returned to Bread Loaf on Sunday, August 16, with Liz. I saw
her shortly after she arrived, striding along the road with Jan
Quackenbush, who had driven up with them. I crossed the road to
greet Liz, noting as I always did her quick, vivid presence, her
precise movements, her clear, intent gaze. I wondered if I would
give myself away. Liz seemed able to see everything. "Hello, Susan." She introduced me to Jan. I remembered his name as the
friend John and Liz were to have dinner with when I had visited
in November. Jan was wearing a Greek fisherman's cap and a light
jacket; Liz was wearing slacks and flat shoes. We chatted briefly;
then they went off to Maple to find John, and I went back to my
room in Cherry. I can do this, I thought. I can act as though nothing is happening.

Illicit lovers need a beard, a cover. Blue was my confidante and
became our protector. After the first night, when she brought John
to Cherry Cottage, Tim O'Brien asked her if John and I slept together. "Oh, no," Blue said. "They just sat on the porch and
talked."

Now that Liz had arrived I redoubled my efforts to act casual,
to keep my secret. Blue assured me that if Liz suspected anyone, it
would be her, not me. John made it clear after Liz arrived that he
still wanted me; the first night she was at the conference, she left
Treman early, as was her habit. He looked at me as soon as we
were alone in the kitchen and said quietly, "Why don't you go get
your diaphragm?" To hear these words and to know what they
implied gave me an immediate physical reaction: I got cold all over
and started to tremble; I find in my journal: *I tremble and can't
talk or do anything or even get my coat and leave; it's amazing;
my teeth chatter, I get cold. And it goes along somehow with the
erotic tension.*

We left together that night and stayed so long in my room that
at last we both fell asleep. I woke with a start at seven and saw
with alarm that it was already bright day.

"John, John!" I shook his shoulder. "You've got to wake up!" I pleaded with him to leave and go back to his room, so that Liz wouldn't suspect anything. I remembered his words, "Liz will find someone else," but I was afraid of an angry scene. I could not imagine what might happen if Liz confronted me. I felt unsure of myself, still *less than*. What if this liaison was to become only a brief drama in John and Liz's ongoing marriage? The risk was too great. I decided that, even though it was painful, I preferred the role of clandestine lover. If I kept my situation secret, I could hold on to my dream, my strongly awakened love, and would not have to face its end.

Later that day Blue told me, "The rumor is that John Gardner fell asleep on the porch at Treman and woke up at six-thirty cold and shivering." When I saw John that afternoon, I asked him about it. "I think I started that rumor," he said.

One night a group at Treman started a political discussion. I was a conservative, surrounded by liberal friends, and generally kept my opinions to myself. John intuited this, and in front of the crowd at Treman, he teased me. "Susan's a closet Republican." He held his glass out and smiled. The group of onlookers turned to me in disbelief. "Susan, are you crazy? You didn't vote for that idiot in the White House, did you?" I began to stammer out my thoughts, from my years at the *Bay State Banner*, when I had discovered that Mel Miller also favored the Republican party and deplored the changes welfare had brought to the black community. I imagined hostility where there was none in the group surrounding me, and all too soon I shut up. John said nothing, only continued to smile. When we were alone later, in bed, he said to me, "I was teasing you and you panicked."

"Yes," I answered. "Every muscle in my back was vibrating."

He kissed me. "It doesn't matter."

I was immediately relieved. It would have mattered to Jack. I had felt he cared more about politics than he did about me.

*   *   *

In the barn stood a grand piano, and quite often evenings would end with David Bain or Bob Reiss playing for the group, which gathered to sing old camp songs, spirituals, popular ballads. David had financed his college education by playing the piano in blues clubs. The later it got, and the more we drank, the more fervently we sang. One night John stood next to David as he played and I saw that John and Liz and I made a perfect triangle around the piano. John wouldn't look at me, and in a short while he and Liz left together, holding hands.

I could hardly bear it. She was young, she was pretty, she was nice to me; she was his wife and I wasn't. What I was doing was unfair, unkind, and dishonest, went against everything I had been taught, and eroded my sense of myself. Yet I had no intention of changing my behavior. I felt caught in an excruciating trap of my own making. It was a deceiving and complicated web, woven of many different, clinging strands. When John and I were together in bed it brought me the ecstatic highs of passionate lovemaking; when I stood next to him at Treman, my glass in my hand, trying hard not to lean too closely into his shoulder, it took me to a heightened and thrilling realm of tantalizing eroticism, where my senses became so acute I thought I might go mad; and now, watching John and Liz leave, I felt a disgust and self-loathing so piercing I might have done anything to end it.

Blue saw the look on my face and gestured from the door of the barn. "Susan, Susan, come with me." She accompanied me to my room at Cherry Cottage and we spent the rest of the night talking together, sitting cross-legged on my bed. She hugged me as I wept. The scotch I drank so thirstily dulled my pain and confused my thinking so I could stand myself. The dishonesty of my actions went against all that I had been taught explicitly, yet was oddly congruent with what I had been taught by example. A family saying as I had grown up was "Least said, soonest mended." It was better not to speak about thoughts and feelings. I used alcohol to cloak feelings that frightened me, and I used silence to keep from my parents things that would displease them.

Now I was applying those lessons. If I kept the secret that John and I were lovers and drank to avoid dark, unpleasant feelings, I could "handle" the situation. As a drinker I had become accustomed to emotional deceit. The secrecy, excruciating as it was, was familiar, an old friend. Well-worn rationalizations ran through my mind: if Liz doesn't know what is happening, it's not wrong, and she won't be hurt. I decided, even though Blue knew about my affair with John, I could not confide in her. She could know the broad outlines—that he and I were lovers—but I could not share feelings and details. I would keep certain feelings even from John. I would manage my life by saying what the other person wanted to hear, and that would make everything all right. I wrote in my journal, *Talked to Blue last night in my room for hours without telling her a damn thing, mainly because I don't know myself what is going on.*

At last Blue left and I slept off my drunkenness, my jealousy, my loneliness. The next night I approached John after supper. "Come to my room?" He had a large pile of student work with him, under his arm.

"I can't; I have too many manuscripts to read." I had totally forgotten his teaching load at Bread Loaf; that he had a responsibility to writers who'd come to work with him was the farthest thing from my thoughts. He kissed the air in my direction and hurried off toward Maple, hugging his manuscripts. I was flooded with fury. I turned without a word and stalked off to my single room. I was standing behind my closed door, biting my fingers, when there was a knock. I threw the door open and found John standing there. I pulled him into the room and grabbed him tightly. "I couldn't stay away," he breathed in my ear. "I couldn't stay away." Then, in a kind of wonder, "You're as excited as I am."

He seemed surprised that I was quickly aroused and as keenly interested in making love with him as he was with me. Maybe he was conscious of our age difference or of the physical imperfections I had frowned on the year before. He still had the age spots on his hands, the dirty fingernails, the potbelly, but now I looked past those to a man whose spirit I loved. His body, imperfect as it was, seemed only his particular, unique clothing, soon known, familiar, dear.

Since I suffered from jealousy, I decided to see if I could make John jealous and carried on an elaborate and public flirtation with Ambrose Clancy, who had come to visit the conference. At Treman I leaned into Ambrose and watched John's face. It worked: later, when John and I walked away from the cottage, John reached for my hand. "When did Ambrose get back from the poker game?"

It was a meaningful question, because what he was asking me was how much did I think about Ambrose. I made an airy answer. "Oh, not that long ago."

John continued. "I saw you talking with him and my heart went . . ." He didn't finish the sentence, but thumped his chest with his hand. He tightened his grip on my fingers. "I ached for you a lot last year," he said. "A lot."

Over and over in bed John asked, "Be my mistress, be my mistress, be my mistress," and I answered, "I will," as if it were a marriage vow. He asked me about Jack. "You have a boyfriend, don't you?" I nodded. "Tell me about him."

I began to talk, to describe Jack and how I felt, but then stopped. John's face had taken on a look of profound sadness, the kind of desolation you can't fake. "Oh, you look so sad," I cried, and kissed him. "Don't look so sad," I pleaded.

I confessed my fears that Jack wasn't faithful to me. "He goes out with other girls, and he tells me he doesn't sleep with them."

"But you know he does."

Now it was my turn to be sad.

"It's all just chance, who you end up with. If I'd met you first instead of Liz, I'd have married you."

The words burned in my heart. Instead of giving me confidence that someday it would work out, that he would marry me, these words seemed to steal my happiness. I had missed my opportunity for joy in life. I had found the perfect man, a man I could love with trust and uninhibited passion, with body and soul, and because of an accident of timing I would never have him. He had married someone else.

That John was married and evading the tensions of his marriage in an affair, that if he married me he might do the same thing, did not enter my mind. I also overlooked his drinking; in fact, I embraced it. Jack was so straitlaced he was sometimes no fun at all. Jack disapproved of my drinking; I knew John would never do that. With him, I could drink as much as I wanted. That this drinking, his and mine, could become a problem for both of us was not a thought I could think at that time.

Instead, I remembered my feeling in the stairwell in New York when I had heard of his marriage, eighteen months earlier. Why couldn't he have waited? Why hadn't I been more forward when I met him in 1979? I realized now, in hindsight, that I had loved him for a long time. That he was available to me now meant he might have been available to me then. Why hadn't I seen this? Why had I been so shy? In 1979 Liz was only his girlfriend. I decided it was all my fault. I should have approached him earlier. *If I'd met you first instead of Liz, I'd have married you.* The words sank into my heart like a thorn. They seemed to embody all the missed opportunities of life.

As the days of the conference ticked by, each one leading to the end of this magical time, I felt sadness and panic. I wished I could stop the clock and tried to be super aware, brightly awake, so I would remember every detail. The next-to-last night of the conference we stood in Treman, as always, a small group, and suddenly John grabbed me in a tight hug, saying aloud, in front of Blue, Bob Houston, and others, "What is this craziness, and in public, yet!" The night of the last dance, the last Saturday night, I stayed close to John, aching for my chance to be alone with him in my room but, once there, discovered he had drunk so much we could not make love. I was profoundly disappointed. He acknowledged what had happened and apologized.

The next day, Sunday, as all the conference-goers packed their bags, started their cars, churned down the mountain, I was heart-sore with a pain I felt I couldn't show. John sought me out and gave me a quick hug, bending his face to my shoulder, not looking directly at me. I nodded as though it didn't mean anything and watched as he ducked into his car, where Liz waited behind the wheel. She put the car in gear and drove off. One of the writers who had helped Carol Knauss in the office came over to say good-bye. As she hugged me I burst into sobs. She drew away, sur-prised—we weren't that good friends, after all—and patted my shoulder. I was bereft.

8

"Why Don't You and Me—and Liz—Have a Really Brilliant Short Life?"

After the conference in August of 1981, John returned to Susquehanna and SUNY-Binghamton and I went back to my life in Cambridge. Those weeks were difficult. I confided in no one. I resumed my relationship with Jack and did not tell him the truth about John and me. John and I began a passionate correspondence in which he implored me to come to Binghamton.

> How I feel is a vast weariness. I can hardly walk. I pick things up and they fall out of my hands. What are we to do? We're far apart. What insanity to fall in love with someone hundreds of miles away! My whole brain and body ache for you, which makes it hard to think. Also I love Liz no less because of you. How horrible! . . . My heart whams when you tell me you really are my flat-out mistress. But what are we to do? I desire you all the time, and I think I always will.

I had signed a contract with a community college north of Boston to teach a section of technical writing as an adjunct professor. While I was willing to be engaged in a serious love affair with a married man, I was not willing to break a contract I had signed. I felt this committed me to staying in Cambridge, at least through the fall, and planned to move to Binghamton in early winter.

This decision made me uneasy. I felt, obscurely, that no matter what I did, I was wrong. John's letters grew desperate in tone, as if he expected me to drop everything and move right away to Binghamton, to be his mistress while his marriage continued. I didn't like this idea. But I blamed myself that he seemed to be so unhappy with my hesitation.

I had lived in the Boston area for nearly eight years and had painstakingly built a life I loved. Why throw all this away to move to a city where I didn't know anyone, just to be John's mistress? Who did he think I was to make such a sacrifice? And who did he think *he* was to ask such a thing? I read and reread his letters, looking for something to make me hope he would break from Liz and offer to marry me.

In his letters John presented himself as a wronged husband, creating a narrative that was comfortable for me to believe and made it easy for me to think I could be the heroine of the drama. He insisted the marriage was over for reasons that predated his seduction of me. I could believe, reading his letters, that I was a better partner for him and was somehow innocent. It wasn't my fault, and I could win in the end: be his savior and get what I wanted, which was him as my husband.

I realize now that what was lacking in his letters was any self-examination. He wrote about the failure of his marriage as something independent of himself; he was constant and Liz was moving inexorably farther away. However, they still lived together, while he wrote to me, telephoned me, and, in one letter, said he thought about me while he made love to her. That he or his actions were responsible for the distance and the difficulties he and Liz were experiencing was never the issue. That his drinking might have caused a problem did not seem to occur to him. Instead, he wrote of his displeasure that Liz would not make love to him when he had been drinking, as if such a decision were her fault. He also claimed she gave him permission to conduct affairs outside the marriage.

This rhetoric was designed to persuade and it did. I was flattered and intrigued and felt justified in continuing my relationship with him. He was also condescending, insisting he didn't want Liz to be hurt or blamed for any of this, as young as she was.

He stated his love for me in such romantic language that I was quite swept away. No one had ever pursued me with such ardor or used such winning language.

> I think how we made love hour after hour, and every breath you breathed at me made me feel like Odysseus' men at the taste of the lotus: the feeling of faintness, almost death. . . . You're the gentlest, kindest, sweetest woman I've ever known. I hope I'm not being too forward.

He said he would write me his biography and asked me to tell him everything about my life, my parents, my grandparents, all my opinions and thoughts.

With one part of my mind I knew that, if he and Liz worked at it, they could quite possibly communicate clearly enough to repair their marriage. With another part of my mind I did not want this to happen. I wrote to him, *I know too that you really love Liz, and I sometimes feel that I'm robbing her, that the sexual feelings you have for me, and the wonderful energy that you direct toward me, really belong to her.* I also told him that, if he asked me to, I would withdraw and let him sort things out. I was relieved when he did not take me up on this noble gesture. I wanted him now, very badly, and was almost convinced that if I took the chance, and moved to Binghamton, he would indeed separate from Liz and make me his wife.

Now and then I wondered, If John responds to stresses in his marriage to Liz by seeking out another woman, might not the same thing happen if he were committed to me? When I had this thought, I fixed myself a drink and waited for it to go away.

In the meantime, I was enmeshed in my own dishonest relationship with Jack. We talked about my possible move to Binghamton, but I did not tell him that John and I were lovers and exchanging long passionate letters. He guessed, however, what was happening. "If you go to Binghamton and end up just having an affair with John Gardner," he told me, "I wouldn't want anything more to do with you."

"Why not?"

"I wouldn't want to be with someone who went whichever way the wind blew."

This feeling of Jack's was quite logical, but it only drove me deeper into dishonesty. I felt wounded by his remark. At one time I had been willing to commit to Jack wholeheartedly, but that time had passed. Now I was continuing to see him, perhaps out of habit, perhaps out of vanity—pleased to have two men in my life who both wanted me—perhaps as a hedge in case John suddenly turned around and said, It's over.

I was almost totally self-centered and very confused, and because I wasn't telling the truth to anyone, I was filled with anxiety and tension, which I tried to diffuse by drinking.

Well, I thought to myself about Jack, he'll only be really angry if I tell him what is actually happening. I'd better not say anything.

Jack and I had never been close emotionally. I had chosen him mostly because he looked so good. I overlooked our difficulties in communicating our true feelings. Once when he was late to pick me up, I got in the car and, instead of saying hello, said, "You're late." He turned away from me and drove in icy silence until I knuckled under and apologized. Our disagreements most often centered around behavior of mine he found unacceptable. "I'll talk to you when you're feeling better" was his standard remark when I brought up painful subjects.

Money was a sore point also, and neither of us was fair or honest. I was scraping along on a shoestring budget and hoped to be taken care of; he saw me as a gold digger. A fall trip to his rental property on Martha's Vineyard began with a quarrel over the ferry fare. I expected him to pay; he expected me to pay. We were unable to discuss the matter and resolve our differences. Instead, as we became less able to speak to each other, our sexual life grew more passionate. This did not seem a good omen, but I had no idea how to be open and honest in a relationship.

John was totally different. He told me almost everything about his life, sometimes more than I wanted to know, and asked me about mine, and listened to everything I said without once making a judgment. I felt he approved of me, and his approval was no small thing. I needed this feeling so badly that it seemed worth the pain of what he was asking me to do: accept a partial place in his life. I felt I could confide in John and be myself and not what someone wanted me to be. Because I had cloaked my feelings for such a long time, letting people see only what I felt they would accept, to think that John accepted me as I was felt like liberation. Later, when I lived with John, I discovered that he did expect certain behaviors. Some of my feelings he would accept, and others he would not. However, in our courtship and our long-distance relationship, I felt we looked on each other as the safe haven the rest of the world denied us.

John's letters were those of a tender and ardent lover. My relationship with Jack was troubling and not emotionally satisfying, and I was lonely and eager for an enthusiastic lover. Even though John could not and would not commit to me, my hungry heart was quick to accept his protestations of love, delivered in his direct, idiosyncratic style. The words seemed so important. We were not perfect people; we were alcoholic and dishonest, convincing ourselves that the physical, spiritual, and emotional attraction we felt was supremely important. I have wondered in bitter moments if John turned to me because I was a drinker and condoned his drinking, and Liz was not and did not. In hindsight I can say that we were both addictive personalities—addicted to each other. He was as intrigued and mystified by it as I. "You know how hungry my mouth gets for yours and how when we hug hello our two bodies come together like electron and proton." The strength of this mutual attraction was undeniable and seemed to mean that our connection should be inevitable. Simultaneously we created and fulfilled each other's romantic fantasies.

I increased my emotional stake in our relationship by writing him letters where I told him stories I had told no one else. These were not necessarily confessions of wrongdoing but, rather, incidents from my life that out of long habit I had kept to myself.

When I returned from my trip on the *Regina Maris*, I had spent an evening regaling friends with tales of my adventures on the high seas. At the end of one monologue my host remarked coolly, "That's enough, Susan." I was startled and decided that if I wanted to fit into the hip Cambridge scene, I had better keep still about my real passions. This was unwise thinking, a pattern of trying to please people.

With John I felt no such restraints and wrote to him freely.

I have done a number of foolhardy things, most notably, I suppose, climbing into the stainless-steel rigging of a tall ship at four in the morning, wearing fifty pounds of foul-weather gear, to furl a sail eighty feet above the deck in an electrical storm. The man I climbed up with was scared; I was crazy. I told him, "You better remember this, it's the most fun you're ever going to have." When we got up there it was as dark as it is when you close your eyes, except for the flashes of phosphorescence in the water below and the St. Elmo's fire to our side. It was pretty amazing, with the ship bucking and rearing like something alive underneath us. The rigging is slippery too, when it gets wet, and you slip a lot (I did) but you catch yourself with your hands.

One nice day, I remember, I went up in the rig and took a nap up on the royal yard. I climbed up on top of the sail, about a hundred feet above the deck, and looked out over the sea and the funny little islands (we were sailing off Newfoundland), and sat on the yard, and hooked my arm around the mast, and fell asleep for a while, in the sun. Melville described being up in the rigging as walking across the surface of the sea on gigantic stilts; he wasn't far wrong.

I wasn't afraid of heights, loved being up "in the rig," as we called it on shipboard, and on at least one other occasion had taken a different kind of chance, in an urban setting. I wrote to John about this as well.

Back to the part where I wasn't scared. The way I got this apartment, which, I should inform you, is the Best Apartment in Cambridge, really a gem, was to finagle a Harvard student ID and assume an innocent air and go to the Harvard student housing agency, which lists the best apartments in Cambridge. So Jamie, my friend who was then a freshman at Harvard, got me the ID and said I had to return it by noon the day I used it. So I was waiting for him in the parking lot behind his dorm (Pennypacker Hall) just before noon on a Thursday in March, when I saw this guy, tall, white, bearded, [wearing a] leather coat, come running through the parking lot, carrying a woman's purse. And behind him I hear someone yelling "Stop, thief!"

It took me a minute to react. It's not like in the comic books where there's a balloon over someone's head to identify them, plus I had an armload of books and papers (I was working for some awful bogus publishers as a proofreader), and I put them on a car and ran after. Jamie came out of the dining hall, just then, across the street, saw me running, and he and his friends ran too. Jamie and I were shipmates on the *Regina Maris*, and he was a good sailor, level-headed and unafraid.

There were about six of us chasing this guy down the street, I was kinda in the lead but I'm not a fast runner, and he was gaining ground, and I was afraid we'd lose him. But there was a student walking up the street toward us, and one of Jamie's friends yelled "Stop that guy!" so the kid kind of bumped into him, and they both fell down, and the thief said, "Stay away from me, I've got a gun, you'll get shot." The kid who'd bumped into him backed away, because he was on the right side of the thief, but I was behind him, and had caught up to him at that point, and threw my arms around his waist and said, through my teeth, into his right ear, "You haven't got any fucking gun, man." And I was right. He dropped the bag, I grabbed it with my left hand, he ran, and we let him go.

A couple of the guys ran after him, but since we had what we wanted there wasn't the same energy. . . . We walked back up the street, and pretty soon here was this middle-aged lady in a black cloth coat and black scarf tied over her hair and around her chin, leaning on a younger man and sniffling. I held up the bag and said "Is this yours?"

I felt safe, sharing these stories with John. I knew he would read and understand and accept. And in his letters to me he was unguarded, open, revealing.

I was a motorcycle racer. (Motah-sickle, we would have said.) In nineteen something-or-other I was the tri-state [sic] champion—Ohio, Penn, and NY. I was a fool. When I was sixteen (when I won it), I wasn't impressed that some guy's head blushed blood down forty feet along a wall. I didn't even look. It was true that that wouldn't have happened to me—I was too smart. Honest. If I knew I was going to spin out, I'd have laid down the bike and saved myself (I did that, time to time). Later I realized that not everybody is cool, and I couldn't comfortably exist in a world where people died, whether bad bikers or good. In those days I thought, if you're not good, you get what you deserve. (I still think only bad bikers die; but that's no longer, for me, the issue.) I did not quit for honorable reasons. I quit because, thoughtfully considering the matter, I knew I couldn't compete beyond what I'd done.

The letter continues with some insights about his drinking.

My culture is a violently whiskey culture, not to mention depressive and desperate, and much as I hate drinking—as I really do—it seems to me, as to generations of my people, the only viable alternative to suicide.

I have what is called, among those who know, the "Welsh blacks," that is, terrible, deep depressions. I don't know why it's common among the Welsh, but it is—maybe other groups have it too, but they're not so arrogant as to mention it. Sometimes, like my father and grandfather and all my uncles I go to the woods and lie there crying for three days. I cannot deny that it's profoundly goofy, but I do it. . . . Once when I was in such a mood (this is the truth), when I was in Southern Illinois, I lay in a sort of cave that was in fact a fox's den. When I came to myself, foxes (little ones) were playing all around me. All I did was open my eyes and they scattered. But I know that for some time (though *I* wasn't there) I had been feeling their presence. . . . It was wonderful and strange.

John's self-concept seemed to ricochet. One letter expressed a high in which he felt he could control the world, could be vastly manipulative:

I kept at the edge of all that, typically [of a conversation between Liz and one of their friends about marriage and marital conflict]. I always try to let the world go its way, never touching the levers, waiting for emergencies.

Another letter revealed an astonishing low.

Who wouldn't die cheerfully in place of the one one loves? I'll tell you the truth—with all my heart I believe it's the truth—I would happily die not just to save my father's life but merely to make him well again.

John's father had suffered a debilitating stroke. I believed what John said, but I was puzzled. I didn't see that his sacrifice should be required or would make the difference he wanted it to make.

John never used the words "divorce" or "I will marry you." I was waiting for those words. He implored me to come to Binghamton but wouldn't offer me what I wanted; we were at a stalemate. He presented my role in his life as part of a continuing triangle; for my part, I looked past those direct remarks that would have showed me, if I had paid attention, that whatever happened he did not intend totally to separate from Liz.

> I, like Achilles, have a predictably short life. I drink and smoke like a maniac; I never sleep. I would like to be a better person. I think about it. But I give you my word, I can't. Why don't you and me—and Liz—have a really brilliant short life?

I ignored this sign of possible trouble and began the process of applying to the graduate program at SUNY-Binghamton so I could begin study in January 1982.

While I felt that I had many friends in Cambridge, I did not confide in them. I tried, once. I sought out one friend, a psychotherapist. Over lunch I threw down my gauntlet: "John Gardner and I are having an affair." Sheila dropped her fork, on her face an expression of shock. I decided she was overly conservative and disapproved of me because she was a married woman. I resolved not to confide more. Much later I found out her true reaction: "I was worried about you. If he'd been serious, he would have left his wife, tied up the loose ends, then pursued you."

I isolated myself with my confusing feelings and, in late October, drove back up to Vermont with Arlene to a "Bread Loaf Reunion Weekend." John and I had planned a romantic rendezvous. He had told me, "As Napoleon wrote to Josephine, don't wash." In the car I greeted Arlene flippantly with, "Well, and what's the gossip?" She gave me a shrewd look. "The gossip, Susan, is all about you."

In the crisp air, the frosty mornings, and the chilly rooms of the inn, John and I met again, and our love and erotic attraction was as before. Liz had stayed in Pennsylvania; Saturday afternoon he got out of bed to telephone her at home and got no answer. "Gone forever," he said, as he rejoined me. That he couldn't reach her and seemed so casual about it was reassuring. Maybe they were breaking up after all. I had begun to work on a way to finance my move to Binghamton. The Massachusetts Council on the Arts now had a small fund that could be given out as financial aid to previous fellowship winners. I wrote a grant proposal and asked John to send me a letter of recommendation.

I returned to Cambridge, still in love with John and hopeful about his love for me. I wrote to him, *I was so happy to see you and be with you in Vermont, it was wonderful, a hundred years of happy nights.*

A few days later, I cautiously pushed open the door of my apartment, knowing the mail fell through the letter slot onto the floor, and sorted quickly through the envelopes until I found a letter from John. I opened it carefully. Like all his letters, it was densely typed, single-spaced, the only handwritten word his signature. I sank immediately onto the couch, not able to take in what I was reading.

I read a Dear Abbey [sic] column that explains when men love other women it's always false and crappy. It explains that the other woman is always just a toy: if he betrays his wife he'll betray his mistress too. Men are shitty, it says. The thing worried me a little. Correction: a lot. I love terribly and seriously—I think you will never meet anyone who loves more of either—but I'm promiscuous. I don't brag. I make no mistakes about whom I love and whom I make love with. In Florida, from where I called you, I got terribly drunk one night and was persuaded by seven girls to go out swimming (I had no suit, neither did any of them, or if they did, they hid them) in the Gulf with the sharks and sting-rays [sic]. I ended up sleeping with all of them, one by one and some by some. I know if I told Liz she'd understand, and I hope you will too. . . . (I didn't tell Liz. It scares me to tell you.)

The piece of paper shook in my hands. I had no idea how to respond. A college friend had once confided being part of a group sex encounter that ended with his feeling empty and sad. "It meant less than a handshake," he told me, shaking his head. "Less than a handshake." I didn't remember that when I read John's letter. Instead, I tried to picture this incident and failed.

The letter continued:

I thought, after I read the Dear Abbey [sic] column, that maybe you'd ultimately like me better if we were only dear friends. Not that that's what I want. I have a thousand thoughts at once, each more complicated than the last. . . . Every which way up is terrible darkness. What would you think of this: you come for a day or two, as you once did before, to talk about your fiction? I will pay your fare. I really will talk with you about your fiction, and also talk with you sensibly about whether or not you should come here to study.

Boy do I miss you. All this gloom and despair is really only hunger. Come. Let's work on your fiction and then figure out what's next.

What bothered me most was *talk with you sensibly about whether or not you should come here to study*. I had been getting mixed signals from Jack, who would pointedly not call for days at a time and then show up with a card or flowers and a special invitation. Now John was putting up a barrier. I had thought he wanted me. Now what? On top of that, this startling confession.

I was surprised by his story, and also disbelieving. I decided maybe he was bluffing and I would call his bluff.

When I read your letter the first time I felt really cold all over and frightened and betrayed (the old "he did our things with another girl" routine; though obviously I know you make love with Liz, jealousy really isn't a mistress's privilege). Then it seemed kind of humorous almost (if you'll forgive me). I mean, seven? I'm kind of curious about it. Is it the most erotic thing you've ever done? Did you approach sensory overload? How did all the bodies arrange themselves and who first grabbed your cock? And what happened the next day? Will you write me a descriptive essay about it? (I'm serious.)

He answered:

That essay you wanted. There's not much to tell, or anyway not much I'm able to figure out how to tell. Certainly I don't do our things with strangers, because it would be impossible. Making love with you my heart and cock are indivisible, and I feel no awkwardness or fear or unease; even the thought that we might get caught doesn't scare me. If we did we'd simply have to deal with it, and obviously part of me wants to. . . . The main thing about making love with seven girls on a beach is that everything is sandy, gritty. A lot of the sex play is petting, which starts with wiping off sand. You're very drunk, of course, or you wouldn't have gotten into it in the first place—at least I wouldn't—and so are the girls. Some of the time they play with each other—it's nice to watch; nice to touch them, too. Some of the time they all play with you. You lie face down and they brush sand off you (we went swimming first), their hands are as soft as feather dusters. I was lying with my legs apart, and I was dusted very clean before I was lured (not unexpectedly) into turning over, to be dusted again, massaged, kissed everywhere, and handled. Two girls, one with wonderful long blond hair, kissed each other and moved their breasts over my skin, chest to groin, and then the girl with brown hair came down on me (as they say), still kissing the other girl; very strange and exciting. When you've come about three times your nuts ache like crazy and you think you'll never come again, but you do. Your chief feeling right after each time you come is terrible vulnerability: you know all these people know this thing about you, and you feel sick at the betrayal of those you really love, people—you and Liz—whom you think to be infinitely less barbarian, not to mention infinitely more beloved. Afterward we went up to the apartment in a condo and showered and slept on the beds and carpet, woke up with headaches, and pussyfooted around. I left early (the time changed that night so I left an hour earlier than I thought I was leaving— 8 A.M.), kissed good-bye at the door by a long-faced not very pretty Irish girl. It was interesting and thrilling, but once is enough for one lifetime. It's hard to be pure animal. I doubt that anyone can really pull it off, however they may try. It's far more thrilling, believe it or not, to be pure animal with someone you deeply love, because then the pure animal part is strangely mixed with the angel part, and everything is clean and sweet and shameless.

I hope it's OK to tell you all this. You asked. I figure you asked partly from curiosity, partly to find out by reading between the lines whether or not I am a shit. I hope I'm not, but I guess you have to decide. I love you terribly, and I'm not sorry about it, though I do feel this one streak of guilt, the fact that my loving you steals you from whomever it is you're supposed to be happy with all your life. I agree with your friend that you shouldn't be wasting time—not because you're getting no younger so much as because you are one of earth's great treasures and shouldn't be misused. I love making love with you, and I love what you are, the writer, the person, the woman, the friend.

This response, the essay I had asked for, took me by surprise. I had been half expecting him to say he had made the whole thing up. I sometimes felt that he showed himself to me in the worst possible light in an effort to drive me away, to see if I would, at last, turn and run at some new, painful revelation.

I would have been more hurt and threatened if he had confided a love or infatuation with another woman. Meaningless sex was just that, meaningless. I was surprised that his desperation should take this form, but it seemed removed: he had been on a reading tour, in Florida; he'd been drinking. . . . I told myself that if I were with him on a day-to-day basis that kind of thing wouldn't happen.

His next letter continued with remarks about this group sex adventure.

> My darling, I have so much to say I hardly know where to start. First, I guess, I wrote that letter about the seven ladies under duress, because you wanted me to, and I do what you ask. But I wonder if I really made clear how I feel: that it was shameful and scary and I never want anything of the sort to happen to me again (or: to admit responsibility: never want ever again to do that). Nature is nature and drunk is drunk, but it's just not true that one can fuck anyone and it's just fun. The heart is never really divorced, at least for me, from the genitals, though one wishes it might be. I felt sick with guilt for days—no, weeks, by now— and I don't think it's pious Christian guilt.

Then, another adventure:

> I also fucked [another writer from the conference]. Went to Washington, sworn never again to make love lightly, but sure enough I did, and it was awful—worse than the seven. . . . She allowed as how she would like to have a child on account of my high IQ, and I would never have anything to do with her raising (or his), and gin-socked as I was it seemed a good idea. When I left in the morning she said she never wanted to see me again except if she wasn't pregnant. She would gladly see me again and again until she was pregnant, and then nevermore. Though it may seem a bit dramatic to mention, when I left her I vomited.

I remembered this woman and how she had targeted John, even stalked him. She had an intense negative energy; I was naive enough to think that John of all people could see through her and leave her alone. Later I asked him why he had gone to see her. He had told me he had supper plans with old friends who seemed infinitely safer than this woman. He shrugged. "I had the shakes, I had to be with someone." He had invited me to come to Washington with him, but I had demurred; I expected him to hide me in a motel room to keep his Washington friends from knowing he was not with Liz, so I told him it seemed too much a mistress-y thing to do. I hadn't realized his terror of being alone in motel rooms, the extent to which his drinking had eroded his control and his self-concept.

In another letter in early November, 1981, John wrote:

> Tonight Liz and I had a long and interesting conversation, painfully accurate on her part (she is certainly the smartest person I've ever known), about our love life. . . . Little by little she begins to think of me as her dear best friend but more like a brother than like a husband. I feel (I told her) the same about her. . . . We talked, jokingly but not so jokingly, about whom I might take as a lover. . . . There was only one person she said she'd be frightened by. You.

I was startled. The irony was striking, and Liz's intuition did seem to be extraordinary. On the other hand, that they should joke about whom John might take as a lover indicated that their marriage really was in trouble. I wasn't sure I could ever joke like that. I began to wonder if I could really understand this triangle.

Then he mentioned a new element: a former boyfriend of Liz's named David Bosnick, who was planning to come to SUNY-Binghamton to study. David had grown up with Liz and, John wrote, *He* [David] *loves her more than he loves his own life.*

John was terrified of being left alone. In one letter, he wrote,

What if it all ends in terrible tragedy—I lose you or Liz or both? Especially both?

His confessions of sexual adventures continued to bother him.

> Having violated my Liz-contract with you, I think I tried to make the violation total and therefore not important, but all that came of it was the ghastly discovery that I love you and only you. No exceptions. I don't know what to do with this. I wish you would fall in love with some wonderful man worthy of you, so you'd be forever out of my life except as a friend. I love you more than anything, and I think if we were together for two months I would be so boring to you that . . . [His thought ends with this elision.]
>
> It bothers me that I can easily tell you all my stupidities and sins, and I can't tell them to Liz, though once I could. She could handle them, I think—the seven ladies and all that. All but the last sin, that I love you.

In late November 1981, I went to Binghamton for the weekend. John and I met in his office at the university, and he took me over to the nearby Holiday Inn, where he had made a reservation for me. As soon as we were alone in the motel room, he began to make love to me. He pressed me into the bed, saying, "I love you, I love you," in a despairing tone of voice, the voice of a man trying to convince himself. This unsatisfying encounter only made me sad.

At his office in the university he turned to the story I had brought with me. This was a new draft of the story we had discussed when I had visited his house in Susquehanna twelve months earlier. At his desk John switched gears from despairing lover to efficient teacher, and we went over the story carefully, line by line. He approved my changes, sat back, lit his pipe, and, in the cloud of fragrant smoke, made comments and suggestions. Here he was at ease, genuinely helping, a solid editor. We avoided talking about whether I should move to Binghamton. It was clear that he was my best possible teacher, the only one I had found, but the ambiguity of the situation was stressful, and heightened by Liz's arrival. We all three went to dinner at Copperfield's, his favorite restaurant at the nearby mall.

The evening was tense. I recalled family dinners where I was on my best behavior, making conversation, hiding from my parents what was in my heart. As a girl I had grown used to keeping up a mannered, polished exterior, and, while I loved my parents, I decided early on not to confide too much in them, especially during my adolescent and college years. Questions, confusions, my awakening sexuality—all these were matters I puzzled over, pretending I could handle them all alone. I was used to strained, polite dinners where those involved kept their own counsel and made small talk to cover their distance and unease.

The dinner at Copperfield's with John and Liz reminded me of that. Liz told me they had recently purchased a new puppy, Teddy, because her beagle had been killed by a school bus. I said I was sorry about Esmé. We changed the subject and spoke brightly of the creative writing program, its faculty and visiting speakers. I smiled and asked questions and expressed enthusiasm, all the while wondering, How much does Liz suspect? and wishing I had the moral courage to put down my fork and say, Look here, there's something the three of us need to talk about. John and I are lovers, and I want to know where we go from here. I couldn't do it. I took my lead from John, who kept his reserve and ate his meal with impeccable manners.

When we got up from dinner, Liz reached for her coat. We had both slung our coats over the back of the fourth chair at the table. As she opened hers to put it on, she stared at the inside lining and gasped. A dark stain of some kind streaked down the lining. "It's blood!"

I leaned over and examined the stain. "No, it's not. It's raspberry syrup."

Liz burst out laughing. "What a difference in worldview!"

We never did figure out what the stain really was or how it got on Liz's coat, but the tension of the evening was somewhat eased.

The three of us drove back to the university campus, where the students were presenting *Damn Yankees*. We had seats in the first row of the balcony. I sat on John's left, and Liz sat on his right. I watched the play with interest; it was a lively comedy and the students were doing a good job.

Afterward we went backstage. The dressing room was hot and crowded; students in various stages of costume, dress, and undress jostled and pushed, leaned into mirrors, accepted congratulatory hugs, bouquets of flowers.

We made small talk, congratulated everyone, and then John went to the parking lot to get the car. At the curb I held the door of the car for Liz. Her long skirt swirled around her ankles. She hesitated, then slid across the wide front seat to sit next to John. I felt tense and wrought up with the weight of many unspoken thoughts. John dropped me at the Holiday Inn, and he and Liz drove to Susquehanna. I had a miserable night alone at the motel. I longed to telephone John, but didn't dare, and spent hours staring at the phone as if I could will him to telephone me. He didn't call, and the next day I drove back to Cambridge.

I felt the affair had suddenly gone awry. The magic was gone; we were only making each other unhappy. John felt much the same. After this visit he wrote to me:

> Whatever may happen between Liz and me, you have fallen in love with a maniac. I wish it weren't so. I love you beyond all words, and I'm afraid that will ruin everything for us.

I was beginning to have serious doubts. If my visit in November set the pattern he intended to follow—that I was expected to be passionate in motel rooms and polite and pleasant around Liz—I didn't want to move.

On December 2, I wrote John a letter where I backed off. *It scares me to tell you this, but I'm afraid, now, of precipitating a break between you and Liz because I haven't yet sorted out my*

107

own feelings about my life. My letter closed with the assertion that I loved him, but my message was ambivalent at best.

Meanwhile, John and Liz were still struggling with their marriage. Liz had spoken about moving out of their house to an apartment, and he continued to assert that he wanted to keep both of us in his life. He lied to Liz, saying that he and I were only good friends, and reported that her feelings were more hurt by that than if he had told her he and I were lovers. He wrote, *Why did we have to be born in a century that doesn't allow multiple husband-wife marriages? . . . How dare I suggest that we all live together?*

I didn't take this seriously, as I knew I would never move in with him if he were still living with Liz. I was willing to be part of a triangle, but not a ménage à trois. That he asserted he still loved Liz seemed to me noble, honest, more direct than the husband in the bad joke who whines about his wife. I denied that this continuing feeling might make a problem for me later.

In a day or two I received another letter: *I really want to be loved, truly and completely, though I don't demand it and am afraid—seriously afraid—I never can be, finally, when my loved one gets to know me well.* John had mythologized his own past and had always interpreted his brother's accidental death as his own fault. He saw himself as monstrous and feared that others, seeing him that way too, would turn aside. This doubt and this grandiosity are typical of thinking distorted by alcohol. Alcoholism is a disease of isolation; the alcoholic feels alone, misunderstood, special, sometimes more lovable, sometimes less lovable, than anyone else and falls easily into self-pity. John was a man of intense sensitivity and intellect but in his wildly swinging self-concept, and in his fear that he would never be loved, I see the effects of alcohol.

One night John telephoned and I spoke of my misery at leaving Cambridge, and all at once he gave up. He suggested that I not come to Binghamton after all.

This gave me immediate relief, which John heard in my voice.

A few days later, the phone woke me one morning at three-thirty: John calling to tell me he and Liz would work things out. She had examined the phone bills scattered on the counter and questioned him about all the calls to me; he had confessed nothing, only that I was a dear friend that he "desperately needed." They had a painful discussion; they agreed to recommit to their marriage. I was out of the picture.

"I understand," I said into the phone, clutching it so tightly my fingers ached. "It's for the best. It's the right thing." After we rang off I sat on the couch without moving, watching the changing light until 8 A.M. My silence and my shock were characteristic. As I had when I was an adolescent, I isolated myself with my secret, with my confusing, conflicting emotions, with my story. I sat miserably on the couch in my apartment, wishing that what had happened had not happened, trying to deny it had. If I told someone, that only made it real. At last I decided it was late enough in the morning that I wouldn't be too much trouble to someone, so I went out, bought a bag of bagels, and went to a friend's house.

"What's the matter," she implored, as soon as she saw me. "You look so awful."

I shook my head. "I can't tell you."

She insisted. "Are you pregnant?"

I ignored her heartfelt concern. I sat at her kitchen table and couldn't tell her anything. It would have given me immense relief to confide in her; I couldn't even cry. I asked about her life and hid my heartache that my affair was over. John had reconciled with Liz; I was desolate. It was, after all, what I thought I wanted.

However, somehow the air was now clear, and even if it was painful, I decided to accept this new role. I knew my relationship with Jack would end if I went to Binghamton, but I felt better about pursuing graduate work if my relationship with John was that of friend rather than lover. He could still be a good teacher, I had seen that in November, and I still wanted to learn what he could teach me about writing. The frightening pressure was suddenly off. I also had a gift, one of those sudden moments of insight that occur in conversation where suddenly you hear what you want to hear.

I had discussed subletting my apartment to a friend from my trip on the *Regina Maris*. David Omar White was a well-known artist in Cambridge. He was then single, in his fifties, an eccentric sort; he needed a place to stay, I needed a subtenant. He listened to my muddled musings about going off to Binghamton. I didn't tell him the truth, of course—I was seldom truthful with anyone in those days—but he could sense my dismay. At last he said, "You know, in my life, all the decisions I made for my art, even though they seemed crazy at the time, always worked out for the best."

I jumped up and caught him in a sudden hug that surprised both of us. Here was my answer. I was an artist. I would commit to my art. I would go to Binghamton to study with John; I would work really hard. I would sublimate all my frustrated love and write wonderful short stories—it seemed so simple. Meanwhile Omar could keep my apartment, and if I were truly unhappy in Binghamton, I could come back and it would all work out. Suddenly I had a clear direction. My mind was made up. I was kidding myself, of course, but I believed it at the time. I told Omar he could have the apartment and I would move to Binghamton.

In the meantime, John and I were still exchanging letters with the understanding that we were only dear friends. He wrote to me that he would be at the MLA conference in New York after Christmas to speak at a panel; I decided to meet him there.

John had been sandbagged into a talk that was a showdown with the "moral majority." He was slated to speak on "Literature and Morality," paired not with another writer but with a politician. The literary equivalent of a brawl was confidently expected, but the organizers of the talk were disappointed. John arrived wearing a banker's suit, an extravagantly expensive silk necktie, and glossy wing-tip shoes. He used his exquisite manners to disarm his opponent and spoke only mildly about art and writing. The expected fistfight, the exhibit of bad behavior by the fierce critic, the motorcycle-riding wild man, did not occur. He had been set up and knew it; he was careful to avoid the snare. His talk completed, a group of us went for lunch: Liz; John's sister Sandy, who had come in from Detroit for the afternoon; Eddie Epstein, to whom John had dedicated *The Sunlight Dialogues*; Harold Brodkey and his wife, Ellen Schwamm; other guests.

After lunch, Liz, John, Sandy, and I walked down Madison Avenue. Liz was swathed in her mother's stunning full-length mink coat. John wore his black topcoat and the hat pictured on the jacket flap of *Mickelsson's Ghosts*. Sandy also wore a dark wool coat; her long blond hair spread out over her shoulders. I remember her scarlet nails and spike heels. As we strolled along, all four of us arm in arm, I remember a transcendent happiness, as if the universe contracted all its sweetness into this one moment. That afternoon in New York, I realized I was honestly happy to be with John, to have him in my life in whatever fashion was best for him. I no longer had to be the compliant mistress; I could be his friend. We came to the street corner where we were to part and I left them, Liz, John, and Sandy, still standing arm in arm. "Be happy," Sandy called to me.

"She will," John said. "She will."

9

"I Threw Snowballs at Your Window"

I left Cambridge on a snowy, blustery day and arrived in Binghamton nine hours later. My car slowed to 40 mph on the hills leading into New York's southern tier as I wiped anxiously at the windshield and prayed that the weak defroster would continue to work. I hadn't asked for directions and wound up on the wrong side of town; John and Liz were waiting for me at John's office. I arrived very late, and we all went to dinner.

Jack and I had parted casually. He promised to stay in touch with me, but we both knew our relationship was ending.

My circle of acquaintances had provided me with friends in Binghamton, with whom I stayed for a few days. John had suggested to his colleagues that they write to me, and I'd had several welcoming letters. I called a real estate agent and rented a furnished second-story apartment on the south side of town, not far from the university.

Binghamton was as much a contrast to the bustling, exciting world of Cambridge and Boston as I had feared. A city of 55,000 souls, it had steadily lost population since its glory days in the 1950s and looked to me like a third-rate copy of Rochester. The shabby downtown was deserted after five o'clock; as soon as I located the only independent bookstore in town I learned it was closing. The nearby grocery store reminded me of the Star Market of my childhood, except that it smelled worse and the produce section offered only woody or wilting vegetables.

The stairs and hallway of my apartment building looked like a cheap hotel from the 1920s, and my carpeted apartment had an odd, musty smell. There were no storm sashes for the ancient hand-cranked French windows. Across the hall from me lived an elderly spinster. She was wrinkled and crook-backed and wore a glossy, ill-fitting wig. She told me she had lived here in the Bingham Arms for thirty years. I pitied her.

In Cambridge I had been used to walking everywhere and spent many evenings browsing the brightly lit bookstores of Harvard Square, going to films, visiting friends. In Binghamton I was thrown back on my own resources. I couldn't keep up a schedule of daily walks because the sidewalks in my neighborhood were sheets of ice. I joined the downtown YWCA and swam endless laps in the small, overheated, and heavily chlorinated pool.

I gritted my teeth, set up my typewriter, and went to work, typing and retyping my stories. I enrolled in John's fiction-writing workshop and attended all his lectures to his undergraduate classes. I investigated the library, wandering up and down the stacks, unable at first to decode the cataloging system. I sorely missed the familiar Boston and Cambridge public libraries, where I had readily located my favorite books.

I was in a financial bind. The Project Finishing Grant I had applied for from the Massachusetts Council on the Arts had been awarded, and I had been given $1,250 to finish a novella I had submitted in outline. This was my only income. John had promised me a fellowship but announced one afternoon in his office, "There's no money. I gave it to David." He meant David Bosnick. I was shocked. What was I going to do? I had confidently and wrongly expected Binghamton to be cheaper than Cambridge, but my studio apartment cost nearly as much as the gem I had left behind in Cambridge, and I was very short on cash. I didn't mention this to John, nor did I protest his decision to give the fellow-ship money to David. He presented it as a fait accompli. I always disliked confrontations. I decided I'd have to manage as best I could on the money I had.

In spite of my unhappiness with my surroundings, I felt im-mensely happy to be near John. Knowing he was nearby so I could speak with him, hear his ideas, attend his classes gave me real joy. I noticed that when he visited campus he dressed up; he had a blue velveteen jacket more appropriate for evening wear that he wore often on days we saw each other. I remember him striding down the ground-floor corridor of the library tower, flinging open the double glass doors that closed it off, and calling my name when he saw me.

I loved being around him and the community of writers he had created at Binghamton. The electricity of his teaching drew a gath-ering of students and teachers deeply committed to writing as art. This was not just a graduate school grind, it was a group of indi-viduals with real drive and passion, who discussed books and ideas with the same energy John did, convinced that writing and thinking were the most important of human activities. John's energy drew the group, and the synergy of the group dynamic supported John's interests; clearly he thrived in an atmosphere where what he loved most was paramount.

I noticed everything: the filled sign-up sheets for student appoint-ments on John's door, with time marked out in half-hour intervals; the Hagar the Horrible cartoon he had taped under his name, with Hagar, the red-bearded Viking, brandishing his sword at his ene-mies but always giving in to his wife; the cartoonish oil painting John had done and hung over his desk, showing hunters in a snowy woods watched by woodland creatures they couldn't see. On John's desk were the same cheap tin ashtrays I had noticed on my earlier visits, and the shelves were crammed with untidy piles of books, manuscripts, folders. It was a busy, bright office. The light reflected off the snow in the parking lot outside, and John's fragrant pipe smoke added atmosphere as he hunched over student work, puddles of water collecting, unnoticed, under his boots.

One snowy night I drove down to Pennsylvania with another student, Alexis Khoury, to have dinner with John and Liz. Alexis was an undergraduate who had come to SUNY-Binghamton to study writing because she had read the same article about John I had read in *The New York Times Magazine*. John had given me careful directions, but as Alexis and I took the exit off Route 81 south, I turned the wrong way and soon became disoriented in the dark, empty streets of the little village of Great Bend, Pennsylvania. It was six o'clock, as dark as your pocket. Alexis and I drove up and down, not finding the route John had told us to look for. At last we spotted a lone pedestrian. I rolled down my window and called to her, asking for Route 171 to Susquehanna. "Oh," she said. "Do you know where they are building the McDonald's?" The only business I had noticed at the highway interchange had been a lonely Stop and Shop. "No," I said, "we're not from here, we don't know nothing." I was irritated enough to abandon my grammar.

"Well," she continued, "McDonald's is a restaurant." Beside me Alexis convulsed with laughter. I listened, impatient, until I got information I could understand.

We arrived at last at John and Liz's, stamped the snow off our boots, and called out. John came out from his study, Liz came downstairs, the house was warm and light, and we all had dinner in the dining room. After dinner Liz disappeared upstairs, and John and I talked, ignoring Alexis. She remembered later, "You and John were pretty intent on each other."

Alexis and I left after ten, and I dropped her off at her apartment and went on to my own. I was thinking things over. Was it enough to be only John's friend? I wanted more.

As before, John and I would meet to discuss my fiction. One afternoon when we were alone in his office, we suddenly ran out of things to say. He drew on his pipe, exhaled, and looked directly at me. "Why don't we have these conferences at your apartment?" I knew right away what he meant. As at Bread Loaf, I knew I would say yes, but I didn't know what it might mean.

I could have said no and kept the relationship we had created of "dear friends," but I didn't want to. I was lonely, I was still in love with him, and we were now living close together; I welcomed him back into my life as my lover.

I was working at my desk alone in my apartment one afternoon when the telephone rang; I was surprised to hear Liz's voice, asking if she could come over. I agreed, with no idea of what to expect. She arrived within the hour, and I waved to her from my window; she smiled up at me and I went down to let her in. She looked around the apartment. We made jokes about the mouse-colored carpet, the general smell of age and old dust; she remarked on the Murphy bed, a feature that dated from the 1920s, that came down out of the wall, transforming a living/sitting room into a bedroom. She exclaimed about the antiquated refrigerator, opened it, and joked about how little it held. At last she sat on the scratchy couch with an air of I-guess-you-know-why-I'm-here and said, "Well."

I held my breath.

"What are you working on? May I read one of your stories?"

I hastened to my writing desk and gathered the first few pages of a story. Its setting was Rochester, its protagonist a school administrator who represses his homosexuality. He has a one-night encounter with a visiting male dancer from New York and pours his frustrated energies into memories and fantasies of a longer relationship with this man, who leaves his bed, never to return. The eroticism of the story drew from my nights at Treman, standing next to John with a drink in my hand, knowing that Liz waited for him in Maple.

I handed Liz the typed sheets and sat down gingerly next to her, watching as she read. "This is really good," she said. I still held some pages in my hand. "More, more." She gestured with her free hand and I handed her the remaining sheets. When she got to the end she looked up. "This is all you've done?"

I nodded.

"You have to finish this. This is terrific. But don't you think . . ." She made a suggestion for a scene that would strengthen the plot line, and I began to relax.

Later, John and I spoke on the phone. "How did the visit go?" he asked.

"Fine," I said. "She read one of my stories; she really liked it."

"That's wonderful," he said. "She's a wonderful editor, the best teacher we've got."

He may have thought it wonderful, but I was highly uneasy. I had no wish·to build a friendship based on false premises with Liz while I was in love with her husband. Liz had always been cordial and now was supportive of my writing. As time passed the intensity of the misery I felt at Bread Loaf had faded, and I was careful to keep feelings of self-hatred and wretchedness at bay. However, I did feel the worst sort of sneak and had no idea what John would do next. In spite of the ardor of his letters, and in spite of our having recommended our relationship as lovers, he made no move to tell Liz the truth, and the triangle we had earlier established continued in an uneasy balance.

If John didn't ask me to move in with him, I certainly wasn't going to beg or even press him for a commitment. For the time being I was content to let things ride. I was prideful. I'd always made my own way; I continued to do so.

One incident might have warned me off, but I didn't let it. John was lecturing, and I was taking notes when he turned his head and I realized the purplish-red mark on his neck was a love bite. I was furious, and for one instant hated him, so keenly did I feel the injustice of my situation. I also felt that he was enjoying himself hugely: the middle-aged professor with the young wife, showing off evidence of the previous night's encounter. I was the more furious because his letters had detailed what he called his "sexual failure" with Liz, indicating they had no love life, and here was vivid evidence to the contrary.

I left the lecture in the middle and ran to the library. I could have gone to my apartment, packed my car, and driven back to Cambridge, but I didn't; I was in too deep. I used all my considerable energies to damp down my feelings until I could live with my situation. I ended up sitting miserably between two stacks in the library, weeping and telling myself I was crying because I couldn't find the book I wanted.

In hindsight, it's astonishing to me how much I accepted, how little I asked for. I saw my choices as all or nothing. I was either with him or I moved back to Cambridge. I didn't understand that there might be a middle way, where I might confront him, share my angry feelings, and insist that he work harder to meet my needs. In this incident, and also later in our life together, I let him dictate the terms of our relationship. This was the path I had always followed. That it was painful was just something I thought I had to live with.

Throughout my life I'd worked hard to keep myself from getting angry. I had gotten way too good at it. I had many passionate feelings and allowed their expression in only a few avenues. Sexuality was one, despair and beating myself up emotionally were others. Writing was a fourth. I could write about painful situations, but I didn't know how to live them and work them through.

I'd taught myself to fear my own anger, and months of therapy hadn't taught me how to feel my feelings, how to express them, how to communicate them in a couple relationship. I think now my therapy couldn't succeed because I was still drinking. Only after accumulating several years of living as a sober person did I learn that to become angry won't kill me, that to express anger will not drive my partner away, and that I can ask for what I need in a relationship. In my thirties I had no idea how to do those things. Even later, John and I had a misunderstanding in which I might have lashed out at him and aired my grievances, but I did not.

* * *

One February night John pitched snowballs at my window at three in the morning.

He'd driven Liz to Philadelphia that afternoon and come back that night. Instead of returning to his house in Susquehanna, he swung by my apartment. The dated building had no individual buzzers for each apartment at the downstairs door. Visitors telephoned first or pounded on the locked door and hoped upstairs residents would hear them. The doorbell would ring loudly in the common hall; at that hour John hesitated to wake the entire building. I had a telephone, but John was impatient. My second-floor window wasn't that high, and his aim was good.

I didn't hear him. Eight years of urban life had inured me to nighttime street noise. In a quiet upstate New York town, I slept only too well. As the snowballs thunked against my single-paned casements, I slept on peacefully.

That he threw snowballs rather than driving around the corner to find a pay phone was characteristic. The professor in a formal black wool topcoat, his shoes slipping on the snow-covered grass, packing and pitching snowballs with his cold bare hands at the window of his paramour on a quiet Binghamton street was a scene that might have come from one of his novels.

He drove back to Susquehanna convinced I was playing games— that I had heard and ignored him. Or maybe I hadn't been there. Was I now betraying him? He spent the rest of the night drinking and writing a long letter about me and about Liz to his university confidante, Susan Strehle, a colleague in the English department who was spending the semester abroad with her husband, Bill Spanos.

Since he hadn't told me, I had no idea Liz was out of town. I had a certain amount of pride. I wasn't going to telephone him if he didn't telephone me, and we didn't see each other until shortly before the next meeting of the evening fiction writing class.

The corridor was dark and empty at six-forty-five. My footfalls echoed in the stillness. I began to feel that something was wrong. I hesitated at the door of his office. The only light came from the gooseneck lamp over his desk. He was reading and put the book—short stories of Chekhov—aside instantly. He didn't look happy to see me. He sat as if weighed down by his coat, his clothes, his very flesh, as if he were, like a character in one of his stories, a "mountain of a man." I sat down and reached for his hand. He pulled away.

"What's the matter?"

"Were you in your apartment night before last?" He looked directly at me, with that intent, clear look.

From his face I knew this was serious.

"Yes. I was there."

"I threw snowballs at your window at three A.M."

I was immediately angry. Who was he to toss a snowball at my window and then blame me because I didn't wake up and invite him in? And why three o'clock in the morning of all times? Just as immediately, I denied and swallowed my anger. I didn't understand that I could love someone and be angry with him at the same time. I felt that if I got angry it meant I didn't, or couldn't, love him.

"I didn't hear you."

He explained about Liz and the trip to Philadelphia. I turned my anger on myself. This feeling was familiar. It was only too easy to assume blame and seemed less dangerous than blowing up at him. I rationalized. If only I'd known. If only I'd waked up. Then panic welled in my chest. He still didn't want me to touch him. What if he didn't believe me? The more I protested my innocence the more guilty I would appear. My feelings were confused and frightening to me. Things weren't right in my own heart, but I ignored that and looked outside myself. I wanted reassurance from him that everything was all right. At last I pushed my foot forward so it touched his. He didn't withdraw his shoe.

"Where did you go for supper?" I meant that very evening. I'd had no idea he had been alone and wished I'd been with him.

"I went to Denny's. It was awful." He made a face.

I decided it was all right. We hadn't talked anything out. I had swallowed my feelings and accepted blame where I was blameless, but I felt we understood each other again. We went to class. He went home alone and I went back to my apartment; Liz was coming back that night. I regretted my lost opportunity to be with him.

John's letters had been imploring. *Come to me*, they urged, over and over. Now that I had, I seemed stuck in the mistress role he had promised me. I could threaten to move back to Cambridge, but since I hadn't lined up any employment there I told myself it wasn't practical. I could demand, deliver an ultimatum, but I wasn't quite angry enough to do that. I didn't have the tools to open a dialogue and work things out in spoken words. Instead, I wrote some poems.

The graduate student hangout was a diner overlooking the Susquehanna River. One always angled for a booth by the window. I was with a group from the fiction writing seminar when I got an idea for a sonnet—I began to scribble phrases and lines on a napkin. "Look at her, writing again," joked Corrinne Hales, a poet and Ph.D. candidate who had befriended me. I smiled, wrote a few more lines, and excused myself so I could run home and finish the poem.

I'd written sonnets before and published one in *American Girl* magazine, when I won a writing contest and saw my work in print for the first time at age sixteen. The sonnet which won the contest was in fairly straightforward Shakespearean style, with the pessimistic theme that it was better to die young than live on to a wretched old age. I had been thinking about my grandmother, then nearly ninety and silent, isolated, despondent.

Now I again used the Shakespearean form and poured out emotion into love sonnets. The exercise was easy for me; by the time I'd done the first two poems it seemed I almost thought in the form and the words flowed readily, needing little or no correction to make them fit the necessary structure of fourteen iambic pentameter lines with their prescribed rhyme scheme.

These poems were heartfelt.

So, love, do you lift me to ideal realms.
Our couch is joy, as loving, God delights
To mold new worlds, planets springing bright.

I addressed my regret that I'd wasted time away from John in Cambridge.

If on a gray day at your desk . . .
You think hard thoughts of me, recalling clear
Long bitter empty months when I refused
Your love—at first unknowing, then in fear—
And in that folly stole much time; my dear,
Despise me not, though fault is mine. I used
To value not yourself but me amiss.
My love—compressed by empty time behind—
The faster flows to you. Each hug, each kiss,
The sweeter is in late-awakened mind.

I characterized my sense of John's love for me:

So vast—through any tempest it holds fast!

I typed up and numbered five sonnets, put them in a plain folder, and handed them to John in his office the next day.

"What's this? A new story?" He rocked back on his heels, pushed at the torn cuffs of his fisherman sweater, looked at me intently.

"Just some poems. Read them later."

I didn't plan it that way, and I had not predicted the outcome, but those poems were the turning point. They expressed my love as purely as possible and, read together, are a heartfelt testament of pure, particular, and passionate feeling. I wrote them for no other audience, and the combination of their strict formal quality with the upwelling of powerful feeling contained within that form convinced him of my heart and my heart's desire more than my decision to move to be with him and more than any spoken words could have done. I had fallen in love at first by reading his work; it was in reading my poems that he was at last assured of my love for him.

That night in Susquehanna, he told Liz the truth: he and I were lovers. She moved out the next morning, and that afternoon I moved in.

10

"I Hope I Never Hurt You"

It was a simple matter to move into John's house. In leaving Cambridge I'd stripped my life down to basics. All I had were my clothes and my typewriter.

He telephoned to invite me out to the farmhouse and that was all I took, my typewriter and a few changes of clothes.

Liz was practical, matter-of-fact. As long as this was happening, she was going to be fair. She had cleared out half her dresser drawers for me, and half the closet. I wasn't sure where she was living. John knew where she would be staying for she had given him her phone number there. Liz seemed to be determined to make her own life in her own way, to have resources to call on.

I was relieved that my status was no longer hidden. I was happy to be with John all the time, not just for stolen afternoons in my apartment. I was hopeful that our situation would resolve itself and that I would become John's wife.

I moved into the house just as it was and didn't change anything. This had been another woman's home, after all, and I was moving in among her things. The house was simply furnished, comfortable, not fussy. Neither Liz nor John seemed to care overmuch for externals, for appearances. Nor did I. John described me once in a letter to Liz by saying that sometimes I looked like Goodwill and sometimes I looked like a queen. This was pretty much true. He had modeled the character Miss Mystery Voice in the musical *Marvin's on "The Distant Shore"* after me. Miss Mystery Voice comes hesitantly onstage, wearing a nondescript tan raincoat. When she takes off the coat she reveals a lovely young woman in a stylish cocktail dress who sings with a beautiful, haunting voice. I was touched; he had me down cold.

I left the photo of Liz's sister still stuck to the refrigerator with its magnet; I even left alone the wooden sign JOHN AND LIZ, WRITERS IN RESIDENCE that John had made and hung on the outside wall by the front door, the door we never used. My mother's house had been controlled by her taste; I had learned to focus on my interior life.

Once John and I were together on a daily basis, the addictive nature of our love came into clear focus. Constant work on writing was interrupted only by lovemaking, and lovemaking yielded only to work.

John's house, a simple farmhouse on a hill, seemed magic, full of his presence. The gravel driveway swept around the left side of the white building and up to a flagstone patio in the back. Beyond the back yard, the land sloped upward to a row of trees. The view from the picture window was of sugar maples in the yard, brooding hills beyond.

I loved being out in the country and felt transported back to those days and nights at Bread Loaf, so steeped in possibility, so charged in memory.

John and Liz's dog, Teddy, a purebred German shepherd puppy, was as handsome as any television dog; his fur was soft and fluffy, and he had a great plume of a tail. He was all puppyish feet and legs, with a great dog smile and lolling pink tongue. My mother had always had dogs as I was growing up, but I'd never had a dog as an adult; Teddy was wonderful. While John worked in his study I took the dog with me for long walks and tried to discipline him; he was badly trained and difficult to control but I adored him.

To an outsider my new life may have looked restricted, but to me it felt deep and rich, a new beginning, an opening outward to another soul, an opening inward to a deeper sense of myself.

My role model was my mother. When she and my father were first married, they lived in the country, outside Wellsville, New York, where he had been born and brought up. Mother put in an enormous garden; it was during World War II, and civilians were encouraged to plant Victory Gardens. She made bread every day. She took a job as a social caseworker but, when I was born, left the workforce to be a full-time mom. Without thinking about it consciously, this was the path I now intended to follow. I'd learned how to bake bread in Cambridge and was given a book of recipes by one of John's friends; while I lived with him I worked my way through it, making one recipe after another. John taught me his favorite treats as well, including Baba Ghanoush, or eggplant appetizer, where, he instructed me, "You add olive oil until you don't think it will absorb any more, and then keep pouring." We both liked to cook, and one of my journal entries notes that I was in the kitchen at two in the morning cooking chicken. For a treat, he would cook Cornish game hens. We ate in the living room, sitting on the floor with our plates on the low glass-topped table, before the fire roaring in the Franklin stove. We drank red wine in elegant balloon glasses with long stems. The china was glossy white with a blue edge. Outside the road was quiet, dark hills sheltered the house; snow fell quietly on the maple trees.

The bedroom was over his study. There was a beautiful bright blue rug, a simple double bed, blue flannel sheets, a blue coverlet. In bed his face opened like a rose. During our courtship I had dreamed of him walking up a hillside toward me, holding out his hands, held together like a cup, filled and overflowing with sweet golden honey. This to me was our life together: his hands, over-flowing with honey.

As he embraced me in bed, or caught me in a quick bear hug in the kitchen before we went out the door on some errand, he would say, shaking his head, "With you in my life, I'll be too happy to write, I'll be too happy to write."

To be around John all the time, to notice the music he liked to hear, to look at the titles of the books he kept in his study, to listen to his thoughts, to touch his hand—these were all sensations I drank in gratefully.

His study was a front room overlooking the road, with its own door to the downstairs bath; it had been designed for a bedroom. He had made a desk from a door laid over two trestles. It faced the road and held his IBM correcting Selectric, his ashtray, was always crowded with paper. On the desk sat a small ceramic bottle stopped with a large cork. Etched into the brown clay was the word MAGIC. "One of my students made that for me," he said. "I had told her I could give her everything but the magic."

Above his desk, between the two windows, hung a large portrait he had done, an older man with pale skin, wearing an overcoat and a hat, standing before a dark background. He insisted his model had been his friend James Dickey, but the portrait looked a lot like himself. There were other paintings: one of the apartment he and Liz had shared in Baltimore, showing Liz on a couch read-ing; a small landscape with a line of men in black all walking up a hill. "Welshmen," he told me, "walking to a *Gymanfa Ganu*," a hymn sing. He had a big oak armchair before the typewriter and a phone to his left; he never let the phone ring but always answered it, saying, "Gardner, John." He had built floor-to-ceiling shelves, which wrapped around the window to the right of his desk. These held his books, manuscripts, galley proofs, music scores, and notes for many projects. To his left was another trestle table crowded with projects, mail from his California publisher, the Lord

John Press, and beautifully produced broadsides of poems by himself, by Liz, by John Fowles and James Dickey. At the back of the room was a closet with music stands, clothes, more boxes, and his French horn in its battered black case.

It was a cluttered, cheerful room, with his churchwarden pipes and tins of Dunhill tobacco and a big black ashtray always piled with dottle from his pipe. He had elegant-looking pipe tools—a pick, a tamper, other arcane paraphernalia—but as at Bread Loaf he tamped the burning tobacco down with his index finger. A bust of Dickens looked down from the shelves, over John's row of published novels and critical work. He used a big cardboard box for a wastebasket; a woven jute rug covered the floor; a paper sign like those property owners fix to their fence posts was tacked to the door and read NO TRESPASSING.

He always put three or four pieces of paper into the typewriter at a time, to cushion the paten, and saved the interior sheets until they were crazily indented over and over from the pressure of the keys. When he began a new story or an essay, he typed its title in the upper left-hand corner of the first page, flush to the left margin, left two lines of space, and then typed his name.

The text began four lines down and filled the first page. He typed fiction and essays double-space, letters single-space. For his novels he used a cover sheet with the title centered midway down the page; then, two spaces down, the words A NOVEL; and two spaces below that, his name.

The books on his shelves spanned many interests, from histories of the Adirondack park and John McPhee's book on Alaska to several on the mad Russian monk Rasputin. He had books on Charles Darwin, about whom he had written a radio play, and several volumes of work by Lewis Thomas. Penguin paperbacks about the Christian Gospels were so broken they were held together with rubber bands. He had books on research into sharks (I remembered his comments at Bread Loaf on sharks and blood in the water), science fiction by Roger Zelazny and others, collections of the Hugo awards (science fiction again), and science fact by Carl Sagan and Isaac Asimov.

As well as fiction by writers as diverse as Cynthia Ozick, Sol Yurick, and John Fowles (whom he considered his only real competitor in the world of letters), he had philosophy as well, a summary text by Albert Levi, *Varieties of Experience*; works by Hegel and Whitehead; a heavily annotated copy of Edmund Burke's *A Philosophical Enquiry into the Origin of Our Ideas of the Sublime and Beautiful*; and work by Ludwig Wittgenstein, his favorite philosopher at that time. As well he had well-thumbed and annotated copies of the *Iliad*, the *Odyssey, Beowulf*, and the minor Old English poems, *Judith, The Battle of Maldon*, and *The Dream of the Rood*.

He also had bound galleys sent to him by publishers, with letters asking for comments, hardbound novels people sent him as gifts, and boxes and boxes of manuscripts to look at for *MSS* magazine. These came to him from writers he knew from Bread Loaf, students from SUNY, former students from other colleges, and casual admirers.

For his work on *Mickelsson's Ghosts* he had a rare copy of a biography of Joseph Smith, *No Man Knows My History*. The house in Susquehanna was only a few miles from where Joseph Smith had once lived. A monument to the Mormon church stands nearby on Route 171, and buses convene there regularly so that devout Mormons can visit the grave site of one of Joseph Smith's young children.

I was interested to find a book I had read and reread during my time in Cambridge, the biography of a Dutchman with documented psychic powers titled *My Passport Says Clairvoyant*, and was intrigued by an oversize paperback titled *The Mysterious World: An Atlas of the Unexplained*. This odd book covered topics as diverse as "spontaneous human combustion," a phenomenon in which a human body suddenly bursts into flame, as well as ball lightning, the magnetism of the earth, and legends of the Yeti of the Himalaya. John also had books on the stone circles and standing stones of England; several privately published books on Remsen, New York, and the early history of Batavia; and a Presbyterian hymnal from the Batavia First Presbyterian Church.

It was paradise. I could have stayed in that house just reading all the books he'd read and happily lived my life.

Above and behind the house was a field leading up to the edge of the woods; I loved to take Teddy with me and tramp over the fields and into the woods, where I found a footpath leading directly into the town of Susquehanna that came out near the home of friends. John had a pond on the property and several bubbling springs, and across the road was a deeper pond that had once been the ice supply for the town. In the quiet evenings, deer came down out of the woods to browse at the edge of the fields, and the air was always fresh and clear.

We kept a low profile those first few weeks. We didn't discuss this, it just seemed to evolve. John left the house only to go up to the university to teach; he neither called nor saw his friends. I now had no reason and no time to hang out at the Park Diner in Binghamton; instead, I came directly back to his house in Susquehanna. In this way we avoided friends and colleagues. It was almost as if we were hiding out.

This went on until one day when John was out of town on a reading tour and I was expecting him at any time. A car pulled in the drive and I heard the kitchen door open; I rushed from the study, and stopped short at the edge of the kitchen. A burly man with dark hair and a dark beard was pushing his way into the house, holding a large package. "I'm a friend of John's," he announced. "These are for him. Where can I put them?" In his eyes was a challenge. Did I dare throw him out?

The package was framed artwork, and the burly man was Jim Rose. I stood back as he put the package in the hall; then he planted himself in the center of the kitchen, looking directly at me and making no move to leave. He smiled and I saw a small gap in his teeth. I said John would probably be right along and asked if he wanted to wait. "Great," he said and, shedding his coat, made his way into the living room. I offered him a drink, Jim settled himself on the couch, and we made small talk until I heard another car and went to investigate.

This time it was John in the kitchen doorway. "Someone's here," I said. "He says he's a friend of yours. Jim Rose."

John nodded, hugged me.

"When I heard his car I came running out because I thought he was you."

He grinned. "Good thing you had your clothes on." In the living room, John and Jim fell on each other like old friends and Jim revealed the true purpose of his visit. John's friends in Susquehanna all wanted to know what was going on. Why wasn't Liz's car in the driveway? Was he by himself? Was he living with a girl? Was he OK? They put their heads together, and Jim was the only one with nerve enough to barge into the house. He created the fiction of delivering the paintings as a ruse and just came on over.

John laughed and poured another drink. We talked, and Jim, as if he were a younger brother checking out the new girlfriend, laughed, told jokes, and looked me over, shrewd behind his genial facade, watching for any misstep. If I wasn't nice enough, if I didn't love John truly, if I was only a celebrity hunter, he was self-appointed to protect his friend.

Later, we visited Jim in his house overlooking a creek in the hamlet of Starrucca. I had been sitting on John's lap in the wing chair. He got up to go to the bathroom and Jim looked me over. He got right to the point. "What's in this for you? Why are you with him?"

"I love him with all my heart."

"Good." Jim nodded. "He needs that."

John kept a grueling schedule. Generally he'd work in his study from 10 P.M. to 4 or 5 A.M., fall into bed, and sleep till ten, eleven, or noon, whenever the phone began ringing. Then it was up and hit the ground running. He could shave, dress, and get downstairs faster than anyone I'd ever known. He made coffee with a special quick-brewing coffeepot, whose speed he intensified by plugging it in before he'd finished putting the innards together; the water boiled up and burned his fingertips, but the coffee was ready one minute sooner.

After coffee, we'd head in to the university, a forty-five-minute drive over curving mountain roads and four-lane highways, where he met students, attended committee meetings, or read manuscripts for *MSS* magazine, conferred with his assistant editors, and contacted writers and printers. Our main meal of the day was in the evening; we generally went to Copperfield's, where he and I and Liz had eaten during my visit the previous November. This dimly lit restaurant allowed smoking, had wide, comfortable oaken armchairs, and mediocre food. I found it very square. In the evenings he taught his fiction seminar, or sometimes we went to movies. Around ten we came home, where he dived into his study and worked all night.

At first I tried to keep up with him. One night he found me curled up, cold, cramped, and asleep, in the easy chair in the living room at 2 A.M. He touched me on the shoulder. "Go to bed," he advised. "You'll make yourself sick."

John's was the only house I'd lived in that had no television. His house was dedicated to and streamlined for work; there were no distractions, no newspaper deliveries, no magazines, slick or literary. He had a radio and a stereo, a quality one, and we listened each evening, at home or in the car, to the news and music programs of National Public Radio.

I took to going to bed when I was tired, at eleven or midnight, and would wake to find him getting into bed with me at four, five, or six in the morning. Thus he worked, in essence, two seven-hour days. One teaching at the university in the afternoon and early evening, and another writing at home from before midnight until dawn.

*   *   *

I was constantly working on my writing, looking over stories I had begun in Cambridge and seeing ways to deepen and extend the range of each one. I continued to work on the draft Liz had critiqued in her visit to my apartment, and I had as well the novella in progress that had been funded by the Massachusetts Council on the Arts.

When John disappeared into his study, I worked at Liz's desk, typing and retyping. When I was ready I shared work with him and we looked at it together, sitting close to each other on the couch. He switched from lover back to teacher, but the eroticism that grew out of his interest in my work was now heightened. John had told me he thought all great fiction was written to an ideal reader, a lover; I was finding this to be true. As I sat at the typewriter, exploring the possibilities of my imagination, I seemed to have both a greater facility with language and a deeper, richer well to draw on. John encouraged this work, and urged me to submit it to the *Atlantic Monthly* and other prestigious journals. He also nagged me to apply for a Pennsylvania Council on the Arts grant, now that I was a Pennsylvania resident. When the *Atlantic* refused one of my stories, he accepted it for *MSS* magazine, the literary journal he had founded in the early 1960s in California and had revived at Binghamton.

John had founded *MSS* in order to encourage the work of writers he admired, writers who had a difficult time having their work accepted by more mainstream literary publications. Remembering the struggles he had experienced to see his own work published, he became committed to helping other artists.

John had gone for long periods of time in his career without publishing. He began writing steadily as a graduate student at the University of Iowa in 1955. Between 1958, when he earned his Ph.D., and 1966 he published no fiction, although he worked on the manuscripts that would become *Nickel Mountain*, and *The Sunlight Dialogues*, and on *The Resurrection*, his first published novel, which came out in 1966 when he was thirty-three. *The Res-*

urrection had a small initial printing, and lukewarm reviews. Following this first publication, John completed a new novel, *The Sunlight Dialogues*. However, in 1968 and 1969 it was rejected by several publishers. While this novel was making the rounds, he began a new one, which he called *The Last Days of a Seer*.

His story, a good one, was that in August of 1969 he was fed up. In his frustration, he packed two finished, unpublished manuscripts—*The Sunlight Dialogues* and *The Last Days of a Seer*—in the saddlebags of his motorcycle, put on his leather jacket, and drove into New York City, where he went to the office of David Segal, an editor at Harper and Row, dumped the manuscripts on his desk, and said, "OK, read." Then John sat in a chair and waited. He said David Segal looked at him, looked at the manuscripts, and said, mildly, "I can't read these, Mr. Gardner, with you staring at me." John said he went away, and when he came back the next morning, Segal agreed to publish *The Last Days of a Seer* under a new title: *The Wreckage of Agathon*.

The Wreckage of Agathon came out late in 1970. David Segal moved to Alfred A. Knopf that year and brought with him the manuscript of *The Sunlight Dialogues*. By this time John had completed *Grendel*. Knopf published *Grendel* first, in 1971, believing it to be more immediately accessible to the public than *The Sunlight Dialogues* which was published in 1972. *Nickel Mountain* was published in 1973. John had been working on it, off and on, for twenty years.

Because he had tried so often and failed to publish, John had a commitment to helping young writers; he knew personally how difficult the process could be.

In early issues of *MSS* he published William Gass and Joyce Carol Oates; he told me he was Oates's first publisher. He also published John Hawkes, W. S. Merwin, and others.

At one point, he told me, *MSS* had been suspended from publication by the U.S. Postal Service for being obscene. The word the censors objected to in a story was "nape" as in, "nape of the neck." John told me he faced ruinous legal fees in order to keep the journal in circulation, so he approached several well-known writers for financial help, among them Norman Mailer. According to John, Mailer sent him a contribution and a postcard on which he had jokingly written, *I've never heard of you* or *your filthy magazine.*

At SUNY-Binghamton, John and Liz decided to republish the journal. John edited the fiction, and Liz edited the poetry. As before, their commitment was to encourage and publish idiosyncratic writers whose work was neglected elsewhere. Sometimes the journal received as many as a thousand submissions in a month. The amount of energy John poured into his editing and correspondence with writers was voluminous and is documented in a special issue of *MSS*, published posthumously, which includes descriptions of his meticulous editing and lengthy letters to his authors.

As his live-in lover, I received the benefit of an extraordinary tutorial from the most gifted teacher I have ever encountered. John had written that he hoped he could continue to help me as a teacher after we had become intimate. He said now we were lovers, even my clumsy sentences took his breath away, and he hoped he would not lose the capacity to critique my work. Instead, living with him lifted me to a new level of creativity.

All that spring I was enrolled in John's fiction writing workshop, the only graduate class I took that term. It met Wednesday nights in a big room in the classroom wing with two tables pressed together. John sat at the foot of the table, away from the door, his back to the windows and the dark night outside; I sat at his left; other students—the seminar had twenty-seven or twenty-eight members—took their places around the table, and David Bosnick sat at the opposite end, near the door. David had a football player's physique and densely curled blond hair. His number-two pencil looked tiny in his massive hand. He hunched, chewing on his lip, at the opposite end of the table from John and me, and I wondered how much the other students knew or guessed of the triangle I was involved in or of David's part in this drama: after I moved into John's house, Liz moved in with David.

John's method was to have students read their work aloud. No one had copies of the work being read; participants were expected to listen and to base their comments on what they heard. The governing criterion was "Did one fall into a vivid and continuous dream? Did the dream hold up? Were there distracting details?" This was, on one level, a sophisticated teaching method. It cut right to the heart and avoided superfluity—there were no problems with photocopying reams of material, no fumbling with papers, and John, having already read the story many times in draft, had less paperwork to do. It was also primitive, harking back almost to the primeval. Instead of shepherds around a campfire, we were students seated around a seminar table in an ordinary classroom with a linoleum floor and fluorescent lights. But I remember the room as dark, pregnant, enclosed, the air thick with mystery, and John as shaman, listening, waiting, encouraging us to listen, waiting for the whisper of the story coming from the heart.

I brought so much new work so quickly to this seminar that one night he took his pipe out of his mouth and announced, "Susan's in a race." He paused. "With all of you."

Of the stories I wrote that spring semester, all but one were accepted and published by various literary journals, and one was anthologized. Those weeks I lived with John were the most fertile and successful time for writing I had ever had.

This intellectual intimacy, of writing stories for him with him as my coach, was as charged and compelling as the sexual intimacy we already knew. That we could be together all the time, not just at stolen moments in my apartment in Binghamton, seemed to relax both of us; our days and nights fell into an easy rhythm. We were both addictive personalities; we had become addicted to each other and now nothing stood in our way.

*   *   *

One morning around four, John woke me up. He was getting into bed, touching me down all my length, holding me so tightly I feared my ribs would crack. He was chill and exhausted, quite drunk, the gin sweet on his breath. "You scared me to death," he was saying, over and over, in between kisses on my cheeks, my chin, my forehead, my throat, my shoulder. "You scared me to death." He said he had left his study to come to bed, shut off the light and climbed the darkened stairs, stood in the doorway of the bedroom—and had not seen me in the bed. I must have been deeply asleep, lying quite still; he had mistaken the form of my body under the quilt for a shadow and gone searching through the darkened house to find me. Teddy wasn't in the room, and usually the dog slept where and when I slept; that night Teddy was in the spare room. He looked up and thumped his tail when John looked in; I wasn't in there. John said he went downstairs again, in the dark, looked in the kitchen, in the living room; was I curled up on the sofa, reading? He looked in Liz's study; was I working? He glanced out in the driveway: my car was still in the drive; at last he climbed the stairs again, heart pounding, and this time got into bed where he could touch me. "You scared me to death," he said, over and over. "I couldn't find you." He was still dressed, his shirt rough against my skin, holding me so tightly I expected to hear my ribs snap like overstressed violin strings. "I even looked in my study." He grinned that grin that made him look an imbecile ten-year-old. "I'll let you go back to sleep in a minute," he said, still kissing and caressing. "You scared me to death."

I'd never scared anyone like that before; no one had ever wanted me in his life so intently before; no one had ever expressed such needing, such vulnerability.

The largeness of his passion for me was overwhelming. I'd never known anything like it. He wanted to see and hear and taste everything about my life; he wanted to pry into every thought, every experience, all my history. This huge desire to know was irresistible. I felt cherished, uplifted; it was as if he worshiped and adored me. Once I tasted that, I craved more.

The sexual side of our life was enthralling, in the old sense of the word, *to hold spellbound*, addictive as any drug, more so. He was totally present to me, the ideal lover.

"My beauty, how perfect you are." He spoke those words over and over, like a poem, as his hands roamed my body, touching everywhere. "My beauty, my beauty, how perfect you are."

I wanted his skin to be mine, his experience to be mine; I worshiped those square blunt hands, knowing the sensual pleasures they gave me, as if they were objects of veneration; I craved his touch the way an addict craves the needle.

Nights sometimes he would follow me to bed at eleven or midnight; we would make love; he would go down to his study; an hour later I would wake to see him standing at the bedroom door, his face a contradictory study: should he wake me? Was this love or concupiscence? "I couldn't stay away," he breathed, as he had done so many months earlier at Bread Loaf.

This was our nighttime life, the molten, erotic core, to which we returned again and again.

I had the sense in living with John that I was entering a deeper and richer life, that I had connected to a powerful energy source, that I could explore a more meaningful life. Both the possibilities of my art and my ability to write seemed to blossom, as well as a heightened awareness, a sharpened sense of what was possible.

I admired and emulated, as far as I could, John's drive and concentration. He felt compelled to hurry partly because of the cancer he had suffered the winter of 1977–78. John had entered the Johns Hopkins Hospital in Baltimore on December 10, 1977, with what he told me he thought was a "psychological" illness. Instead, he was shown a slip of paper that read: *John Gardner. Diagnosis: carcinoma. Prognosis: terminal.*

This cancer had come at a time of turmoil in John's life. He had separated from his first wife, Joan, in October of 1976 and left their home in Bennington and his teaching position at the college there. In early 1977 he accepted two teaching jobs, one at Skidmore

College and one at Williams, where he taught on alternate days. He lived in what he called a "hunter's cabin" in the small town of Cambridge, New York, where Liz began to live with him. In the fall he began to teach at George Mason University in Fairfax, Virginia. He kept up a hectic schedule of teaching, writing, and lecturing, and when at last he entered the hospital in December at the end of that year and received the cancer diagnosis, he told me he was "pleased."

He also told me that because he was certain he was going to die, he allowed the surgeons to do an experimental procedure on him. The surgeons removed a cancerous tumor from his colon and created a temporary colostomy. When his healing had progressed far enough, they performed a colostomy takedown and reconstructed his large intestine in the normal way. He wrote about this surgery and its aftereffects in his novel-in-progress *Shadows*, which remained unfinished at his death. He stayed in the hospital only six weeks and got better so fast, he told me, "they thought they had the wrong patient."

It was Liz who helped him to heal. "Every night, as soon as I got out of intensive care, even if I was drugged out of my skull, Liz came to the hospital and made love to me. My surgeon, a woman, knew about it and saw that it helped me and didn't say anything, but once we got caught by a nurse who, if she were a boy, could have been an inquisition-style Jesuit. The doctors had told everybody—my family, Liz, everybody—that I was going to die. But I didn't. Liz saved my life."

At the hospital just up to his surgery, and as soon as possible afterward, John worked on the text of *The Art of Fiction*, a book that distills all his years of teaching writing. In May 1978, he delivered a paper at the International P.E.N. organization in Stockholm, and in August he returned to Bread Loaf, where he electrified his audience: "I used to be afraid of death. Now I've faced death and I'm not afraid. I don't give a shit about dying."

Since his recovery, he felt pressured to continue his headlong creative drive, telling the reporter from *The New York Times Mag-*

azine that he concentrated hard on his work because of his sense of mortality. In Illinois he had seen his friend the sculptor Nicholas Vergette sicken and die from cancer; friends of his have told me that so many of their circle faced cancer in those years it was like an epidemic. In the months I lived with him, John returned to Johns Hopkins for a checkup and for removal of a cyst that had developed under the skin near his shoulder blade. He told me it had been "reaching toward his heart." His doctors found no evidence of cancer there or anywhere in his system.

This compromise to his health compelled his drive, but I felt there was another cause as well; Priscilla once made the chilling comment to an interviewer that it was as if John were living two lives. His record of publications expresses a startlingly dual path. He could have, and did, achieve renown as a medievalist, and his scholarly publications alone make a list many professors would envy. That he branched out also into creative work—novels, opera libretti, poems, and plays—shows an immense intellect, an enormously fertile mind.

He didn't write because it was a "career," like being an electrician, or to build his ego. He wrote to be part of "the great conversation," as he told the reporter from *The New York Times*. He wrote and rewrote because he wanted his work to last a thousand years, as had the Greek, Latin, and Anglo-Saxon poetry he loved. He told interviewers, "Fiction is the only religion I have." Indeed, when his work was honored, his focus was always on the work ahead, not the work completed. His question to colleagues and students was always, "What are you working on?" He meant, What are you working on *now*? What was published was over; he always looked ahead.

In addition he had an amazingly well-stocked mind and took genuine pleasure in reading books others might consider esoteric. Earlier, he had written to me:

Spent all Monday and today reading and thinking, trying to change my life. Mostly reading a biography of Bismarck—a strange, lucky choice. He was a raging egocentric fool, a world disaster; a good mirror for the side of me I must beware of. He was also a wonderfully poetic soul—that was the side of himself that he repressed. Tomorrow I plan to cook most of the day and read Xenophon, one of the more pastoral books, maybe the one on horsemanship. I've decided not to write anything for a while, just answer my mail and calm my soul a little. . . .

I'm teaching Beowulf in the epic course. . . . I don't want to be limited—don't want to be mainly a medievalist—but the minute I start unlocking the secrets of that weird, weird age, I can see in the way people start watching me that I've done it again, revealed my special lunacy. In fifteen minutes I traced the whole history of Christian Platonism, the four levels of scriptural interpretation, the medieval reputation of Virgil, *Zählenkomposition* (counting words and lines, etc., and slipping in geometrical symbolism, as when in *Beowulf* and *The Dream of the Rood* the poet's word-counting between key images arranges the poem into the Golden Section), and then I started the line-by-line analysis of *Beowulf* itself (most of it my own invention, or anyway most of it first pointed out by me in early so-called scholarly books). . . . And as if that weren't enough, that night Richard Loomis lectured here (translator of David ap Gwylim), and I got into a heated debate with him about fourteenth-century Welsh poetry.

A man with tastes like this is bound to be lonely.

When we talked about books and authors I discovered one of John's favorites was Isak Dinesen. Not her autobiographical work, *Out of Africa,* but her stories, *Anecdotes of Destiny, Seven Gothic Tales*, and others. John loved the mythic cast of her mind, the lofty diction of her storytelling. He particularly admired her story of the apostle Peter, who, after betraying Christ, vows to go without sleep. He loved to quote the opening of that story—"Will the narrator be believed . . ."—and used motifs from it in his last short story, published posthumously, "Julius Caesar and the Werewolf." I began to read Dinesen too, found her a powerful influence, and used one of her stories, "The Sailor Boy's Tale," as a model for my own work.

John developed a method of writing where he worked on a book as long as he could, until, he told me, he couldn't "see" it anymore. Then he turned to another manuscript and worked on that. He said this enabled him to use the passage of time as an editor. When he turned to a book he had set aside for weeks or months, he could suddenly see that a subplot, a character, an incident didn't work and would have the moral courage to cut it out and brutally revise. Even, he told me, if he had worked "weeks" on that section or even that paragraph. He told me that when he was working on a novel his schedule was to sleep five hours, wake up and work, and then take a two-hour nap. He told me of often spending twelve to eighteen hours at his desk.

We talked about his own books, and he pointed out how his method of writing and rewriting over a period of time sometimes caused one book to bleed into another. "For instance, in *Freddy's Book* I wrote about a monster, a hugely big man, and that bled into *Mickelsson's Ghosts*, because Mickelsson is a big man and lifts weights." We talked about *Freddy's Book*. Reviewers had criticized it because it is a frame story with an odd structure: the opening he had read at Bread Loaf, where Professor Winesap receives Freddy's manuscript, is not referred to again at the end of the book. Many readers found it incomplete. "I should have written another cocktail party scene," John joked. "Freddy could have leaned into someone's shoulder and said, 'I have a father who's a monster.' "

John had written to me, "I hope I never hurt you." There were times when he hurt me quite a lot. One morning we woke to the sound of a car in the drive. It was bright day, about nine o'clock. John snapped awake instantly. "It's Claire Perillo," he said. "I forgot it was Thursday."

"So what?"

"She's the cleaning lady. I don't want her to see you."

"You what?"

He hauled hips out of bed and dressed. "You stay upstairs," he commanded.

"What?" I was balanced on one foot, trying to get the other foot into my corduroy slacks.

"She never cleans upstairs. When she's done downstairs, then you can leave."

"Are you crazy?"

He was already heading down the stairs. I struggled into a pullover and followed at his heels through the hall. When he got to the kitchen, he shut the door behind him. That stopped me in my tracks. He had slammed the door in my face: he was serious. I could hear him talking to someone in the kitchen. I didn't have the nerve to follow him. Instead, I hestitated, turned, and went back upstairs.

In the driveway the Honda Civic started up and my heart sank. He'd actually done it; he'd driven off, telling me to stay upstairs, like a good dog. There was no way to get out of the house without Claire seeing me. She'd already seen my car in the drive. But seeing a car and seeing a person are two different things. Did *I* care if she saw me? The thing to do was waltz downstairs, say hello to Claire, give her a big smile, get in my car, and peel rubber out the drive. I didn't do it.

John had told me to stay upstairs. I stayed upstairs. I had once asked a Massachusetts governor questions he didn't answer, I had climbed the rigging of a tall ship in an electrical storm, I had chased down a purse snatcher who said he had a gun, but I was now so disoriented by all the changes in my life that I did what John told me.

I pulled the covers up over the bed and walked softly into the spare bedroom, the guest room, where we had a mattress on the floor, made up as a bed. I sat behind the closed door, on the mattress, and listened to Claire downstairs. The hum of the vacuum cleaner was quite loud. The sun moved across the walls. I thought about making a run for it, but there was no way to know where she was downstairs.

I waited. John said she never came upstairs.

I heard footsteps on the stairs, the clunk of the vacuum cleaner being dragged up.

The door to the spare room, my hiding place, was closed. I could only hope. I lay down on the bed in my clothes, face in the pillow. I listened as she moved around in the next room, our bedroom, as she stripped and changed the bed. I listened as she ran water in the adjoining bath, scrubbing out the sink. I listened and I hoped, lying face down on the pillow. Then I heard footsteps, and the door opened.

Claire didn't speak. I kept my head in the pillow. I knew she was standing, with her hand on the knob, looking at me. My shoulder blades burned. I hardly breathed. At last she closed the door. I listened as she went back downstairs.

The kitchen door closed, I heard her car start up and she drove away.

I got up, came downstairs, gathered my things, and drove back to my apartment in Binghamton. I wanted to forget the farmhouse, forget what had happened, forget what John had just done. I buried my feelings in work and spent the afternoon typing and retyping a draft of a short story, hoping time would give me distance on my experience.

As I had in early February, I kept my hurt feelings to myself, at least for a while. I did not know how to confront John to talk about my feelings, and I still saw my situation as all or nothing. Either I was with him and accepted everything or I cut and ran back to Cambridge.

John was treating me just as badly as his fictional Mickelsson had treated his girlfriend Donnie, in *Mickelsson's Ghosts*. In retrospect, I'm amazed at how much power John had, how much power we gave him, Claire and I, two grown women, accepting and acting on a fiction that wasn't even voiced. John didn't have to say anything, only to leave the house, pretending he was alone, and both Claire and I pretended I didn't exist.

The rhetoric of his love letters fell away before this abusive, sorry treatment, but I was by now committed to my choice. He wanted it both ways: he wanted me in his life; he wanted Liz in his life and he wanted to pretend to be happily married to her. Somehow he didn't mind that Jim Rose knew about me and reported on his new status to all his friends, but to make a statement to the cleaning lady seemed too much.

Throughout that winter and early spring I kept my apartment in Binghamton, and for a while there was a lot of going and coming. Liz would move back in so she and John could talk, be together, sort out their feelings; I would move to my apartment. Then Liz would move out and go back to David's apartment in town, and I would return to the farmhouse.

While I was at the farmhouse I used the table in Liz's study; a big open ground-floor room, with an Oriental rug and a hanging lamp, a knockoff of a Tiffany, over the writing desk. At the other end of the room stood a potting table facing the picture window and crowded with plants clustered under a grow light. I used her desk but my own typewriter, like John's, an IBM correcting Selectric. It was a terrific machine but very heavy.

When Liz and I changed places, which was often, John carried my typewriter out to my car for me and carried her typewriter into the house for her. He would stride out of the house wearing his dark blue slacks and his oatmeal-colored fisherman's sweater, his face carefully neutral, as he balanced the heavy machine on his shoulder next to his ear and lowered it carefully into the back seat of my car.

I respected John and Liz's breaking up process. I envied Liz her status as his legal wife, but I was not jealous or fearful. I was not afraid that he might come home from an afternoon or evening with her to throw me out of the house permanently. The electricity of John's and my connection seemed to me total, unbreakable and gave me a confidence, even an arrogance. I decided it was in my best interest to be patient, to take the high road. I was convinced that John had made his choice, had chosen me, and I clearly remembered the anguish in his letters and his description of what he called his "sexual failure" with Liz.

Her poem "Married Love" had been accepted by *The New Yorker* and was published later that spring. The poem is poignant and personal. Its theme is the failure of a marriage. To me, Liz's choice to publish was a statement that her marriage had broken.

I was confident, but this did not make me immune to pain. One night John and I sat together in the living room, an icy rain chattering at the windows, the roads outside slick and glassy. He was drinking gin, I, whiskey. A fire glowed and snapped in the woodstove. I had recently returned from a trip to Cambridge, and had brought with me as a treat for him a bottle of fragrant body lotion. I poured some out into my palm and lifted it for him to catch the scent. He inhaled and said, "It smells like Nancy."

Nancy was a former love, a woman he had written to me about. He described her as a female guru and an effective faith healer. He was married to Joan but had pursued Nancy for four years, offering over and over to marry her; at last she had finally refused him.

When he mentioned her, I sat back in my chair and looked at his face. I was very nearly accustomed to this casual cruelty. I had known of his promiscuous nature from those first conversations at Treman and recalled his comment about the chaperone to whom he had been assigned on a reading tour: "I woke up and I was inside her." The list of his conquests seemed endless: the photographer assigned by a publisher, wives of close friends, fellow writers. I had become used to the idea that I was one love of many, if not in fact, at least in his imagination.

He waited a beat; he probably expected a response, a cry of pain, a slap across the face. I didn't give him one.

He began to talk. He went on and on about his life and his loves. He still loved Joan, he pined for Nancy. He told me he would never love me as he had loved, still loved, these ghosts from the past; I would never be good enough.

Then he went on to Liz and how smart she was. I could never

measure up. His intellectual life with her was going to continue. He and she would still teach together at SUNY and edit *MSS* magazine; he would still look to her as first reader for his novels; I couldn't be, no one could be, as good an editor for him as Liz was; she was perfect. He needed her for his work; he would always need her. It was as if she fed his brain and I his body.

I sat in the chair across from him, stunned. I took it all in and believed it. These wounding words seemed true. With unerring skill, he had found my weakest, most sensitive point. I had never doubted my intellectual ability. I was the girl who knew Latin and French, who aced the advanced placement tests and entered college with twelve credits, I was the girl who could astonish Ron Hansen at Bread Loaf by knowing Newton's theology. While at times I had doubted my attractiveness, had fretted about my weight—more than one boyfriend had commented, "If you'd only lose ten pounds you'd be perfect"—I had never doubted the strength of my intellect. And yet here was John, the man I adored and idealized, telling me Liz was smarter than I and for that reason he could never let her go. She would always meet a need that I could not.

As he told me all this, I could not protest. To a certain extent I still have this characteristic. If someone close to me makes an accusation, however false it may seem to an outsider, in the moment I believe it, experience the crushing blow. Over time I have learned to step back, to consider, to think over what has been said and consider its truth. Then I respond, after I have thought over what has happened. I don't answer angrily in the moment. I still lack the instinct to lash out.

I did not protest or lash out that night. I listened to what he said, and it seemed that my life was ruined. I was addicted to him, committed to him, willing to accept his promiscuity as a painful condition of life with him, but this was too much; that Liz would always be part of our lives, that I wasn't smart enough to read his work. At last I collapsed in tears. I threw myself out of the chair I had sat in, facing him, and fell at his feet. He scooped me up with his hands, pulling up on my torso so I was kneeling on the floor before him, tears sheeting down my face, gasping for breath. He had his arms around me and at last bent his head to my shoulder, stopped all the wounding words, and began to lick my face, his broad tongue warm and wet, lapping tears from my eyes, my cheeks, my throat.

He lifted me, still weeping, and supported me up the stairs. In the bedroom he pulled me to the bed and undressed me. I was emotionally exhausted and spent, not caring any longer what happened to me, and in bed he made love to me over and over, caressing, hugging, kissing, raising me to climax after climax in the midst of the exhaustion, pain, and despair. I clung to him as if I were drowning, the pain and pleasure mixed so I could no longer tell them apart. This man I'd staked my life on was dangerous and irresistible, toxic and tonic, wounded and wounding. "I want to draw you into me," he said. "I hold you so tight because I want to draw you into me."

I escaped into sleep, still clinging to his body, and when I woke the next morning I blamed the whiskey. The whole terrible scene had happened, I imagined, because I had been drinking Jameson. I resolved to stick to gin or red wine so such a scene would not happen again.

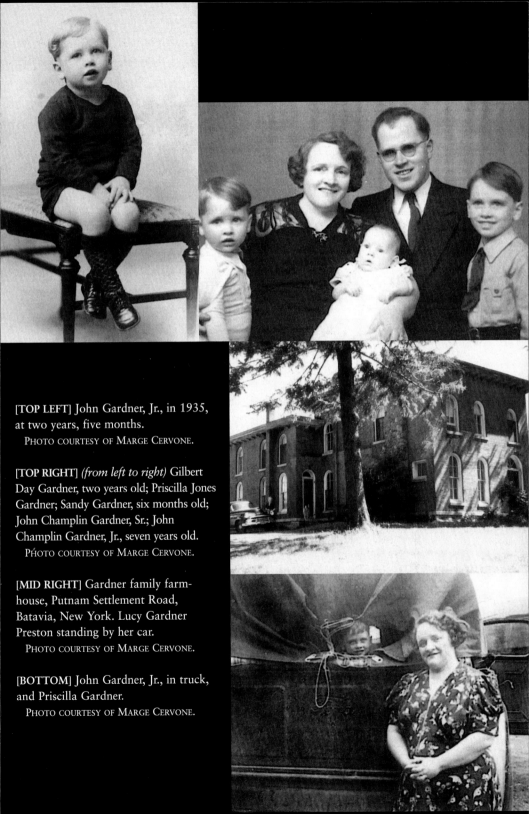

[TOP LEFT] John Gardner, Jr., in 1935, at two years, five months.

PHOTO COURTESY OF MARGE CERVONE.

[TOP RIGHT] *(from left to right)* Gilbert Day Gardner, two years old; Priscilla Jones Gardner; Sandy Gardner, six months old; John Champlin Gardner, Sr.; John Champlin Gardner, Jr., seven years old.

PHOTO COURTESY OF MARGE CERVONE.

[MID RIGHT] Gardner family farm-house, Putnam Settlement Road, Batavia, New York. Lucy Gardner Preston standing by her car.

PHOTO COURTESY OF MARGE CERVONE.

[BOTTOM] John Gardner, Jr., in truck, and Priscilla Gardner.

PHOTO COURTESY OF MARGE CERVONE.

The New York Times Magazine

'Morality in
fiction is
accuracy
and truth . .
however
dismal.'
—John Updike

'Gardner's
making a
shrill pitch to
the literary
right wing.'
—John Barth

'Almost all modern
fiction is tinny,
commercial and
immoral.'
—John Gardner

'I can't suit
every taste.'
—Saul Bellow

The Sound
And Fury
Over Fiction

New York Times Magazine cover, 8 July 1979.

BREAD LOAF 1980

[TOP] Faculty and Associates: *(rear, from left to right)* Tim O'Brien, Bob Houston, Michael Arlen, Stanley Elkin, unknown, Stanley Plumly, Ron Powers, Pamela Hadas, Steve Orlen, Seymour Epstein, Ron Hansen; *(middle)* Nancy Willard, Linda Pastan, Judy Moffett, Gail Godwin, Howard Nemerov; *(front)* Hilma Wolitzer, Marvin Bell, Bob Pack, Molly Cox-Chapman.

PHOTO BY ERIK BORG, COURTESY OF BLUE ARGO.

[BOTTOM] Staff: *(rear, from left to right)* Warren Baker, Gary Glover, Jack Bridgman, Steve Bauer, Virginia Bates, Andrew Litz, Betsy Sachs; *(middle)* Bruce Porell, Susan Thornton, Joyce Renwick; *(front)* Linda Yorton, Elizabeth Mansfield, Blue Argo, Ben Reynolds, John Bryan. The dog is Byron, owned by Jack Bridgman.

PHOTO BY ERIK BORG, COURTESY OF BLUE ARGO.

The Bread Loaf Inn.
PHOTO BY BLUE ARGO.

Treman Cottage.
PHOTO BY BLUE ARGO.

Gail Godwin.
PHOTO BY BLUE ARGO.

Howard Nemerov.
PHOTO BY BLUE ARGO.

Donald Justice.
PHOTO BY BLUE ARGO.

BREAD LOAF 1980–1981

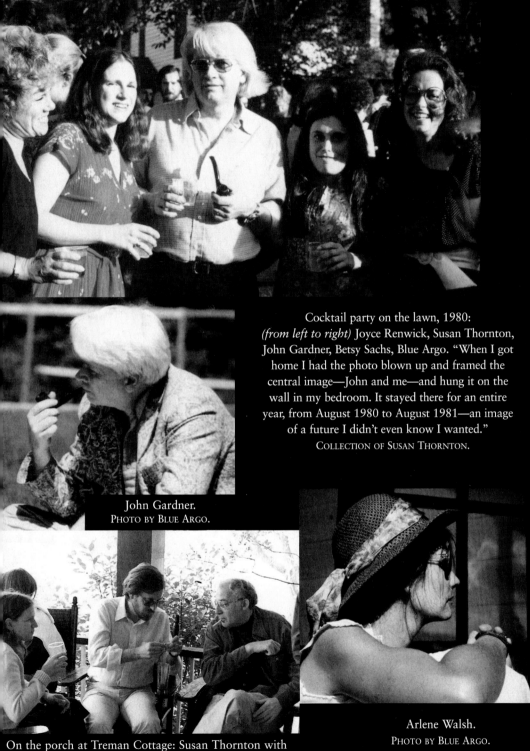

Cocktail party on the lawn, 1980: *(from left to right)* Joyce Renwick, Susan Thornton, John Gardner, Betsy Sachs, Blue Argo. "When I got home I had the photo blown up and framed the central image—John and me—and hung it on the wall in my bedroom. It stayed there for an entire year, from August 1980 to August 1981—an image of a future I didn't even know I wanted." COLLECTION OF SUSAN THORNTON.

John Gardner.
PHOTO BY BLUE ARGO.

Arlene Walsh.
PHOTO BY BLUE ARGO.

On the porch at Treman Cottage: Susan Thornton with Ambrose Clancy *(center)* and Stanley Elkin.
PHOTO BY BLUE ARGO.

BREAD LOAF 1980–1981

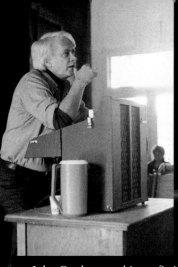

John Gardner teaching a fiction workshop in the Little Theatre at Bread Loaf, 21 AUGUST 1982.
PHOTOS BY DAVID STANTON.

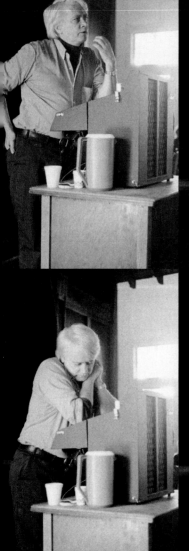

In San Diego, California, early August 1982: *(left to right)* Susan Thornton, John Gardner, Leslie Reynolds, Larry Kapiloff.

PHOTO BY GEORGE MITROVICH.

John Gardner and Ron Hansen in Bread Loaf Barn, 1982.

PHOTO BY DAVID STANTON.

[LEFT] Teddy dressed up, at Bread Loaf.

PHOTO BY PATRICIA LAWLER, COURTESY OF BARBARA SCHIAPPA.

[RIGHT] John Gardner and Susan Thornton in front of Treman Cottage, 1982.

PHOTO BY DAVID STANTON.

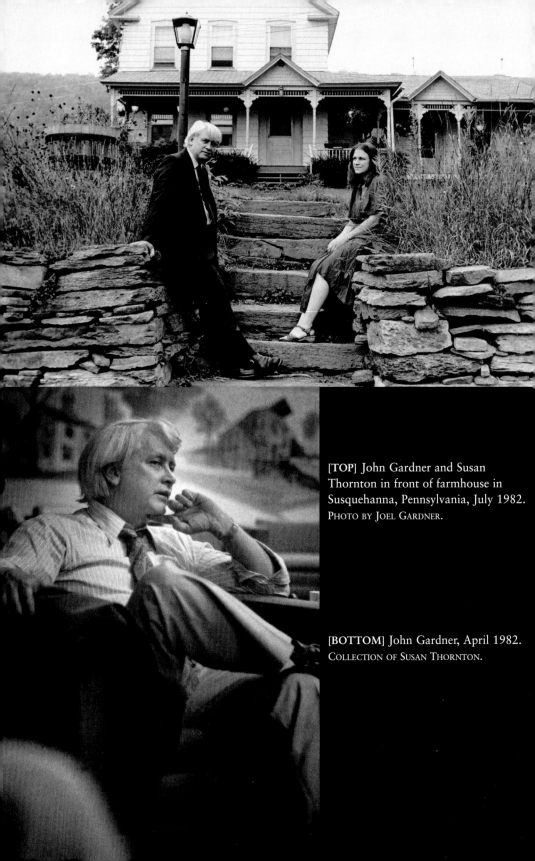

[TOP] John Gardner and Susan Thornton in front of farmhouse in Susquehanna, Pennsylvania, July 1982. Photo by Joel Gardner.

[BOTTOM] John Gardner, April 1982. Collection of Susan Thornton.

11

―――

"A Cat's Paw Has Two Parts"

How dare I suggest that we should all live together? John had written to me. I didn't take him seriously, but I should have. Even though Liz and John and I did not share the house at the same time, our lives were inextricably woven.

Did Liz hate me?

One evening John was on the telephone with her. "Yes, OK." He nodded and smiled, then hung up. "Liz sends you her love." I reported this to my mother, who remarked, "A cat's paw has two parts."

I was sufficiently puzzled by this comment that I wrote it down in my journal.

My envy of Liz ebbed and flowed like weather. In December I had written to Sue Watkins:

> Have been reading about Talleyrand, the French diplomat and aide to Napoleon, a bad person for me to read about now; he lived under one roof with his wife, his mistress whom he loved, and her daughter (from a previous association) whom he also loved. He had a secret staircase built to the daughter's bedroom

(she was forty years younger than he) and she bore him a child, never acknowledged legally, when he was in his late seventies.

At the time I wrote this letter to Sue I did not acknowledge or understand the psychological abuse inherent in this man's life. Instead, I was drawn to the sense of flouting convention, of living outside standard boundaries. Such a situation seemed to me intriguing rather than annihilating. I probably identified more with the man than with the women involved. I was pretty sure I didn't wish to live as had Talleyrand's wife and mistress, but the sense I had with John that "anything goes" was exhilarating rather than frightening. I didn't understand that I might be in danger personally; instead, here was a new challenge. I had always thought I could handle anything. I now understood how a man could exert such a force of personality as to keep two or more women in his life without hiding his connection to any of them. The force that pulled me to John seemed irresistible, a current tugging under running water, despite whatever bad behavior he indulged in. I focused on how I felt when I was alone with him, when he turned that personality on me full force, and I luxuriated in it, breathed it in like ozone.

Liz was a big part of our lives. She received mail at the house, came out to do her laundry, and telephoned continually, with requests large and small. Even our clothes commingled in the drawers of her dresser. Sometimes I wore her socks because it was easier than hunting for my own. I lived in a strange, reckless space. I hardly recognized myself.

At times I liked Liz; she was quick, witty, immediately intuitive. I admired and appreciated her dark good looks, her verbal acuity. It was an odd situation, sisterly, competitive, edgy. We were extremely friendly on the surface, but Liz was not above a catty remark. One sunny afternoon she spied my blue-jean skirt hanging out. "Is that mine? It's huge!" Another time John reported that he and Liz had been strolling through a local department store. "I was looking at a blouse and thinking it would look nice on you," he said. "Liz saw where I was looking and snapped, 'I don't think it comes in a size twenty.' "

Amid the emotional upheaval of those winter weeks, John had a phone call from Shannon Ravenel at Houghton Mifflin. Had he forgotten he was to be guest editor for *The Best American Short Stories 1982*? Where were his selections and his introduction? The material was past due. John had indeed forgotten. No problem, Shannon said, she'd already selected twenty stories; she'd send them on and he could write the introduction.

John wouldn't agree. If his name was going on the book, he'd choose the stories.

My problem was that he wanted Liz to help him. He asked Liz to move back into the farmhouse so they could work around the clock on this project. I knew nothing was as important to John as his work and had decided to do whatever it took to expedite it. Here was my first test. Could I step aside and let him be, to complete this literary project? I had the wrong credentials; I was only John's student. Liz's poetry was widely published; she co-edited *MSS* magazine. Clearly she knew more about contemporary American literature than I did.

I knew I didn't have what it took to hang around the house, keeping myself busy while John and Liz collaborated. Nor did I have what it took to horn in, to read and judge stories myself and interpose my opinions. I could imagine them both turning on me: "Susan, how could you choose such a dumb story? This is an important collection." If I stayed, where would the three of us sleep? Would Liz or I be the one to end up on the couch or in the guest room? I didn't even want to consider that question. It was easier to let them be, to pretend I wasn't hurt, to accept a secondary role. I hid my pain and agreed to move back to my apartment.

In the introduction to the completed collection, John wrote:

What happened (to speak of the mechanics of this collection) is this: Shannon did the preselecting and sent me her results months ago. I put off looking at her work, hoping for the best and being frantically busy, as I always am, for no good reason. Finally, when time was up, the deadline for this book less than a week away, I opened her thick packages of tear sheets and began to read. It was evident at once that we did not exactly agree on things. It was not that she chose badly, only that she'd chosen none of the stories that, in my casual reading, I'd liked best that year. So I ran to the library of the university where I teach and there discovered that all the year's magazines had been sent to the bindery. After a phone call, Shannon sent me her truckload of magazines—I asked her not to bother sending me the "slicks"; most of them I'd looked at already, without much pleasure—and my wife Liz and I read ourselves blind.

When John and Liz had mailed the selected stories back to Shannon, and I moved back into the house, I read rapidly through the journals still lying in untidy piles around the living room and put together my list of the hundred stories I liked best, to make the Other Distinguished Short Stories list, always a part of that collection. I did this without mentioning it to John beforehand and solely to show him that I could. Pleased with myself, I presented this list to John and was so innocent that I was startled and hurt when he said casually, "Oh, Shannon already made up her own list. She's going to be publishing that one."

I was patient all through February and most of March, as I moved out and Liz moved in, as Liz moved out and I moved in, but in late March I had had enough. First there was a telephone call I overheard one night at the farmhouse. I was in the living room and John stood in the kitchen on the phone to Liz: I heard him pitch his voice higher and almost shout, "I'll never love anyone else the way I love you!"

Second, Ray Carver and Tess Gallagher were planning to visit for a week; they were to drive down from Syracuse, where they were both teaching. John had been Ray's teacher in Chico, California, and they were now friends. I knew Ray's work. I had begun to read it after I moved to Binghamton. I found it puzzling and remarked once to John, "But nothing *happens* in his stories." I was working hard on stories where events somehow changed the characters; they moved forward or retreated from new knowledge.

John looked at me, startled. "You know, you're right," he said.

John announced that he wasn't ready to have these old friends know he and Liz had separated, so I was to go back to Binghamton and Liz would move out from David's apartment to live in the farmhouse while Ray and Tess were visiting. It was just to keep up appearances. It didn't mean anything.

I didn't like it, but as I had earlier, I agreed. On one hand, I felt some relief. With all the turmoil in my life it was easier to hide in my apartment and pretend I was just a graduate student than to stay at John's farmhouse, playing hostess for people I'd never met. I felt that Ray and Tess would be expecting to see Liz, not me, and they might harshly judge John's new situation. On the other hand, I knew if John were sure of me, supportive, I could have done anything. That he asked me to move out meant he wasn't as committed to me as I was to him. Later, when I told my mother what had happened, she remarked, "That must have been some visit. In the middle of a breakup."

I used denial to cope with jealousy. The thought that John and Liz would sleep together for a week, might make love, was a thought I literally couldn't think. Because I had decided their sexual relationship was over, it had to be.

I waited out the week and, after Ray and Tess had gone, moved back into the farmhouse. I was profoundly angry and had decided in my heart that I had had enough.

In a day or two, John suggested a trip up to Brockport, New York, so he could visit with John Maier and ask his help on his translation of the Gilgamesh epic.

The Gilgamesh epic is an ancient work from the Near East and dates back to 2600 B.C. The stone tablets, marked with cuneiform text, were excavated in Iraq in the late 1800s. John had been intrigued by this work since the late 1960s and had based large parts of *The Sunlight Dialogues* on ideas contained in *Gilgamesh.*

John Maier was on the faculty at SUNY-Brockport and had been working on a translation of the Gilgamesh epic during the 1970s. He began work with John on a version for the nonspecialist in 1976, after they met at the Brockport Writers' Forum.

The story of Gilgamesh embodies ancient themes: heroism, love, friendship, and death. Gilgamesh and his friend Enkidu create a name for themselves as heroes and forge a lasting friendship. The gods decree that Enkidu must die, and Gilgamesh is devastated. He defies ancient wisdom and journeys to the land of the dead to seek his friend. Many scholars have seen this work as only pessimistic, with its overwhelming message of death and loss. The central theme of the epic is that death is inevitable; only the works a person achieves can gain a kind of immortality.

John had committed to teaching an undergraduate class in the epic at SUNY-Binghamton. In the fall term of 1981 he taught *Beowulf* and the *Iliad*, in the spring of 1982 he lectured on Dante, and he planned to complete a new translation of *Gilgamesh* for the class for the fall of 1982. His goal was twofold: to complete the joint project he had worked on with John Maier and another scholar, Richard Henshaw, and to have a new translation for his students, one he had a part in creating, and was the best he personally could do. He had once described the scholarly work he did on Chaucer, *Beowulf*, and the Greek and Latin epics he used as the basis for his own twentieth-century epic poem, *Jason and Medeia*, as akin to rebuilding a ruined cathedral. Now he had set himself the task of reinterpreting *Gilgamesh* for a new audience.

John's role in the project was to decide on the final reading of the lines of the poem. He worked from previously made translations and from photographs of the stone tablets. John Maier had translated the Akkadian sections with Henshaw's help. Other languages in which the epic is written include Sumerian, Hittite, and

Old Babylonian. It was this last section that John found most interesting.

It was early spring, with the air still chill and abundant snow covering the ground. John Maier and his wife lived in an ordinary split-level tract house in a development in Brockport. One opened the ground-level hollow-core door into another world; the interior of the house was distinguished by statuary, plaques, and relics of Babylonian art. We were to use a small guest room on the lower floor. The Maiers' son was away at school; his room was also vacant.

Once we had arrived in Brockport, I saw my opportunity. We were only minutes from Rochester and my parents' home. Because we were away from John's house I felt a certain empowerment. I remembered who I was. I allowed myself to burn with anger, recalling his shabby treatment of me. He was treating me like the mistress he had said he wanted; it was not enough.

John's example of a literary heroine for women was Sheherazade, because, as he remarked to Blue Argo, "a woman in a man's world needs to be cunning." I might have used more of that quality. My next move was honestly felt and direct.

That night he and John Maier talked over the manuscript and the translation, and I waited until John Maier and his wife had gone to bed. *My* John was still up; I knew he would work all night. Papers and books were spread out over the Maiers' dining room table. I confronted John in the kitchen, where he was digging the last three cubes from an ice tray for a martini. "Which one is that?" I asked.

He looked at me. "My second."

I decided he was sober enough to talk. I laid out my grievances. "You asked me to come to Binghamton. I did. You said your marriage was ending. It doesn't look like it. You say these things, but you don't act like you're serious. I'm good enough for your local friends, but when your literary friends come, you kick me out of the house."

John opened his mouth to speak; I didn't let him get a word in. "And a few weeks ago you closed the door in my face so the *cleaning lady* wouldn't see me. You closed the door in my face! And I stayed upstairs, hiding from her as if I were some kind of refugee."

John looked away from me, biting his lip. I paused for breath and played my trump card.

"You're not treating me right; I don't like it; it's over. Tomorrow morning I'll call my mom. She can come get me and take me to Rochester, and later she and I can come to your house and get my stuff and I'll just go back to Cambridge. You said you wanted me with you, but you're not treating me like you mean it. You and Liz should just patch things up since that's what you appear to want most."

I turned my back and went off to bed in the Maiers' son's room.

Just before dawn, John opened the door of my room and asked if we could talk. He sat gingerly on the edge of the bed and said I was right, he hadn't treated me properly. He said he hadn't been working on the translation that night; instead, he'd waked up John Maier and had been up all night telling him that he and Liz were divorcing, that he was committed to me. This surprised me and seemed significant. I began to melt when I saw his contrite face, as he sat on the edge of the bed, careful not to crowd me, looking at the carpet as he spoke. That he had made a complete turnaround from hiding me to talking things over with an old friend convinced me that this was different. "It's important to verbalize these things," he said. He turned to look directly at me. "Please stay with me. Don't go back to Cambridge. I did treat you badly; you're right. I won't do it again." He asked if we could make love, and I agreed. He ran the flats of his fingers down my legs. "You don't know what it means to me, your flesh."

I decided I could trust him to commit to me. We drove back down to Binghamton and on to Susquehanna, and I felt confident. In the car, as he drove, John reached over from time to time to squeeze my leg, to smile at me.

* * *

We had been back in Susquehanna, at the farmhouse, only a few days. One night I was in the living room reading, curled up under a blanket on the sofa underneath the drafty picture window that looked out onto the empty hills. I heard John answer the phone as he always did—"Gardner, John"—then a moment of silence as he listened; then I heard him say, "Yes, sir, she's right here." That got my attention immediately. I heard the scrape of his chair. John came to the doorway of the living room. "Susan, it's your dad."

On the phone my father said, "We've had a hard time getting ahold of you. We wanted you to know your mother is in the hospital; her surgery is scheduled for tomorrow."

Over the winter and spring of 1982, as my relationship with John deepened, I did not tell my parents what was happening. They had my phone number in Binghamton, but as I spent more and more time with John at his farmhouse, they weren't able to reach me. Mother, at seventy, suffered from arthritis and osteoporosis and had fallen the previous New Year's Day and broken her upper arm. The break had not knit, and the doctors wanted to pin the bone. Dad called my apartment over and over at various times of the day and night and couldn't find me. At last he remembered I had said John lived in Susquehanna.

I listened to my father's voice and felt my face flush with embarrassment and emotion. Although I was thirty-two, I suddenly felt much younger. I was chagrined that I had made them worry, concerned about my mother, gratified that my father had been smart enough to call John, and thankful John had a listed phone.

If mother had not had to be hospitalized, I don't know how much longer I would have kept from them my altered status. I had long had the habit of keeping my sexual affairs private; besides, what could I tell them about John and me? That I was living with a married man?

I apologized to my father, choosing my words carefully. "I'm sorry you had a hard time reaching me," I said. "I'll drive up tomorrow."

The next morning I got up early. John kissed me good-bye at

the back door; then, as I drove around the curving driveway to the front of the house, he walked through the hallway to the front door, opened it, and stood in the doorway to wave.

At the hospital, Mother and I had a difficult conversation. Although she was debilitated from the surgery, wearing a hospital gown, and confined to a hospital bed, she had an authority that threw me into confusion.

She watched me, her eyes wide in her pale, luminous face, and stroked the rough hospital sheet with her long slender fingers. "Your father and I couldn't find you."

My chagrin returned in full force. It was clear she didn't want sympathy. That she had had surgery wasn't the issue; indeed, she seemed to have forgotten about herself. She wanted instead to know about me and what was happening, what I had been keeping from them.

I told her I had been pretty much living at John's and began to cry. An attendant nurse was instantly alert; she hurried over and demanded whether I had a cold; she was worried that I would infect my mother with some virus. I explained that I was crying and I didn't have a cold. She watched us for a minute. "Oh," she said at last. "Just emotion."

I got myself under some control. Mother wasn't angry, wasn't going to tell me what to do, she had just wanted to be able to reach me; that was the cardinal rule I had broken.

"Well, dear, if that's what you want." She watched me narrowly and waited for me to say more. We had never really been intimate. I had never shared with her details or feelings about my love life. I could have told her the whole story, but I didn't. I held back. The habit was too strong. I was living with John and I loved him; that was all I was going to tell her.

I stayed in Rochester two days and then returned to Susquehanna.

The night after my return, John and I were sitting in the living room. Jan Quackenbush was there too. Jan was the friend John was to have dinner with that November when I had visited before;

he had brought Liz up to the Bread Loaf conference in 1981; he was a playwright whose work had been well received and widely noticed in Europe and New York. Jan had come over for dinner to talk about the Laurel Street Theatre; we'd finished eating, and the room was still and dim, with the black night pressing in on the windows. Teddy whined and prowled on the porch; the fire crackled in the woodstove. Plates and wineglasses still stood on the low glass table before the three of us. John leaned forward in his chair and looked at me intently. "Will you marry me?" His voice was strong and firm.

It seemed fitting that Jan was there, as witness.

"Yes," I answered, just as firmly. "Yes, I will."

12

"The Best Man in the World"

In April, at John's parents' house, I wanted to call my mother in Rochester. As I picked up the telephone, John spoke to me in a low voice. "Use our calling card." I was momentarily puzzled. The toll call to Rochester couldn't be more than forty cents. Then I reconsidered his parents' lives and used our calling card number.

John was a junior or, to be more precise, he was the fourth John Champlin Gardner in his family. To distinguish him from his father, his family nickname was Bud, or Buddy, and his father, John Senior, was John.

Every weekend in the spring and summer of 1982, we went up to see John's parents, sometimes on the Harley, sometimes in the car. This trip took between five and six hours. When we were in the car, to pass the time as John drove, I read aloud to him. Our favorite book was *Endurance* by Alfred Lansing. This nonfiction study, published in 1959, describes Ernest Shakleton's expedition to the Antarctic, 1914–1916. As I read, John listened with rapt attention to the unfolding story of the survival of twenty-eight men stranded on pack ice off Antarctica for more than a year.

*　　*　　*

Shortly after I met John's mother and father in the fall of 1981, John's father had suffered a stroke. His right side was paralyzed and he lost his speech. At first we visited in the nursing home; later we visited at their house outside the town of Batavia. Just before John Senior was released from the nursing home, John made an appointment at the local lumberyard, had planks delivered, and built a wheelchair ramp up to the front door of the house. He also planted an enormous garden.

John's parents lived in the brick farmhouse they had always owned, the house of his boyhood. They had divided it up into apartments for rental income, and the big square building now housed three families. A duplex apartment was made from the former living room with a new kitchen and upstairs bedrooms, a second-floor apartment had been made out of the additional bedrooms, and John's parents took the meanest space for themselves, living in their former foyer, sleeping in what had been the dining room, and cooking in the truncated kitchen.

The door opened directly into the converted foyer, crowded with its upright piano, rocking chair, armchair, and couch along the far wall. John Senior sat, head bowed, in the upholstered chair facing the piano, his good hand resting on the handle of his four-pronged cane. John's mother held court on the sofa, surrounded by her boxes of stationery and Kleenex, a portable phone, and small spiral notebooks that she covered with her looping, downward-sloping script.

On the broad back of the knobby upholstered sofa leaned a small framed photograph, fading with age, of a redheaded six-year-old: Gilbert. The camera had caught a mischievous look; the boy's smile was vibrant. Whenever I came through the flimsy screen door, this photo was the first thing I saw. I had overheard at Bread Loaf, not from John but from one of his friends, Joan's complaint that when she and John were married and returned to Batavia, John's mother always set a place at the table for Gilbert. I had wondered if this were literally true or just expressed her sense that

Gilbert was a constant presence. I asked John if his parents' re-
minders about his brother bothered him. He avoided the question
and shrugged. "I never had anything to compare it to."

Above the sofa hung a mural showing Jesus as a boy of twelve
preaching at the Temple. Christ is depicted as clear-eyed, with his
hand extended, the image favored by calendar makers who serve
kindergarten classrooms and want children to have a positive image of their Christian God. His older listeners are awestruck, leaning forward, listening intently. The Biblical text illustrated tells of
his hearers' wonder that a boy so young would teach with such
authority, not as one who has merely studied, but as one who
knows.

I found this sentimental image significant. John's parents were
devout members of the local Presbyterian church; however, not
every Christian home contains religious art. This image meant
something to them. I wondered what it had meant to John as a
boy, and if its presence had fostered his intellectual courage.

Priscilla told me John Senior's stroke had caused great consternation in their church. How, members of the congregation wondered, could this tragedy have befallen such good people? Was God
good?

On the kitchen wall, over the stove, was a mural John had done
as a boy, a country landscape with brightly colored mountains,
woods, and a stream in the distance. Now it was darkened with
age and had been cut by the remodeling. Priscilla boiled water for
tea on an ancient stove whose weak gas flame took forever to heat
her favorite battered kettle. The breakfast nook, which looked out
over the yard and a willow tree, had been John's childhood bedroom.

His parents slept in a double bed in the former dining room,
darkened by curtains and heavy furniture. Next to his mother's
bureau hung a photo of John and Joan in their early twenties, both
in profile, looking in the same direction. With his dark and her
blond hair, the pose and the gold frame, they resembled film stars
of the early 1950s. I noticed that Priscilla hung it where she would

see it every day, but no one else would unless snooping in her bedroom.

John's father could not tolerate tobacco smoke, so John would stand in the doorway, pipe in hand, blowing the smoke out the tattered screen past the weeping willow and toward the curving driveway.

I remember John's sensitivity and tact as he waited outside the door of the tiny bathroom, only a toilet and sink, closed off from the hall by a folding door. "You OK in there, Dad?" I would hear him ask. Then, when his father rang the bell he used as a signal, John would help him up and adjust his trousers with matter-of-fact love and good humor.

When John was growing up, his parents often read aloud to each other and the family at home, choosing the narrative poems of Scott, Longfellow, Tennyson, and Browning. In John's library in Susquehanna was a yellowing volume of Browning's complete works, so worn that his uncle had clumsily rebound it in thick leather to hold it together.

John also read aloud to his bedridden grandmother, Priscilla's mother, who lived with the family in her last years.

On our visits to his parents, John read to his father. He began with *Kim* by Rudyard Kipling but found the dialect and the convoluted opening chapter difficult. "You like this, Dad?" John Senior shook his head. "I'll get something else." On the shelf John found *The Magic City*, a children's book by E. Nesbit. John and his father loved it, and that was the book he chose for reading aloud on all our trips to Batavia.

One day the speech therapist came out with her list of words. John Senior worked his mouth carefully, concentrating. "Gar-den-er," the therapist pronounced. "Gardner," he answered promptly. "Gardner." He was clearly pleased; at last a word he could say. The therapist shook her head. "Gar-*den*-er," she repeated, emphasizing the middle syllable. John Senior tried again. "Gard-*ner*." The therapist frowned and went on to another word.

John Senior had been a local celebrity, well-known throughout western New York. He was a lay preacher who traveled to different churches and read the scripture or gave the sermon when the regular preacher was away or on vacation. He had no theological training or formal education beyond high school but nonetheless was much in demand. He was tall, striking; he practiced to train his voice, used an actor's gestures. He loved an audience. Outside of church, he entertained at Grange halls. In rural communities, the Grange is the social center, a combined town hall, senior center, youth clubhouse, and music hall, often the only place farmers can gather free of charge to meet, chat, be entertained. John Senior and Priscilla had often provided that entertainment. He recited stirring bits of Shakespeare, for example, Marc Antony's speech from *Julius Caesar*, and from his favorite poets, or told outrageous shaggy-dog stories he made up himself. Sometimes he read poems that Buddy had written. He held local audiences entranced with emotional recitations in his deep, resonant voice.

Priscilla was an entertainer too, but she mostly sang, choosing anthems or spirituals. Now and then they had put on plays together, which Priscilla directed, or traveled with their two-person show, *An Evening with the Gardners*.

John's sister, Sandy, told me that when John gave readings from his work in western New York, after *The Sunlight Dialogues* had been published, on one occasion an older lady approached him. With awe she looked up. "Are you *the* John Gardner?" Instantly John guessed her meaning. "Oh, no." He shook his head. "That's my dad."

I worried that Priscilla wouldn't like or accept me. Now I have more empathy for her position. She and John Senior were in their seventies and early eighties. Here was their middle-aged son, with grown children, already divorced, now divorcing again. They weren't enthusiastic but were willing to accept this, to let John be. Priscilla didn't say anything directly, but one afternoon she deliberately brushed past me with her bowlegged, lopsided walk, reached out, and briefly squeezed my hand.

Priscilla had an odd gesture; she now had to speak and interpret for her husband, but she had the habit of touching his forearm, plucking at his sleeve. When we were alone, John asked if I'd caught it.

"How come she does that?"

"It's the gesture of the betrayed wife. He was always unfaithful to her. See, it's like, *Look, I'm still here, don't forget me.*"

John was always a teacher. To his apprentice writers he said over and over: show the gesture, your reader will understand the emotion. He drew my attention to his mother because this was an example of his thesis, a fine point he wished me to note to enrich my understanding, my ability as a writer. He was also telling me something about his parents.

Priscilla was eight years older than her husband and had been his high school English teacher. This imbalance in their lives, that John Senior was the daring precocious high school student who seduced his teacher, that Priscilla was older and not the beauty her sister Lucy was, had played itself out in family tensions through the years. John Senior had reenacted the part of the seducer, the thrill of courting and winning the forbidden woman, in adulterous affairs throughout his life.

In John's story "Redemption," his father's womanizing is presented as an escape from grief over his son's death. "He became . . . a hunter of women, trading off his sorrow for the sorrows of wearied, unfulfilled country wives." When Dale Hawthorne at last returns home on his motorcycle from seeking escape with other women, he kneels in the living room, embraced by his wife and his daughter. Young Jack watches from the doorway. When his aunt calls to him, he enters the room and kneels to embrace his father. The boy is dizzy, nauseated, and whispers, "I hate you," too softly for the others to hear.

*   *   *

My sense was that in dramatizing his father's infidelities as springing from grief over Gilbert's death, John was rationalizing, trying to be kind. From what he told me, John Senior's love affairs had been habitual and constant. While John did not grow up in an alcoholic home—his parents did not drink or allow liquor in their house—it was a family where adults evaded responsibility and escaped pressure in other ways, his mother in the grueling work of a farm wife, through religiosity and gossip, his father through motorcycle riding and sexual adventures.

This was John's model of a husband and father: a celebrity who evades responsibility, seeks consolation in sexual affairs outside of marriage, and who, because of his charm, his way with words, or whatever reason, is always accepted and forgiven.

John never articulated resentment toward his father for anything said or done. Instead, he always described him as "a much better man than me." John didn't want to express or even feel darker emotions toward his parents, but occasionally I sensed his true feelings.

One night at home in Susquehanna, John described an incident from his childhood on the farm. He said that one day in haying season, when he was six, John Senior lacked a helper. He took his son John, stood him up in the tractor, tied his hands to the wheel, started the engine, released the clutch, and jumped off. The tractor started moving, with John, six years old, tied to the steering wheel, more or less holding it on track. When the tractor reached the end of the row, John Senior caught up, jumped back on, turned the wheel around, so that John's hands were crossed over each other, still tied on, and again let the tractor run. So it continued, row after row, until the harvest was made. As he told this story to me, John held his hands in front of him, crossed and then recrossed them, grinning, but he didn't look happy. I was horrified, imagining what it felt like for a six-year-old child, hardly tall enough to reach the wheel of the tractor, to be tied there, having to keep his balance as the machine lurched across the fields: the noise of the engine, the heat of the sun, and the hardness of the metal seat pressing against his back, with his father following on the ground behind him, leaving him to run the tractor. . . .

John had written to me:

> When I was a kid I got up at four in the morning to get the cows. It was nice, in a way—though I always, of course, resented it, and swore I would someday get free of farming. At 4 A.M. it's dark. You take the dog—usually a collie or shepherd—and you drift in half a dream down this mile-long lane to the upper pasture, and you look in meadows and groves for the cows, and then you yell them and stone them back to the barn, by which time the sun is beginning to come up, and it's beautiful. Your pantlegs [sic] are sopping wet with dew and your shoes squish, and on the way you eat raspberries and cherries, the wild kind, and then back in the barn you grain the cows, eating some of it yourself— made, in those days, of real grain and alfalfa and mollasses [sic] and sorghum (I can't spell) and then you go back to the house and sleep for an hour. Then you get up and eat breakfast and then go out to plow or disk or cultipack for eighteen hours, with breaks when your sister comes and brings you lunch and supper (or as we said, dinner and supper). . . . You think everything is possible—you can be president or a great Welsh poet, and it's true. Comes the day you accidentally kill your brother, and it's incredible that the pastoral life is over—no reason it should be, but it is. Your father the best man in the world lies in the gutter with the manure, crying, and you know it's your fault, though it was all an accident, and you know for all time you're monstrous.

John found his freedom from farming through his drive and his intellect. He joined the Boy Scouts and worked his way rapidly up to Eagle Scout. He was made "Mayor of Batavia" for a day. Like his fictional Jack Hawthorne, he took the bus into Rochester and studied French horn at the Eastman School of Music, and he traveled to Indiana to DePauw University, over his father's objections.

"Dad told me, You won't like those people at the university," John said.

He further estranged his parents by his marriage to Joan just a few weeks short of his twentieth birthday. John Senior's plan had been for his eldest son to take over the farm. That John escaped him, by enrolling in the university, by marrying, frustrated his hopes. Now he would have to wait for his last son, Jim, to grow up, and Jim was a child of six. In the end, Jim didn't take over the farm after all, but followed his own path. When John informed his parents of his plan to marry Joan, "My father went into a blistering rage. He refused point-blank to come to the wedding. Mom and Aunt Lucy had hard work to turn him around."

After his marriage John transferred to Washington University in St. Louis, grateful for the encouragement of his mother-in-law, who, he told me, typed some of his early manuscripts. "I built a study out in the garage," he said. "It was so small my elbows touched each wall and it filled up really quick from my pipe smoke."

In his senior year, John was elected to Phi Beta Kappa and won a Woodrow Wilson fellowship, which supported his enrollment in the creative writing program at the University of Iowa. In three years he completed his M.A. and his Ph.D. and accepted a teaching position, first at Oberlin College, in Ohio, and then at Chico State College, now the University of California at Chico.

John spent his professional life at various colleges and universities as far away from Batavia as he could get, yet he still visited Batavia regularly and, his mother told me, came back especially to see her when she had hip replacement surgery.

But beneath this surface of devotion ran darker currents. The image that stayed with John after Gilbert's death is that of his father, face down in manure in the gutter of the barn floor, weeping over the death of his son. To me, this image is striking. It says to me that Gilbert was valued over John and that John Senior focused on his own grief and guilt, failing to understand the damage done to his eldest son.

John's anger toward his father surfaces briefly in his story "Redemption." In describing Dale Hawthorne's return to his family, John wrote:

> in a month he was again reciting poetry for schools and churches and the Grange, and sometimes reading Scripture from the pulpit Sunday mornings. Jack, sitting rigid, hands over his face, was bitterly ashamed of those poems and recitations from the Bible. . . . Jack scorned the poems' opinions, scorned the way his father spoke directly to each listener, as if each were some new woman. . . . Sometimes his father would recite a poem Jack himself had written, in the days when he'd tried to write poetry, a comic limerick or some maudlin piece about a boy on a hill. Though it was meant as a compliment, Jack's heart would swell with rage; yet he kept silent, more private than before. . . . One of these days, he told himself, they'd wake up and find him gone.

I saw this latent rage in something John told me about his first marriage. At one point he suspected his father of a sexual interest in Joan. This theme of incestuous love surfaces in John's last novel, *Mickelsson's Ghosts*, where Mickelsson witnesses Tillson, the humpbacked, goatlike chairman of the English department, and Jessica Stark, Mickelsson's lover, in an office at the university, after dark, making love.

In addition to long-standing family tensions, John also experienced the frustrations of a middle-aged son dealing with elderly, failing parents. One day at home in Susquehanna, he hung up the phone from a conversation with his mother with a look of disgust.

"What's wrong?" I asked.

"She told me, *Dad had a good movement.*"

Another time I heard him shouting into the phone at his mother. "No, no, that can't be true! What do you want me to do about it? Why are you telling me?" His mother had confided her fears that his sister was suicidal. Sandy was then living in Detroit, working as an English teacher and experiencing an acrimonious divorce.

Priscilla had a morbid streak. One afternoon in Batavia at his parents' house John picked up a list of hymns—"Amazing Grace," "A Mighty Fortress Is Our God," "All Hail the Power of Jesus' Name"—in his mother's handwriting on top of the upright piano. "What's this?" he asked. "It's the hymns I want at my memorial service," his mother answered. John looked at me, and raised his eyebrows.

Priscilla told me she had taken audiotapes made of John Senior when he was reciting poetry in his glory days and played them for both of them to listen to, she and her now-mute husband. "We had a good weep," she said. I felt this action showed both malice and selfishness. Because John Senior was disabled, he needed Priscilla constantly; she was no longer a wife he could evade or discard. Indeed, with her sister Lucy she was his primary caretaker and had him just where she wanted him, at home.

13

"Rochester Girl"

In early May we went to Rochester, where John met my parents formally. As he put his foot on the bottom step leading up to the front door, he hesitated. "I've been in this house before."

I looked at him, startled.

"Alec Wilder lived here, didn't he? The composer?"

My parents had moved into the house in 1970, and I had no idea who might have owned it previously.

John looked around. Next door stood the former carriage house, now converted into a residence, far back from the street. I knew a member of the Rochester Philharmonic had lived there for some years. John nodded. "Alec Wilder was a friend of my parents. I'm sure I've been here before."

We went inside, where, in my mother's elegant living room, furnished in silk and damask, with its collection of Steuben crystal and cloisonné, John was suddenly a lot less confident. He sat forward on the couch, pushing back his hair, swiping at his upper lip, fiddling with his pipe, scuffling his feet, acting like the farm boy from Batavia he may have suddenly felt himself. He mumbled, staring at the vivid Oriental carpet, that he and I were "together." In that setting he couldn't say *living together*, although my parents already knew. He continued that we were "working toward marriage." My mother remarked later, "He acted like a young suitor." My father clapped his hands on his knees, rose from his chair, and announced he would take us all to dinner. In the back seat of my parents' car, John held my hand. We made an appointment at St. Paul's Episcopal Church to meet the minister who would marry us; I began to make wedding plans; we set a date: Saturday, September 18. The church secretary told us we were lucky to get any Saturday in September, planning a wedding so soon.

As we left, John told me, "When I see a living room like your parents', I know I'm around people a lot different from me. You know what?" he teased. "I'd like to get all my old motorcycle buddies together and show them what's happened: I, John Gardner, Batavia farm boy, have finally gotten a 'Rochester girl.' "

Mom didn't think much of the Gardners. They may have represented to her the small-town mentality she had fought off by moving my father from his hometown of Wellsville, where they lived first, to her hometown of Rochester. Mother's family had been well established in New York State since the Revolutionary War. My mother and my grandmother had both belonged to the DAR, the Daughters of the American Revolution, but both quit that organization in the wake of the 1940s scandal when Marian Anderson, the gifted African-American soprano, was denied the right to sing in the group's hall. Neither Mom nor Grandmother wanted to be part of such a racist decision, and neither ever rejoined.

On Dad's side, my grandfather, Lewis Henry Thornton, had been a pioneer in the oil industry as it developed in Pennsylvania and New York. He was also a newspaper publisher and achieved wide renown throughout New York State. His name was bandied about as a gubernatorial candidate, but in the summer epidemic of 1910, just before my father's birth that September, he contracted infantile paralysis, or poliomyelitis, which left his legs useless. In search of treatment, Lewis Henry and his wife, Winifred, traveled to Warm Springs, Georgia, where Grandfather befriended Franklin

Roosevelt. In the 1920s, both men were at Warm Springs for a new underwater treatment. Family stories are that Winifred liked Franklin well enough but didn't care much for Eleanor. Winifred, after all, was a Republican State Committeewoman and the granddaughter of one of the founders of the Republican party.

Unlike Franklin Roosevelt, Grandfather did not pursue his interest in politics but spent his remaining years building his business in Wellsville. Later he became a trustee at the University of Rochester, where my parents met and courted.

In choosing boyfriends, I was always conscious of my family background, and it seemed quite unlikely that I should end up with a farm boy. Growing up in Rochester, all I knew about Batavia were strident advertisements on the local radio for Batavia Downs, a local racetrack.

In contrast to John's father, my father was a faithful husband. He told me often, "After I met your mother, I never looked at another woman." Dad disapproved of men who cheated on their wives. His policy at his company was never to hire a man whom coworkers would describe as an unfaithful husband. "If a man cheats on his wife, how can an employer trust him?" Dad asked.

If my parents disapproved of John as a man who had been divorced once and was planning another divorce in order to marry me, they chose not to say anything. Much later my cousin Sandy Ernest told me, "Your mom was really worried about you. She saw the drinking, the infidelity; she was worried about the debt, the cancer surgery, the age difference. She was really worried."

While my father was devoted to my mother, I had the sense that Mother was dissatisfied with her choice of husband. There was always an edge of discontent, an imbalance of affection. I felt often that Dad loved Mom more than she loved him. He tried to purchase her affection, showering her with gifts: a mink coat when she was pregnant with me, a huge aquamarine ring the day I was born, trips to New York City, where he installed her in a corner room at the Biltmore and she could buy new spring and fall outfits, and the most lavish gift of all: a cruise on the Cunard Line's *Ca-*

ronia to London to be present in the crowd for the coronation of Queen Elizabeth II.

On that trip they left me with my grandmotherly caretaker for over six weeks. I was three years old and missed them terribly. Now that I am a parent, I doubt the wisdom of their decision. Their absence was not required by work or financial necessity; it was a pleasure trip. I can understand why they went: they were in their forties, they had the money, it was the trip of a lifetime. However, I also remember the sadness, puzzlement, and isolation I felt, when I was left at home for the coronation and during subsequent trips to Europe. I turned often to Florence Joseph, our housekeeper, whose presence was more constant—and sometimes more comforting—than my mother's.

The irony, which I discovered later, is that in attempting to buy my mother's love, my father borrowed against his share of the family business. Rather than withdraw surplus capital, he made himself loans he could not pay back, and this contributed to the failure of the business in the late 1960s. My mother stuck with him after the business failed and went back to work herself at the age of fifty-eight, but she was not happy about it. She used the money she inherited from her father, a banker who had invested in blue-chip stocks, to keep up their standard of living, and used her salary to meet some expenses. Mom and Dad attempted to assuage their marital and financial tensions with alcohol, but it didn't work.

In the meantime, I was making my own way, more or less, but had remained determinedly single, and Mother was restive. On trips to Cambridge she had met Jack and hoped desperately that I would marry him. When I announced I was leaving Cambridge for Binghamton, and thus leaving Jack, she was angry and made no secret of her feelings that I was throwing away an excellent potential husband. Her disapproval only heightened my confusion in the late fall and winter of 1981. With John at last committed to me, in the spring of 1982, I was relieved and genuinely happy, looking forward in spite of all the difficulties.

*   *   *

My parents could tell I was immensely happy with John, so they befriended him. Dad, always a great reader, grew curious about John's work. With great anticipation, he checked *The Sunlight Dialogues* out of the library but was sorely disappointed. Some time later my cousin Harry mentioned that he was reading it also. "I hope you have better luck with it than I did," Dad remarked.

With John I felt confident enough to step out of my self-imposed isolation, and I let him into my life as I had let no other person. I took him around Rochester and showed him the girls' school I had attended, whose remaining buildings are now part of the Rochester Museum of Science; together we traced the path I had walked to school. He showed genuine interest in these landmarks of my youth.

John and I went to Seneca Lake as well, where my parents had owned a summer cottage, and I introduced him to all my parents' friends; we ate dinner at the cottage of my godmother, Catherine Elliott. As we drove away, a fierce thunderstorm came up. I squinted out the windshield at the driving rain. "Maybe we should go back and spend the night," I suggested. Partly I was worried about the driving; in a car, I'm more anxious about rain than snow. Partly I wanted more time with these dear family friends.

John turned and looked at me. "I'll bring you back here." I was immediately relieved. This was why I loved him, after all. He saw through my veiled remark to the heart of my anxiety—that our marriage would cut me off from my beloved family. I had lived in emotional isolation for so long that my love for John felt miraculous. Both of us used alcohol to cloak feelings that scared us, but we felt sufficiently safe with each other that I could share with him experiences and feelings I had shared with no one else, and he could do the same with me. I felt this shared intimacy was an unbreakable bond, rare enough that I could make certain sacrifices to keep it in place.

One night in Susquehanna, John looked at me and said, with wonder in his voice, "Most people love me *because* I'm a writer. You love me *in spite of* the fact that I'm a writer." It was true. I didn't give a damn if he wrote or not, as long as he was happy. I loved being with him, loved the vivid turns of his mercurial intelligence, his odd remarks and insights. When he didn't write—and he didn't work on a major book that summer, only shorter projects—he was a lot of fun to be around. He spoke of giving it up, turning to carpentry or pig farming. I let him talk, figuring he'd make his own decisions. I saw his role as providing me with an intimate connection I had never had before, and therefore an enhanced, enriched life; I saw my role as facilitating his happiness.

Through the spring John quite often went out of town on lecture tours. I still had my apartment in Binghamton and often I went back. I felt more comfortable there, partly because John had sent Teddy off to a dog trainer who worked with him at his home. I was hesitant to stay at the farmhouse without Teddy.

From my journal, while I was in Binghamton: *John called this morning at 3 A.M. from Texas. We talked for two hours. He asking: "Do you love me?" Said he saw a girl on the news who reminded him of me and he burst into tears. Tried to call previous night, he said, but couldn't get through. Very upset.*

A woman gave him her book to sign. On the page for his signature was written in pencil: "I'm available. What's your room number? What time?" He said, in that tone of voice that made him sound an incredulous imbecile, "and she was pretty." There were all these people around. He signed the book John Gardner, *closed it, and handed it back to her.*

I was pleased. I felt this meant he had turned over a new leaf. He might be faithful to me after all.

Asked how I felt, did I desire other men. I said I'd thought about that and I'd already made my decision: I didn't. He said "Good," emphatically.

Said he holds me so tight he's afraid he's going to hurt me. He said if we married, what if I don't love him? What if I always thought I could have done better?

He said I was brought up to be classy. Could I be a farm wife?

Then he fell asleep holding the phone, with the long distance line still open. "John, John," I said urgently into the receiver. "Wake up and hang up the phone."

Could I, as a city girl, adapt to country life? I had never had the ambition to live on a farm, had never really thought about rattlesnakes, woodchucks, or deer or how to control animal pests when you have a garden in the country. He had resolved to make our farmhouse a real farm, and in the summer of 1982 we bought two goats. We had no way to get them back to our house except in the back of the Honda. John's solution: lead them to the car, open the door, shove them up onto the leather upholstery of the back seat. The car, which had smelled bad because of Teddy's constant presence, now smelled a great deal worse.

We also bought two piglets and took them home too—again, on the back seat of the car, each tiny piglet squirming in its burlap sack. He built a movable pigpen in the back yard, with the idea that as he moved it around the margin of the yard, the pig manure would form a natural barrier against the rattlesnakes that infested the area. He instructed me to keep out of the woods and away from certain ponds during the hot dry summer, when the snakes came down from the hills to drink. His one-character, one-act play *Days of Vengeance*, which he wrote for his mother to present, was based on a newspaper account of a local widow who had killed a rattlesnake in her house.

We put in an orchard of dwarf fruit trees, and he told me a folk belief of his family. As I steadied one tree, John tamped dirt around its root ball. "My grandfather cut his thumb and let a drop of blood fall onto the root ball of every tree he planted." He looked up at me. "You plant a hundred and fifty trees, that's a lot of cuts."

I discovered, that spring and summer, in our trips up and down the mountains on various errands or to see friends, that the country had a unique beauty. The hardtop roads swooped up and down like a roller-coaster ride. From the dizzying tops of the steepest hills the views were breathtaking; then one plunged down again as if through a leafy green dream into verdant valleys or enclosing, spooky woods. Through it all curled the Susquehanna River, a broad silver ribbon, and next to it abandoned rail tracks. I looked past my initial apprehension of poverty and misery that I had seen in Susquehanna, and while that impression remained, I learned to savor the natural beauty of the setting John had chosen for his life.

We had an infestation of gypsy moths, which made their shaggy gray nests in nearly every tree. By midsummer the surrounding woods looked as though fall had set in early; the insects had eaten away the leaves and, in some cases, killed the trees.

The standard method to get rid of these pests was to burn them out. John made up torches; I poured the gasoline with a liberal hand and shinnied up the tree. John passed me the torch and I lit it. The resulting flare nearly took my eyebrows off. I managed to burn the gypsy-moth nest and jumped down. "A little less gasoline next time," John advised mildly.

Later he reported this incident to Liz. It was typical of him to tell her stories of our daily life; in this case I think he wanted to upset her. He saved the best detail for last. "And where was Susan?" Liz asked. "Oh, she was up in the tree," John said, and gloated when Liz turned pale. Here was the arena where I could best her, in foolishness and derring-do, and John knew it. He liked having two attractive young women in his thrall.

Similarly, he held her up to me. "Liz is so smart," he commented, one night at home, holding his pipe away from his face, crafty as one of his fictional dragons. "She'll probably go on for her Ph.D."

He watched me narrowly. In that instant I resolved that *I* would go on for a Ph.D. just to show him, and I did. This calculated, seemingly offhand remark later impelled me through an M.A. and a Ph.D. in less than four years.

He also reminded me and others over and over that it was Liz who had come up with the quote with which to decorate the gazebo he had built in the side yard. "I asked her for an eight-word quote and she didn't even pause. She just rattled it off: 'And all seasons shall be sweet to thee.' " He smiled, proud.

Could I come up with a quote like that? I felt hugely inadequate. And yet I didn't say anything, and he went right ahead with his plan to use the quote she had contributed, even though she had moved out of his house.

To a certain extent, of the two of us, Liz and me, I was the more malleable, conventional wife. While Liz lived with John she earned the M.F.A. degree, kept up her ties to *The New Yorker*, where she had worked as a personal assistant to author Ved Mehta, and persisted in her efforts to craft and publish her poetry. When they married, she kept her name, Rosenberg. She didn't have much use for the Featherweight sewing machine John bought for her; she taught alongside him at the university; she dove into her editing for *MSS* magazine. She was nervous about the Harley and often insisted on following him in the car while he rode ahead on the motorcycle; then she fretted that she might come upon his body if he crashed too far ahead of her. She hated airplanes. She had bought John a bicycle for a birthday present; when I saw it gathering dust in the garage I just shook my head. Couldn't she see that he was not the bicycle-riding type?

In many respects I was more domestic than Liz, or perhaps less squeamish. She told a story on herself that, while John had been away on a reading tour, her dog Esmé had stalked and killed a rabbit, then dragged its carcass into the house. Rather than touch the dead rabbit, Liz closed off the door to the hall and left the rabbit stiffening on the carpet until John came home two days later to deal with it.

I, on the other hand, came bursting into John's study one morning shouting, "Teddy's trying to kill a woodchuck!" and then raced out to watch the suspenseful fight: the dog lunging for an opening, his hackles raised; the woodchuck on his hind legs, spitting and sparring; and Teddy's jaws closing on the woodchuck's neck and shaking until its spine snapped.

I put the dead animal in a box myself and then hoisted it all into a garbage bag. When John picked up the bag later to put it by the road he said, "Is there something dead in there?" I explained about the woodchuck. "I thought it had a funny feeling," he said.

In many respects John and Liz had a parallel drive to succeed while I was willing to take a secondary role as wife, homemaker, and, later, mother. Yet I too wanted respect for my intellect, to be more than just a bed partner. I kept up with my own writing, I went to John's fiction workshops, and I attended his lectures on the epic, often taking notes. He commented on this once, indirectly. "You know," he remarked offhand, "I'm not telling those kids anything they can't get on their own out of the library."

I nodded, understood that he'd seen me taking notes, and kept right on. I was greedy to know what he knew, to understand everything in his well-stocked mind.

With a farm and farm animals came the desire for a garden, and with the idea of a garden came the need for a gun. Deer grazed in the fields alongside the cows, often, in winter, feeding on shrubs beneath our porch. Woodchucks could eat their weight in radishes. While John wasn't a hunter, he wanted to have a garden, and woodchucks were a pest. He asked: "What if I buy a gun?"

He was testing me. Would I become hysterical and accuse him of trying to kill us both? Remind him that he was crazy and not to be trusted? He had told me no woman he had lived with had allowed him to have a gun in the house. He was watching me closely: I shrugged.

When I was fifteen a family friend had taught me how to handle and shoot a gun at my parents' summer home. Warren instructed me carefully, showed me all the parts of his .22, and watched as I took aim and fired at bottles he'd set out on a stump behind his mother's property. When I had finished, I lowered the gun and put on the safety as he had taught me before I turned and handed the gun back to him. Warren nodded approvingly. "You did that just right." My shooting wasn't spectacularly good or spectacularly bad. I'd hit at least one bottle. At the time, that was enough.

John drove out to Marieder's country store in Lanesboro and bought a hunting rifle, a 30-30, and left it in the closet off his study, and I didn't think anymore about it. I felt I had to trust him, that he was fundamentally sane, and there was no point in getting upset about owning or not owning a gun. I had the unshakable confidence of the young, the untested, the deeply in love. I was in denial about his drinking, and we hadn't yet had a really bad scene.

We bought the farm animals, he expanded the garden, put in an orchard, spoke about vineyards. He wanted to start a second family. How did I feel about having a baby? He began to press me about pregnancy while his divorce was in process. I was more conservative; I did not want to become pregnant until I was actually married. He was impatient; I felt he was constantly reaching out for changes. In retrospect I see he wasn't making the right ones. Nor was I. I needed to become sober, in order to live a sane life, and so did he. The fundamental change he needed was to enter a treatment program, to seek help for his obsessive drinking.

I see this now even in his autobiographical novel fragment *Stillness*, published after his death as *Stillness and Shadows*. His mouthpiece in that book, Martin Orrick, speaks constantly of making a change but seems immobilized by personal circumstances. I didn't understand the burden of guilt and shame that overwhelmed John, his sense that his drinking was long gone out of his conscious control, and the panic and fear he lived with on a daily basis. I knew he drank daily, mostly at night, but he didn't show the signs of alcohol in ways I expected. John didn't complain of hangovers, his hands were steady, he woke up alert and pushed himself to keep his fantastic schedule, but he never went without alcohol. I watched him while he was composing a short story and noted in my journal that he worked all day in his study, drinking coffee. He didn't stop to eat until suppertime, when we had red wine with dinner. That evening he went back to work in his study and drank martinis as he typed.

The miracle to me now is not what he didn't do but how much he managed to accomplish.

Alcoholism is a disease of the spirit; alcoholics who reach rock bottom often feel, as John did, a sense of impending doom, a sense that they are dying. Friends and strangers alike remarked of his last weeks that he seemed sad, as if something terrible was happening to him and he was unable to stop it.

In hindsight I can now see behavior which I feel was twisted by alcohol and by his sense of being set apart: the artist as someone different, who does not need to adhere to middle-class standards of behavior, the man who can act outrageously and be forgiven, the man who can demand and receive special treatment.

In the middle of May, John went out by himself to California, to give the commencement speech at San Diego State University. This had been arranged by Leslie Reynolds, who was the Director for University Relations and Development. She'd read John's work, loved it, and invited him out as speaker; she met him at the airport.

"When I got there, he was standing by the baggage claim, wearing a blue work shirt and khaki slacks, tassel loafers, holding his pipe. He said it had been a long flight and he was waiting for a chance to load up his pipe. He was so down-to-earth, so unpretentious, I took to him immediately."

In the car Leslie announced plans to drop John at a motel, but he shook his head. He told her he didn't want to be by himself and asked if he could come to her house for dinner. She agreed and set up an impromptu dinner party with her then-husband, Larry Kapiloff, a California State Assemblyman, and the vice president of the university and his wife. They ate on the deck of Larry and Leslie's house in Leslie's crowded urban neighborhood. The view from the deck is of back yards, other houses, the winking lights of the airport, the ocean in the distance. John had a lot to drink, and with his charm, his wit, his many fascinating stories, he was the man of the hour, until he had to pee. He leapt from the table—"Hold that thought"—and moved to the edge of the deck, turning his back to the party. He unzipped and peed off the deck into the shrubbery, turning back over his shoulder to add comments to the conversation, which was so interesting he couldn't bear to abandon it. "He had his back turned, but we could hear him," Leslie told me, laughing. "Larry and I thought it was great."

"What about the other guests?" I asked.

"Oh, they didn't like it so well."

Alongside the general unmanageability of his life, this is only a small example of inappropriate behavior. The major problem was his emotional dishonesty, the still-entangling involvement with Liz, the way he pitted Liz and me against each other.

As spring came, the roads cleared, which meant we could take the motorcycle instead of the car. I loved the motorcycle. It was a big black Harley, a Hog. Sleek, sturdy, powerful, it was better cared for and in much better condition than the Honda Civic sedan, which had an undependable engine with over 120,000 miles on it and brown leather upholstery torn by Teddy's teeth. The Honda overheated and stalled; in city traffic we drove with one foot on the brake, gunning the engine at stoplights to keep it going. We looped Teddy's old leash around the frame and the exhaust to keep the rusted tailpipe in place.

The Harley, by contrast, seemed to hold the road, to leap forward with animal swiftness. John's hands were always sure on the controls; I felt safe against his back, my hands clasped around his waist as we drove miles into central Pennsylvania to a speaking engagement, or to New York City, or up routes 17 and 390 to Batavia and Rochester to his parents' and mine. On a trip to Stroudsburg, Pennsylvania, in April, I got bored with the consistent speed of 55 mph on the four-lane highway. The wind was constant, droning; I caught my hands in John's belt, leaned my head against his shoulder, and dozed off, lulled by the rhythm of the road, buoyed by an immense trust that all would be well.

John's entire family loved motorcycles, either riding them for pleasure or commuting to work. At John's parents' I met his Uncle Howard, then sixty-seven, when he rode up on his motorcycle to say hello. Before his stroke, John's father had spent the summer building a custom-designed motorcycle with a sidecar so that he and Priscilla could ride together. He might better have spent the money reroofing the house. Priscilla was at that time nearly eighty. A photograph shows her, wearing a helmet, sitting in the sidecar, smiling, and John's father, seventy-two, astride the motorcycle.

At home, John tossed his motorcycle jacket onto the couch and I decided to fix the badly torn silk lining. I got needle and thread and painstakingly patched together the ruined, shredded silk, making tiny stitches I knew would last. That summer the advertising slogan for Harley-Davidson was THE EAGLE SOARS ALONE. At the Harley dealership I found an emblem I liked, showing an eagle with talons and outstretched wings, mouth open in a scream of challenge. I bought the cloth emblem and spent a warm summer afternoon on the porch, beneath our hanging fuchsias, carefully sewing this eagle onto the back of my blue-jean jacket. Now I felt a proper biker's girlfriend.

As I was sitting on the porch, sewing, a car pulled up and Frank and Anne Ryan got out and introduced themselves. I was hesitant to meet John's friends, as he insisted that everyone loved Liz so much they would hate me for sure. Frank was small and slight, bearded, wearing blue jeans and a turquoise stud in one pierced ear; Anne was slightly taller, with curly salt-and-pepper hair. They were both friends of Jim Rose and Jeanette Robertson, part of the group that centered on the Laurel Street Theatre; Frank was a musician, and Anne a graphic artist. Frank nodded at all the hanging plants I had put up along the porch. "We wanted to meet the lady of the flowers," Frank said, and bowed. Anne smiled. I realized these people weren't going to hate me at all.

Not all John's friends liked me. I had met Harold Brodkey and his wife Ellen Schwamm in New York City in December of 1981 at lunch after John's lecture at the MLA. I'd read Ellen's book,

Adjacent Lives, but didn't know Harold's work, although I knew he was a writer too. On a trip to New York in March we stopped to see them at their high-rise apartment with its stunning view of midtown Manhattan.

Ellen kept me busy in the kitchen with small talk while John and Harold huddled together by the window. I wondered what they were talking about so earnestly and excused myself from Ellen to edge closer. Harold was hunched over John's open palm, pretending to give him a psychic reading. "A terrible mistake," I overheard. "You must not break up your marriage." John was watching Harold skeptically; I didn't think about Harold's point of view, that only three months previously I had been introduced to him as merely one of several luncheon guests; I decided the Brodkeys were not my friends.

I became watchful and guarded after that, but another friend of John's whom I too adopted as a friend was Jeanette Robertson. Jeanette was a graphic artist, and an actress, for whom John had written a play, *Helen at Home*. Jeanette had a soft voice, a girlish laugh, dimpled white hands with long, pointed fingers; she was closer to John in age than I, and I sensed at once that she was a true friend: she loved him for himself and didn't want anything from him—nothing sexual, no promotion of her work, not even the play he had written for her, though she was thrilled to have it. She kept the signboard that advertised it in a prominent place in the entryway of the home she had built on her remote country acreage. I came to regard her and Anne as older sisters, women who were part of John's life, new friends who were safe.

John continued to press me about pregnancy. This was vitally important to him. I began to rethink my earlier hesitation. Pregnancy would confirm my commitment to him, and if I were pregnant John would have to marry me; he was that old-fashioned. I think we both wanted an excuse. I was thrilled that he loved me enough to want that commitment. I was ready to make a family life and agreed to stop using contraceptives. John was elated. One morning I woke up with nausea; "Is it morning sickness?" he asked eagerly. "It's a stomach bug," I snapped and ran for the bathroom.

I had thought this would take some time: I was wrong. In June I missed my period and hurried to the drugstore to get an at-home pregnancy test, new at the time. I waited only the minimum number of days, counting each one with a steadily mounting joy. As I stood in the bathroom at my parents' home in Rochester and watched the blue circle come up I felt a wild elation. I drove to Batavia to tell John and watched my smiling reflection in the speedometer of the Honda.

John broadcast the news far and wide. We told his parents, his son, Joel, and daughter, Lucy, my parents, his friends, my friends. My mother said, "If you're happy, dear, we're happy."

"You think having this baby is going to turn you into a slave, into a drudge," John said. "Well, you're wrong. You're gonna have to fight me to take care of this baby. When my kids were small I put their cradles in my study. I'd type for a while, feed the baby, type some more, change the baby." It was clear he couldn't wait; he was overjoyed at the news. "The baby's going to sleep in bed with us," he said. "There's something magic about a man and a woman and a baby in bed." He patted my stomach. "How's the baby's place?"

I had no morning sickness, only a tiredness so extreme in those summer afternoons it felt as though a giant hand pressed me into the sofa. John moved quietly around the house. I slept and woke and slept again, now and then hearing his step in the hall.

Susan Strehle recommended her obstetrician, Dr. Moore, and I went to his office for a test, which confirmed my own. He gave me a prescription for prenatal vitamins and a date for a follow-up appointment. I began to think about our September wedding date and how I would look. Maybe we should have a smaller wedding. The doctor gave me a small pocket calendar with a wheel I could use to calculate my due date, February 10. I looked at the date again and again. It seemed magic to me, something wonderful.

*　　*　　*

John still occasionally went off on reading tours without me, but now I felt more established in his life. Also, Teddy was with me constantly, back from the dog trainer but as unruly as ever. On one such occasion, John was gone and I was alone in the farmhouse when the telephone rang. "This is Joan Gardner, John's old ex-wife." The voice was confident, intense. "Is John there?"

"No, he's not, but I can take a message."

"Tell him I beat George Scheley's ass." Now the voice was elated. She spelled the name, not a difficult one. Evidently there had been a lawsuit, a win for Joan. This was something he would understand from his former life; she wanted to share the news.

I dutifully took down all the information. There was a pause.

"This isn't Liz," Joan said. "Who is this?"

"This is Susan."

The voice turned arch. "Well, over the years, there have been a great many Susans."

In June, just about the time I discovered I was pregnant, the IRS put a lien on John's checking account. John's trouble with the IRS had begun while he was married to Joan. He called it a "book-keeping mistake." For several years he had not paid income tax. The debt, with penalties and interest, had mounted to nearly $500,000. He fictionalized this in *Mickelsson's Ghosts,* commenting on Mickelsson's discovery that financial ruin is, like everything else, a process.

Every check John wrote was refused by the bank. We were constantly on the phone with creditors, the grocery, the trash collectors, the university bookstore. John had a business manager in Buffalo, Willard Saperston, who handled all his accounts. The university paycheck and all the bills went directly to him. The idea was that Willard took care of the details and John could concentrate on his work. Willard telephoned us to say, "This is totally illegal, way out of line. I'll fix it as soon as I can." In the meantime, we had no cash and many irate callers. One day a royalty check came directly to the house. We drove up to Binghamton, cashed the check at Marine Midland Bank, and spent the afternoon driving all over Susquehanna County making bad checks good with cash. I remember one farm wife of about forty-five, pushing back her rickety chair, tapping her bunioned foot in its flip-flop, licking her thumb and making us wait as she counted the hundred dollars in cash we had owed her son for helping with the farm animals while we were away on our constant trips.

John often drove up to Binghamton to meet and talk with Liz. One afternoon, just after his car pulled out of the drive and I knew he would be gone a good long time, I got up from the study where I had been working, went up to the closet between the bedroom and the spare room, and got out Liz's wedding dress.

The dress hung not in the closet off the bedroom but in the closet off the spare room. It was a handwoven wool dress, hung not on a conventional hanger but on a rod to keep the fabric smooth.

John told me he had commissioned it from a woman he knew who was an art weaver. Every time he told the story, the price of the dress went up. First he told me it cost him fifteen hundred dollars, then two thousand dollars, then twenty-five hundred. He said when the box arrived at the house and Liz opened it, she burst into tears.

I spread the woolen fabric out on the mattress in the spare room and could see why. It was beautifully woven, in a series of natural colors, pale brown, beige, and ocher, which would have looked lovely, given Liz's dark hair and coloring, but the dress itself was not well made. It had not been tailored, but cut and sewed in a boxy unsophisticated T shape. It might have made a beautiful wall hanging, but it was hardly something to wear.

I picked up the dress and held it against me, looking at myself in the mirror. Then I put it down, took off my clothes, and pulled it over my head. For a moment, as the fabric slid over my face, I remembered the Greek legend of Medeia and wondered if I had made a terrible mistake. Would the dress burst into flame?

I pulled the scratchy wool down over my body and looked at myself in the mirror. The fabric bunched at my waist, strained over my hips, rode up on my shoulders. I squirmed and pulled at the confining wool. The dress looked awful.

Then I looked at my face in the mirror, pale, pretty, desperate: the face of a young woman trying way too hard.

I pulled the dress over my head, put it back on its rod, and replaced it in the closet.

In his short story "A Rose for Emily," William Faulkner had written something that puzzled me. About his heroine, who poisoned her faithless lover and slept for the rest of her life next to his decaying corpse, he wrote, "She clung to what had robbed her, as people will."

Until I experienced the highs and the lows of my love for John I did not understand. However, now I think I do. In my life with him I clung to my fantasy that only an accident of timing had kept me from being his wife. I remembered his words at Bread Loaf. "If I had met you first, I would have married you." I dramatized this sense of loss for myself when I tried on Liz's wedding dress. His death robbed me of the wedding I had planned, but his actions while I lived with him held out intimacy with one hand while denying it with the other. I felt obscurely that I was being robbed, but I clung to that which robbed me.

14

———

"A Person Should Wear His Life on His Face"

In June, *Mickelsson's Ghosts* was published. When the crates of books arrived one hot morning, it was like Christmas. There it was, a big thick book, the high-quality paper crammed with tiny print, and a photo of John, looking pleased, impish, in his hat and dark coat. The illustration on the cover is meant to evoke a worn tombstone, with cavernous eye sockets. John was dismayed at the cover price of $16.95. "How can they expect people to buy books at that price?"

As soon as the book arrived, John drove up to Binghamton with a copy to give to Liz. John had originally dedicated it to Marcus and Helen Vergette, the son and widow of his dear friend Nicholas Vergette, the sculptor from Carbondale, Illinois. When Liz protested that he had never dedicated a "major novel" to her, only *On Moral Fiction*, which she said was "nothing but rant," and *In the Suicide Mountains*, which was a "kid's book," he changed the dedication of *Mickelsson's Ghosts* when it was in galleys. The book is dedicated "To Liz" and the jacket copy reads, "He is married to the poet L. M. Rosenberg." He came back to the house looking gloomy. "When she saw the dedication, she cried," he said. "I cried too," I replied.

Anatole Broyard, in the daily *New York Times*, praised the book:

> There are different ways of enjoying a book. For most of *Mickelsson's Ghosts*, John Gardner's new novel, I felt like sprawling out in a big chair and just having a good time with it, taking the pleasure as it comes. It seemed to be doing just about everything a novel can do. It offered characters I liked, but who troubled me, so that I wanted to see them feeling better, doing better. It gave me the kind of sense of place that one doesn't often find in serious novels today: A thick texture of landscape, community, friendships, infatuations, intrigues, insanities. . . . It's as if the world had suddenly become unbearably vivid again, after all our disillusionment and irony.

The Wall Street Journal called the book "An ambitious, morally searching murder mystery." Edmund Fuller wrote:

> Mr. Gardner's most ambitious work since *The Sunlight Dialogues*, it is on the same scale with similar questions about what is real and what is surreal. That earlier big book succeeded better. If here his reach exceeds his grasp, the book sometimes escapes control, those are the perils of a bold attempt.

Fuller called the book "overlong, complex, almost always interesting, morally searching, [and] flawed."

Novelist Larry Woiwode, writing in the *Chicago Tribune*, praised parts of the book: "Besides its central delights, *Mickelsson's Ghosts* contains some of the best dramatizations to be found of high-powered classroom encounters." Woiwode expressed disappointment in the prose, calling it "lumpy . . . propped by journalistic dashes. . . . [It] falls for periods into a flat-footedness close to cliché." He closed, however, by calling the book "the most substantial of Gardner's achievements."

A bad review came in the local paper, where the reviewer found only two pages to praise and ran an accompanying article condensing the worst of the reviews that ran in the national press. We kind of expected that, as John had made some digs at his adopted city, but the worst was *The Saturday Review*.

Under the title "What's So Moral About John Gardner's Fiction?" Robert Harris wrote:

> It is a good bet that John Gardner enjoys writing his novels far more than the public enjoys reading them. *Mickelsson's Ghosts* is dreadfully long and padded, and it often degenerates into drivel.

The reviewer took to task the National Book Critics Circle for their choice, in 1976, of *October Light* for its annual award, and stated, "Gardner's connection with ideas has always been dilettantish." He called ideas in the novel "creepy" and closed by saying:

> *Mickelsson's Ghosts* is a sham. Stripped of its excesses, however, it does have enough substance to have made a good Raymond Carver short story.

My first thought was that John mustn't see this—it would hurt his feelings. The final comment, that Ray Carver would have told the story better, in his flat, minimalist style, seemed a deliberate affront. The reviewer must have known of Ray and John's friendship. I didn't consider that through his long career John had weathered many attacks from critics. Instead, I reacted as a child who wants to protect a friend: I wadded up the magazine and thrust it as deep as I could into the trash barrel, hoping he wouldn't ask about it.

I needn't have bothered. A few days later we went up to the university, where John got his mail and then let himself into his office. I came in a few minutes later and saw him standing at his desk, reading. On his desk was a new copy of *The Saturday Re-*

view, open to the review I had tried to hide; Liz had let herself into his office with her key and left the magazine there with a note.

"Did you see this before?" His face was sad and drawn.

I nodded. "I put it in the trash at home. I didn't want you to see it."

"I guess Liz is mad at me."

I felt I had been right; reading the review did hurt his feelings, and Liz had left the magazine in order to get back at him for their separation. "I guess so too."

John had hoped this book would renew his reputation, would be as well-received as his earlier novel, *The Sunlight Dialogues*, and in a deliberate strategy had included frank descriptions of sexual love in order to correct an omission that had been noted in previous books. Friends sent encouraging notes; Ron Hansen wrote that the book seemed to levitate off his shelf, but the book sold poorly, and early reviews did not live up to the comments in the *Publishers Weekly* advance review that the book was "as rich in feeling as in thought" and might be "Gardner's most impressive work since *Sunlight Dialogues*." John was immensely disappointed and spoke about giving up. The composition of this huge novel had depleted his reserves of creative energy, and he had hoped for a larger payoff, both financially and critically. He kept his distress to himself and focused on the work he still had left to do, the *Gilgamesh* translation to be ready for the fall term, the revisions for *Becoming a Novelist*, but his disappointment ran deep and ate away at him.

On June 27, we invited friends over for dinner. It was a Sunday, and a play would be given at the Laurel Street Theatre. The theater group was a local institution with a twenty-year history of producing musical comedies. Now it was divided into two groups, those who wanted to continue producing musicals and well-known plays, and a new group, centered around John and Jan Quackenbush, who wanted to produce original dramas. The night of our dinner party, the theater group was putting on *Lizzie Borden of Fall River*, a melodrama based on the famous nineteenth-century murder case, and John thought it a deplorable waste of energy and talent.

We invited Joanna and Jerry Higgins, who lived not far from us in Little Meadows, Pennsylvania. Joanna, who already held a Ph.D. in literature, had taken the astonishing step of giving up a secure university teaching position in Hawaii to return to SUNY-Binghamton solely to work with John on her writing. This deliberate casting away of status left most of her former professors shocked and dismayed.

At the door we welcomed our guests, and Joanna smiled, transforming her looks instantly, softening and warming her narrow, precise face. Jerry, wearing a sport jacket and tie, shook my hand and presented me with a well-chosen bottle of Bordeaux. He was tall, reserved; he worked in Binghamton as a stockbroker. Jeff Ford came too. Jeff was a graduate student who had sent John a postcard of Herman Melville that John tacked to the wall above his desk. "He's got it," John had told me about Jeff. "He works all day at some awful job and comes home and stays up all night and writes; he's really got it." I think John saw in Jeff a younger version of himself. Of the students that year he was the most like John—from a working-class background, already married, pushing himself through graduate school, and composing weird, wonderful, looping stories that mimicked the structure and content of *The Thousand and One Nights*.

I prepared a simple meal: baked chicken, a rice dish. John walked around the table, holding the casserole so guests could serve themselves. We ate in the dining room at the elaborately carved wooden table, watched over by the silvery, brooding suit of armor, a gift from Charles Johnson. John was drinking steadily, mostly gin. Conscious of my pregnancy, I wasn't drinking at all. I watched as he fixed himself a large martini, drank it thirstily, then got up. "Anyone want another?" he asked, lifting his eyebrows. No one did. He made another, drank that, then a third. We drank Jerry's wine with dinner, and John had more gin.

After dinner we drove over to the play and John took a seat at the rear of the auditorium. The play had barely begun when John got up and went outside. I heard him scuffing his feet on the gravel, talking in a too-loud voice with the young man who directed parking. The lead was played by Irene Allen, who had a seat on the board of directors of the theater. At the climactic scene she confronted the audience with her hands and skirt dripping stage blood; I found it obvious and overdone. John peeked back into the auditorium, then ducked his head and went outside again. I heard him making jokes, smelled his fragrant pipe tobacco. As soon as the play was over he hustled me to the car. "Let's get out of here." Ordinarily we would have gone backstage to speak to Irene and the other actors. That John wanted to leave so suddenly made it only more obvious how much he hated the play. We came back to the house, and John headed straight for the liquor cabinet. After a few minutes, Joanna and Jerry and Jeff joined us at home. By this time John had already fixed another big drink. His eyes were beginning to glaze over and his face was flushed. His hand was unsteady as he splashed the gin into the glass.

There's a point at which a drinker who is alcoholic can't stop. The Japanese have a terrifying proverb:

> The man takes a drink.
> The drink takes a drink.
> The drink takes the man.

That night the drink took John.

Joanna described this later as "fierce, awesome drinking." John sat in his odd, almost medieval chair with its unnaturally high arms and nodded forward over his pipe. When he got up to go to the kitchen for more ice, he stumbled and nearly fell. He brought out the gin bottle, now almost empty, and left it by his chair. He asked

Joanna and Jerry pointed questions about their life, told them about my pregnancy, and insisted they think about having a child of their own. I was uncomfortable with his intrusiveness. At one point John went upstairs; we heard him fall down in the bedroom. Jeff glanced at me and then away; I looked at the floor. When John returned, he sat heavily in his chair, rocking it a bit, filled the bowl of his pipe, spilling the tobacco, took a long time to puff the pipe alight, then forgot it. His forehead and hair became smudged with black as he rubbed at them with his sooty fingers. I began to wish our guests would leave. Joanna glanced at her husband and they stood to make their good-byes; later she described the light from the chandelier as glaring, the atmosphere "jittery and precarious," herself as scared and badly shaken, ashamed that she hadn't confronted John about his drinking.

John leaned against the doorjamb, hugging his chest. "Staying longer?" He turned to Jeff. "Come on in my study." He staggered to the liquor cabinet, hooked up a full bottle of Jameson Irish whiskey and his glass, and motioned Jeff to follow him.

It was now close to two in the morning; I was tired after the afternoon of cooking, the long evening of dinner, and the play, and wanted to get some sleep. Let John and Jeff stay up and drink, I was going to bed. No sooner had I gotten settled than I heard heavy footsteps and John talking loudly. I pulled on a wrap and came out of the bedroom. John and Jeff were coming up the stairs. John pointed to a reddened spot on his cheek. "He popped me one in the face," John declared joyfully. "He hit me in the face." I doubted this. John's eyes were overbright and didn't focus; his grin had a manic quality. Jeff hung back like a guilty schoolboy.

Jeff wrote later that he stayed and kept drinking because

> All that day I had the ridiculous feeling [John] was going to tell me something important. There was something I wanted from him, but I couldn't figure out what it was . . . [John] talked of his disillusionment with writing. He shook his head at the viciousness of the critics. He talked about giving up. He told me his most

personal problems. It frightened me to hear him so unsure of himself. He slurred his words. I felt like I had to get out of there.

When Jeff started his car, he was too drunk to drive and backed solidly into the ditch that ran along the gravel drive. I heard the car engine, then a grinding noise as the body of the car came to rest on the top edge of the ditch. Our kitchen door opened and closed, and I heard John and Jeff talking. I got dressed and went outside. It was three in the morning and pitch-dark out.

John decided all he needed was a chain to hitch Jeff's car to ours; he would get behind the wheel of our car and pull Jeff's car out of the ditch. He went into the barn to look for a length of chain, stumbled, and fell, hitting an iron pipe that jutted from the concrete barn floor. The pipe just missed his eye and made a bad gash up the side of his nose, and across his forehead. I came out of the kitchen to find John on his hands and knees at the doorway of the barn. Jeff was in his car, futilely grinding the engine and attempting to rock the car out of the ditch. Blood was falling from John's forehead like rain.

I became hysterical. However much drinking went on at Bread Loaf, I had felt safe. I stood over John as he swayed back and forth on his hands and knees. "I broke my head," he said. I was frightened most of all because he seemed so matter-of-fact, as if he didn't feel any pain or distress. I caught some of his blood in my hand and ran to Jeff's car. I wrenched open the door on the passenger side and thrust my hand in his face. He turned to me, startled. "See, see what you've done!" I shouted. I went back to John. Now he was standing, blood smeared over his forehead and across his hair. He swayed back and forth with the chain in his hand; he had found it after all. He headed toward our car, leaning forward as if walking in a heavy wind, now and then stumbling to the side but catching himself. He was determined to attach the chain to the rear axle and continue with his plan of towing Jeff's car.

By now my fear was out of control. I became convinced that if he persisted, if he got down on the ground to tie the cars together with the length of chain, if he got behind the wheel of our car, drunk as he was, and gunned it to pull Jeff's car out of the ditch, something would go terribly wrong and someone, John, Jeff, or I, would be killed or seriously injured. "Can't you just stop?" I shouted. "You can't do this. You're way too drunk to do this. You ought to go to the hospital to get your head looked at, for one thing." I wanted help, reinforcements, sober grown-ups. I felt terribly alone out in the driveway, lit only by feeble squares of light from the windows of our kitchen and John's study.

He wouldn't stop but stumbled toward the Honda with the chain in his hand.

I ran into the house and called our next-door neighbors, Jeannie and John Rodriguez. "I've got to get John to the hospital," I said. "He's fallen and cut his head and I don't know how to get there."

Teddy was up and out, nosing around amid this chaotic scene. I saw Jeannie first, her stocky figure and bright, strawlike bleached hair. Her husband was taller, reed-thin, dark. His face was tense and worried. Teddy saw them coming down the hill and charged, the hair standing up on the back of his neck, his great mouth open, showing all his teeth. Jeannie shrieked. Teddy circled them, barking fiercely. I ran to pull him away.

"John fell and cut his head; he wants to start our car and pull Jeff's out of the ditch; you've got to help me stop him," I shouted, as I pulled on Teddy's collar. Teddy whined and tried to bite at my wrist as I shoved him into the house and locked him in the kitchen.

John had the car keys in his hand. "Give me the keys," I demanded.

"No, I won't. You're overreacting. This will work. I can get the car out of the ditch."

"No, you can't." I lunged for his hand, grabbed it, and tried to pry the car keys from his closed fist. I couldn't move his fingers. He pushed on my shoulder with his free hand. Gradually he forced me down until I was kneeling at his feet, struggling to keep my balance. I fell over sideways, then sat down hard on the stony ground. John kept pushing at my shoulders. "You're not getting the keys," he said, "You're not *getting* them."

"What are you doing to that girl?" Jeannie shouted. "What are you doing to her? Stop it, stop it."

Suddenly he let me up and stepped back. Surprised, I scrambled to my feet, and then his fist came up out of nowhere and landed a solid punch on my arm.

I knew right away what that punch meant; it meant: Leave me the fuck alone. I can do what I want to do. You're way out of line here.

At the same time I was seized with a sickening fear. I was pregnant, with John's baby, and he had just hit me. Every nerve in my body told me this was wrong. A pregnant woman has an atavistic sense of what is needed for herself and her child. My feeling was gut-level and primitive: I saw him as threat; I wanted to run. At the same time I wanted to manage the unmanageable, to neutralize the danger, to make the effects of his drunkenness go away.

John backed away from me and I stayed clear of him as well.

"I'll take you home in our car, Jeff." I was pleading now. "Let me take you home. You can come back tomorrow for your car. We can get it out in the daylight."

Jeff agreed, and suddenly the venom and the danger seemed to evaporate.

I got my set of keys. Jeff, much subdued, got in the passenger side of our car, and I drove to Binghamton with fierce concentration. Jeff sat quiet beside me. He gave me directions to his apartment and with great relief I saw him stumble up the outside stairs. I was still very angry.

I headed back to the farmhouse, not knowing what I'd find.

At home the house was quiet. By now it was starting to get light. I tiptoed upstairs and found John asleep on his back on the mattress in the spare room. Dried blood caked his hair; his shirt and trousers were dark with blood spots. The gash on his forehead was deep and open.

I went back downstairs. I got water for Teddy, put plates and glasses in the sink, and was starting to do the dishes when the phone rang.

I picked it up at once, frightened. It was Jeannie. Her voice was hushed. "What's happening over there?"

"John's asleep. What happened after I left?"

"Oh, Susan, it was awful. We came in the kitchen and he got ice out for another drink. He accused us of terrible things, vile betrayals. He said awful things, things he shouldn't have said." Her voice broke. "We've been neighbors and friends now for a long time. He just said some awful things."

"I'm so sorry."

"It's not your fault."

My heart sank, for I knew only too well what John could be like when he got going. I hung up the phone and looked at my arm. I remembered the punch, but there wasn't a mark. I finally went upstairs and lay down in our bed and fell asleep.

The next day was hot and bright. When John got up he went downstairs to take a bath. I walked into the bathroom; he didn't see me. He was exploring the wound on his forehead with his fingertips. When he realized I was in the room, he took his hand away.

He got out of the tub and got dressed and I did something very unusual for me: I confronted him about his drinking.

I had never seen my mother confront my father, or my father confront my mother; this was not done in my family. Nor did anyone ever mention drinking or its effects. One morning at my parents' summer home when I was a young adult, my father had an ugly, ragged gash running the length of his shin. "What happened?" I asked, alarmed. "I fell off the dock," Dad answered, in a tone of voice that said, "Don't ask any more." He had quite clearly fallen from the dock the night before, alone and drunk. No one mentioned it again. That he might have drowned—but had not—was accepted as a matter of course, and the subject was closed; Mom pretended not to see the cut or to hear my question. A grown-up was expected to take care of his own wounds.

The day after John fell and cut his head, I was angry enough to take a chance, to overrule my conditioning, to state the obvious.

"Look what happened last night," I said. "We can't end up like you and Joan. We just can't."

John stared at me as if he didn't understand.

"Don't you remember? You hit me."

He looked momentarily startled, then glanced at my arm. There was a mark on my lower forearm where Teddy's rope had grazed me when I walked him, and he'd lunged away; the rope had given me a brush burn.

"Is that where I hit you?"

"No," I said. "It isn't." I looked at my arm. Maybe he hadn't hit me that hard. How upset should I get over a punch that didn't leave a mark?

I tried again. "We can't end up like you and Joan," I repeated. He looked at the floor. He had written to me about the dreadful physical fights he had had with his first wife. Once I had asked him if it were really true, what he had written to me. He was drunk that night, and answered, shaking his head, not looking at me: "There was blood on all the walls." Now that I had seen blood in handfuls, I was more inclined to believe him.

What I feared about confrontations, that they didn't change anything, was coming true. John was listening, but he wasn't hearing me, and it wasn't doing any good to talk. I began to think I might as well have stayed quiet.

The phone rang. John answered, listened for a moment, then said, "Oh, no, I had a wonderful time." He leaned into the counter, his tone happy, jovial. I stood behind him and fumed, knowing he was speaking to Jeff. John half turned toward me. "I'm only sorry that we frightened Susan. I had a wonderful time."

"What about your face?" I asked after he hung up. "We should go up to the hospital, get it stitched up."

He shook his head. "It's nothing. A person should wear his life on his face." He took a Band-Aid out of the medicine cabinet and stretched it over the cut.

My attempt to confront had ended in a stalemate. I didn't get what I had wanted, which was for life to get more sane, because I didn't understand that it was alcohol that made life so insane.

Later that day, Jeff and his wife came down from Binghamton to get Jeff's car. In daylight the problem of getting the car out of the ditch was easily solved. Jeff's wife sat behind the steering wheel, John and Jeff pushed, and the car popped out. Jeff and his wife drove away in their separate cars and John and I walked back to the house.

When we saw Liz and David that afternoon, Liz took one look at John and demanded, "What happened? What did you do to yourself?" She insisted John remove the Band-Aid so she could see the cut. He sighed and lifted the flesh-colored plastic strip. When Liz saw the wound she gasped, stepped back, covered her mouth with her hands. I looked miserably at my foot. "And you didn't go to the hospital?" She glared at me.

John shook his head. "Can we not talk about this any more?"

I wrote to Sue Watkins about what had happened—"John went off on kind of a toot last night"—minimizing my fear and distress. I did not tell her or anyone else that John had hit me. Like other partners of alcoholics, I turned to denial. "That won't happen again," I told myself. "I won't let it happen." How I was going to prevent another such evening, I didn't know. All my energy went into denying how unmanageable alcohol was making my life.

That night should have been John's wake-up call. He'd always been a writer, he'd always been a drinker. As he neared his fiftieth year, alcohol was becoming his master, not his servant. What if he couldn't write without drinking? Alcohol made him despair, yet he continued to turn to it. What if he quit drinking, and the despair continued?

I could have given him an ultimatum, as I had in March. I could have said, You're going to get treatment or it's over. I could have put him in the car and driven him to the hospital.

I didn't. Partly, I didn't know what one did with drunks. I had no understanding of detox centers, of thirty-day programs of hospitalization, of Alcoholics Anonymous and how it works. I was at a loss. All I knew was that he'd hit me. I was pregnant with his baby and he had hit me. I couldn't leave him, because I didn't want to; nor could I tell *anyone* what had happened.

I remembered his letter: "As much as I hate drinking (and I do), it seems the only solution."

He had also written, "She [Liz] won't make love to me if I have whiskey on my breath." The message was clear.

Only when people want help can they get it. John didn't want help; he didn't want to change.

15

"You've Got Nothing Alive in There"

A few days later, on Friday, July 2, we drove into New York to do publicity for *Mickelsson's Ghosts*. John's publisher, Alfred A. Knopf, put us up in a small hotel near the Plaza and arranged interviews with National Public Radio and with Curt Suplee of *The Washington Post*. It was a long hot drive into the city in that rattletrap Honda with no air conditioning; John wore his banker's suit and complained of the pinch of his wing-tip shoes.

We met with Curt Suplee in the restaurant of our hotel. I sipped at a ginger ale and kept quiet as Curt conducted his interview and John smoked and drank "like a maniac," as he'd described himself in his letters.

"The martini count approaches double digits, the pronunciation turns muddy and the pipe drops occasionally from his mouth ('Gotta get these teeth fixed!')," read Suplee's published article. John talked, smoked, ordered so many martinis that at last the worried-looking waiter chose not to listen, pretending he didn't hear the order.

When Curt finally turned off his tape recorder, gathered his notes, and left, John got up, unsteady, reached out for support to a nearby table, and pulled the tablecloth right off. He spun, awkward but still on his feet, a gyroscope off-kilter, and raised a warning finger and an eyebrow, mock stern. "Don't be embarrassed," he counseled.

During this trip to New York we visited Robert Blue, a composer with whom John was working on a musical adaptation of *Grendel.* John was doing a libretto and Robert the score. We met for lunch at a Chinese restaurant. John refused the fortune cookie. "Just before I went into Johns Hopkins Hospital, I opened a fortune cookie at a Chinese restaurant," he said. "The slip of paper was blank." He left the table to use the men's room, and Robert and his girlfriend backed me up against the counter by the cash register. "You've got to do something about John. Does he always drink like this?" Robert said.

I was angry, frightened, offended. John's drinking at lunch seemed no worse than usual. What could I do?

I was alcoholic also. I abstained from alcohol during my pregnancy, but denied that alcohol was a problem in my life, or in his. I didn't know it was possible to live a life without drinking. I thought I drank to cope with the unmanageability of my life; I didn't understand that drinking created this unmanageability and that it was possible to live a clearer, more ordered life. It was his tragedy, and mine, that neither of us understood the ravages of alcohol.

We stayed overnight in New York. A week later, on Friday, July 9, in Binghamton I had a routine examination at my obstetrician's office. I had been pregnant for about eight weeks. Before the appointment, the nurse telephoned and told me they planned to do an ultrasound examination and that I should not go to the bathroom before I arrived. "I know it's uncomfortable," she said, "but we want you to have as full a bladder as possible. It helps with the picture. You can go to the bathroom as soon as we're done."

When I arrived the nurse took my blood pressure and weighed me. In the small examining room I undressed, put on a gown, and went into another room, where the nurses arranged the ultrasound equipment. I lay on the table and Dr. Moore came in to do the test. I watched as he ran the sensor over my abdomen, not under-standing what he was looking for. When he was done I left to go to the bathroom and came back to the first examining room. The doctor hurried in with the results of the exam.

"You've got nothing alive in there," he declared.

I was alarmed and didn't want to hear this all by myself. "Can you wait until John comes and talk with him too?"

"I've got nothing to say to him. When you get cramping and bright red blood you go right to the hospital and call me." He left me alone. I sat on the table, fighting back tears. Now, after all these years, I understand what had happened. He was looking for a fetal heartbeat and didn't find one.

I dressed and went out to the waiting room. Across the room from me a woman rested her hand on her gravid belly; to her left, another leafed through a magazine about baby care. The room was brightly lit and painted with cheerful colors; the receptionist an-swered the phone; the doctor was nowhere in sight. John wasn't late, but I had some time to sit there as the appointment had been so brief. The lady across from me smiled over her magazine; I turned away, biting my lip. At last I saw John's face at the door. As soon as he saw me his expression changed. I stood up and hurried to his side. "Let's just get out of here," I said.

On the way to the car I told him what Dr. Moore had said. He hugged me and then looked over my shoulder. "Maybe it will take longer than we thought."

We were getting ready to stage the play *You're a Good Man, Char-lie Brown* at the Laurel Street Theatre. The Tuesday after the doc-tor's appointment, Liz and David came to Susquehanna for a rehearsal of the play; Liz and John were co-directors. This meant constant meetings and evening rehearsals through June and early July where both met to work on this play; I had accepted this as just another part of my life. To cope with it, I'd said I'd work on the play backstage, as property mistress, and David had accepted a role in the play. Jim Rose had a part, and Jeanette, and other friends; it was our social life, and it was fun. If there were tensions, we pretended they weren't there. We were artists, after all, and artists weren't supposed to have conventional lives.

I felt sympathy for David. At times I wanted to seek him out, have a heart-to-heart talk while John and Liz were occupied with each other, but I didn't dare. I had enough to do just to hang on in this exasperating situation. David and I had something in common; we were both waiting on other people to make decisions that affected our lives. I wanted John, David wanted Liz; we each had to wait while John and Liz made up their minds. I used to joke about not living in a triangle, but living in a rectangle. David was devoted to Liz; he put a good face on a difficult situation; he was excellent company, a surprising and genuine wit. I liked him as a person.

After the rehearsal, Liz and David came back to the house for a snack. We sat and talked about the play, the actors, the music, about *MSS* magazine, about books, art, music, writing, all the many ideas and activities we always talked about, but I couldn't concentrate. I was thinking about what Dr. Moore had said, and I was beginning to feel cramping.

At about 11 P.M. I excused myself and went into the bathroom, where I found the bright red blood that the doctor had predicted. As soon as I saw it, the cramping started to get worse.

I came out of the bathroom and called to John. He came instantly to my side. "We have to go to the hospital. It's what the doctor said would happen."

After that I couldn't talk anymore. Suddenly there was a lot of confusion. Time seemed to slow down as though none of us could think properly. John had to explain. Then there was the question of the animals, for by then we had the goats and pigs and Teddy, and we had to settle them for the night. John and David went out to take care of that while Liz picked up the dishes and I stood miserably in the kitchen. Then John realized we didn't have nearly enough gas in the Honda. No gas stations in town or at the highway interchange were open after 9 P.M.

We finally decided that John and I would drive the Honda Civic and Liz and David would follow in their Honda Accord in case John and I ran out of gas. John drove and I sat in the passenger seat and we didn't say much of anything. In spite of the needle on empty, we got to the hospital. When Liz and David saw us pull into the emergency entrance, they continued back to their apartment.

John and I walked into the emergency room where, with typical understatement, I said, "I'm having a little bleeding." What I should have said was, I'm hemorrhaging. By then it was after midnight. A kind, calm nurse took me into an examining room. When she got me up on the table and realized what was happening, other nurses crowded around me and I began to cry. "I'm not crying because it hurts," I kept saying, "I'm crying because I'm sad."

At last they let John in to see me, stripped of my clothes and wearing a hospital gown. I clung to the sleeve of his jacket. "One of the nurses recognized me," he remarked. "She asked for my autograph." I couldn't believe that someone had done such a thing at such a moment.

Dr. Moore was summoned; by the time he arrived it was after one in the morning. When he came into the room, John put his arm across my chest as if to protect me. Dr. Moore declared he had to do a dilation and curettage right away. I was frightened of him, frightened of the D and C procedure; once again I did not fully understand what was going to happen. I didn't know if they were going to put me under or not, and I was anxious either way. The anesthesiologist kept asking me over and over what I'd had to eat and when I had eaten it. I was too scared to show how scared I was. Dr. Moore remarked that he'd been up since 5 A.M. and had done four procedures and delivered a baby that day; that only intensified my fear. John looked at me, and I saw he was worried too. I might have insisted that another doctor be called in, but I felt powerless and tugged under by events: the suddenness of the pain and loss, the anxious midnight drive to the hospital, the quantity of blood I was losing.

At last the nurse pulled John away, the anesthesiologist did something, and I realized I was going to lose consciousness. At last I spoke. "If I sleep too long, tell John to go on home." This was the only way I could express my terror and my irrational fear that I might die.

I came to in the recovery room. John was pressing his face to the bars around my gurney and holding my hand. "Where's the doctor?" I asked.

"He's gone. It's all right. How are you?"

I relaxed. I was relieved to be alive. I was happy to see John. We talked for a time. I worried about Teddy, about the animals; I told John to go home. We were supposed to go to Rochester that day. I knew I couldn't manage that and asked John to call my parents.

After John had gone and I was alone, waiting to be transferred to the maternity floor, something strange happened. I felt a caress on my face, the gentle touch of a hand. No one was there, not John, not a nurse. But I felt a soft stroke much like my mother's: personal, intimate, loving.

16

"Your Sister's Here"

The sun streamed into the room and lit up the rough white sheets of the bed on the maternity floor. A nurse came in and said, "Your sister's here."

"My sister?"

Right behind her, Liz stood in the doorway, her dark curly hair falling to the side as she tipped her head slightly to her right shoulder. The expression on her face was compassionate, encouraging; I saw a flicker of uncertainty. She had lied to the nurse so she would be allowed to see me.

"Come in, come in." I shifted over on the bed so she could sit on the edge. I had been so lonely. I was to go home today but John hadn't come yet. There was no one else who could have consoled me at that moment except Liz. No one else in Binghamton understood my situation as she did. Only she could have comforted me by the simple gift of her presence.

We sat and talked for quite a while. I told her about the D and C and said that John had gone back to the house. "He came over to our apartment first," she said. "He told us that you sewed up the lining of the motorcycle jacket for him. Then he started crying.

He said that was so important. It means you think the motorcycle is OK."

I nodded. "What was it like for you when he was in the hospital that time?" I meant the surgeries John had had for colon cancer. "How did you get through that?"

I had seen the evidence on John's body; the long scar, half an inch wide, that ran from his sternum to his pubis, and another scar, a square inch of shiny hardened skin on his left side, where the temporary colostomy had been.

She shook her head. "I don't know *how* I got through it. All the doctors said he was going to die. They all said he was dying, that we should say good-bye. I've blocked a lot of that out." She changed the subject. "Do you want to take a little walk?"

I pulled on a hospital bathrobe and got out of bed. We walked along the corridor. "It's too awful they put you on the maternity floor," Liz remarked. We approached the nursery. "I should warn you, there's a baby in here named Gardner."

Sure enough, behind the window of the nursery lay a swaddled newborn, his face red and puffy, eyes squeezed shut; the name at the end of the tiny cot read GARDNER.

We went back to my room and the phone rang. Liz smiled and stepped out into the hall. John said into the receiver, "It's your faithless lover, it's your faithless lover. I fell asleep; I've just waked up; I'm sorry it's so late."

"No, no," I said. "I'm glad you got some sleep."

"I'll be up to get you as soon as I can."

"It's all right," I said. "It's all right."

Liz came back into the room and I said, "John's coming right up."

She nodded. "See you later."

When John arrived he had Teddy in the car; the dog leaped into the curving drive where patients are discharged. "Down, down," John said futilely, as I aimed pats at Teddy's head and back as he capered at my feet. At last I got in the car. Teddy bounded in behind me and from the back seat leaned forward to lick my ear and the side of my face with his long pink tongue. "What do you want, do you want ice cream, anything?"

"Let's just go home," I said. When we got there I called my mother. "We know, dear, John called us." She hesitated. "He was crying so hard I couldn't understand him at first. He kept saying, *She was so brave, she was so brave.*"

I hung up the phone and asked John what had happened. "She answered the phone, and she just sounded so—so motherly." He started to cry again and I hugged him. "I just couldn't help it."

Later I found a letter on his desk he'd written to some old friends, telling them of the changes in his life and what had happened. "Why couldn't this little one have survived?" he wrote. "Why couldn't this little one have survived?"

Neither of us knew how to cope with our grief. At home I was filled with sadness to see the prenatal vitamins on the kitchen counter. I considered taking them until they were all gone because I knew they were good for me—it made me too sad and I threw them out. I wrote to Sue Watkins, telling her of our "bad luck" and downplaying the horror and fear I had felt. In my ignorance, I blamed myself for allowing the doctor to do the ultrasound, thinking that it had harmed the baby. One hot morning I went for a long walk in our garden and came back to the house; John was in his study at his desk. He rose to embrace me. "How are you?"

"Sad," I said. He held me and patted my back. There wasn't much to say.

That weekend was the opening of *You're a Good Man, Charlie Brown*. Harold Brodkey and Ellen Schwamm came from New York City to see it. I put on a convincing show of health and good spirits. "We thought you were frail," Harold said to me.

That we lost the baby seemed to plunge John into an abyss of gloom. It had seemed crazy to various friends and colleagues that he was rushing into a new marriage and a new baby. One or two had quietly advised abortion, being rational, thinking we needed time to sort out our lives. John had wanted so to change his life; maybe it wasn't going to work out. Neither of us knew, as I know now, that one quarter of all pregnant women will lose the pregnancy in the first trimester. We thought it was abnormal, a portent, a sign that perhaps presaged a worse fate.

17

"I Kissed Her, I Just Kissed Her"

Saturday, Harold and Ellen said good-bye and went up to stay with Liz and David. That night was the cast party at Jim Rose's. Cast parties were always the high point of the production, maybe even the reason for having them. This one, at Jim's tiny little house on the bank overlooking the creek, seemed to go on forever. All the actors and their families had brought food; we had beer, liquor, abundant ice; the party spilled noisily out of the house and onto the lawn. I was still exhausted from my miscarriage, from the stresses and the fear I had felt that night in the emergency ward and, later that same week, from the dress rehearsals and production of the play. At Jim's party, John showed no sign of wanting to go home. Around two in the morning I fell asleep on the daybed in Jim's living room in the midst of all the noise, drinking, and confusion.

About four in the morning I woke up. The lights were still on. I heard voices, but I didn't see John.

I stood up, rubbed my eyes, found Jim in the kitchen. "Where's John?"

Jim's face was flushed, his dark curly hair stuck to his forehead, and he held a half-empty drink in his hand. "Uh, he went home."

"He went home?" I didn't believe him, but I was vaguely alarmed, uncertain of what might be happening.

I went out onto the front steps. There on the flagstone sat John, holding a drink, shouldered much too close to a stocky blonde I didn't remember having seen before. He looked up and saw me. "I kissed her." He shook his head, looking at the ground, waved his hand, holding the drink. "I just kissed her." His words slurred, his eyes didn't focus; he looked down and away.

The blonde eyed me as I sat down next to them on the cold flagstone. My throat closed with rage. She was not a girl he knew in Washington; I was no longer hiding away in Cambridge, full of doubt and fright; instead I had been fifty yards away, asleep on a cot in Jim's house. Then I became impatient, just wanting to get back home where I could lie down in our bedroom. What I had told Jim was true: I loved John with all my heart, but he seemed to be pushing me away, poisoning the relationship. I sat silently on the step while the blonde looked me over and John stared at whatever double vision of the tree in Jim's yard he could make out. Then the blonde got up, dusted off her bottom, and sashayed off.

"Come on, let's just go." I tugged on John's arm. He stood up unsteadily, swaying on his feet, and followed me. Jim managed to drive us home.

I did not confront John, remonstrate, or argue. It was too difficult for me to do so, and the one time I had, after his fall in June, hadn't helped. My role model was my mother. My mother never confronted, never argued, never questioned my father; she just accepted and got her own way through indirection. Also, she enlisted my help in keeping secrets. When I was in high school, she had purchased an energetic purebred boxer puppy. This dog had ruined the silk-upholstered love seat in the living room by shredding the cushions with his sharp claws as he searched futilely for his ball. "Your father will be furious," she told me. "You have to help." We knelt before the ruined love seat and I held the edges of the silk together as she stitched the fabric. Then she turned the cushion over. As long as no one looked underneath, it would be fine.

Within a month she had the entire sofa reupholstered, using the excuse that she had tired of the color. Dad never mentioned the expense; he never did. He just shrugged and made another drink.

I had adopted her method of handling a partner. I accepted John's behavior, kept quiet, and denied how badly it made me feel. Now that I was no longer pregnant, I could drink again, and if my emotions got too painful, I poured myself a glass of red wine or fixed a gin and tonic, went back to the short story I was writing, and tried to forget those of John's actions that were hurtful.

John had written to me, "I'm what the worst sort of woman is imagined to be, a huge sick howl of 'I want, I want!' " He sought to fill the emptiness inside him with work, alcohol, travel, interviews, lectures, reviewing, translating, teaching, and the kisses of a blonde he'd never seen before. He knew this about himself, and even wrote about it jokingly in the play, *Marvin's on "The Distant Shore."* The main character of that play, Marvin, a goofy looking science-fiction writer, has a lead song for which John wrote the lyrics: "Hug me, kiss me, I'm a shy young man." To a certain extent, that was John's theme song. Hug me, kiss me, love me. He looked outside himself for the consolation that could not come from within.

In his cups one night he had said, "You have to be here every night. If you're not here to sleep with me, I'll find someone else." This was not something John would have said sober. Sober he was fair, thoughtful, considerate. Drunk he was threatening. Why would I not want to be with him? It was a ridiculous question, arising out of some strongly rooted fear, his fear that he could not be loved if his beloved "knew him well" and the deeper, ancient wound, that he was a Cain who had killed his brother. His meanness in that instance sprang from his suffering and shows distorted, alcoholic thinking, the grandiosity, the sense of being cut off from community, being lost.

At least once, though, I found out he meant it. An old friend who lived in California, Gloria Goldblatt, was visiting family in Ithaca;

she called me and proposed that we meet them for dinner. John demurred; he was working hard to finish the *Gilgamesh* translation. I decided to drive up alone to Ithaca, a trip of a little over two hours, to meet Gloria and her cousin, but I was uneasy. "You're sure it's all right?"

"Of course," he said. I felt he was lying. I was torn. All my life I'd kept up with my friends, old and new. I hadn't seen Gloria in a long time; a trip to California to see her didn't seem likely in the near future. What was my life if I couldn't leave John alone for an evening to go see an old friend? Was that a partnership or a prison? I left in midafternoon and drove up to Ithaca; it seemed an endless drive. I met Gloria, her husband and daughter, her cousin; we went out to dinner; I couldn't relax. From the restaurant I telephoned John; he said he was working, he was OK. I was still uneasy and couldn't focus on the conversation. At last I excused myself, made my good-byes and drove home.

When I got to the house, the Honda Accord was in the driveway. Liz and David are here, I thought, but when I let myself in the house was quiet. Why didn't I hear conversation? I stepped into the living room. Liz and John were sitting quietly, across from each other, she in the easy chair, he on the couch. I said hello to Liz and sat down by John; he leaned his head onto my shoulder. He looked immensely tired. I cursed myself that I'd gone away at all, and I was furious and also frightened that Liz was there. Had he called her? Had she called him? I didn't ask.

It didn't occur to me that John and Liz might have gone to bed together in my absence. I was convinced they had only talked. Even that made me sick. I didn't confront him. I didn't insist he evict Liz from our lives; rather, I felt guilty that I'd gone off on my own and left him.

I blamed Liz, believing she had called him. I didn't imagine that John had called her. I told myself she was making me crazy with her tenacity, her continual staking of claims on his life, on his time. Yet on other occasions my heart warmed toward her. Shortly after my miscarriage, John and I had gone to see the film *E.T. The Extra-*

Terrestrial. This sentimental story of the abandoned, childlike creature who bonds with earth children struck a painful chord in me. From the opening of the film I was stricken with grief. I didn't connect my sadness with my recent experience, but Liz did. When we saw her the next day, John reported that we'd seen the film; "Susan cried through most of it." Liz understood immediately. "He walked just like a toddler, didn't he?" she remarked, meaning E.T., and bent down to imitate the bowlegged walk of a two-year-old. I smiled because she looked so comical. "That's what made you sad," she said. Her insight touched me, and I was near tears once more.

It seemed impossible for John to set borders on his relationship with Liz as they moved toward formally dissolving their marriage. I was passive as well, making no demands of my own, waiting instead for him to set boundaries, waiting for them both to come to some accord it seemed they could not reach. The house was not my own; I'd chosen none of the furnishings; my possessions were still at my apartment in Cambridge. My feeling of displacement was intensified one day when I came home to find the wicker basket we used as a clothes hamper missing. It was Liz's; she'd taken it up to Binghamton. On the other hand, the house had been Liz's also, and she had probably purchased the basket; I was an interloper. My situation was very unclear.

I mentioned this to Mary Pat Kopp. "Geez, Susan, why don't you say anything? I mean, your house isn't a Kmart."

I didn't say anything because early in the spring I *had* said something and was sorry later. I was restless using Liz's study, surrounded by her books and possessions, and Liz showed no inclination to come and move them out. I knew that at some point Liz and John would get to the point of dividing their things, but it hadn't yet happened and I didn't like using her study surrounded by all her books. One morning I asked, "Can't we just box them all up and put them out in the barn till she's ready to come get them?" John answered by turning and stalking out of the house. Alarmed and unsure of myself, I resolved to hold my tongue.

John showed this inability to set boundaries on my behavior as well. One weekend his son Joel, then twenty-two, came to visit. Joel was fair and blond with a gentle manner and quiet voice. His photographs had been used to illustrate the text of *Mickelsson's Ghosts*. We traveled far and wide over Susquehanna County that weekend as Joel took photographs. One night John and Joel wanted to stay up and talk; I went to bed. In the bedroom I felt lonely, so I dressed and came downstairs and interrupted them in the kitchen.

John looked at me but didn't say anything. I was selfish, insistent as a small child. I wanted to be with John every minute, to be in on every new adventure. I had no sense that I was intruding on a private moment with Joel. He didn't say, Honey, this is my son, we need some time alone. Instead he included me in the conversation. If Joel was disappointed by my lack of tact, he was too polite to show it.

John couldn't set a limit to my behavior that night, nor, as he worked through his separation from Liz, did it seem that he could set any limits on his continuing need to have her in his life, or on her need for reassurance that she was still loved.

18

"I'm a Great Artist and You're Just an Accountant"

Shortly after the production of the musical *You're a Good Man, Charlie Brown* came a board meeting of the theater to discuss the current season, look at the balance sheet, and plan future productions. I attended with John, even though I didn't have a seat on the board. The June production, *Lizzie Borden of Fall River*, in spite of John's hatred of it, had done well under Irene Allen's direction; it had come in under budget and had even made a little money. So had *Charlie Brown*.

In discussing the next summer season, Irene suggested doing more popular plays, established hits, not turning completely away from the original works by local playwrights John wanted to do but, rather, creating a balanced season so the company didn't risk any big losses.

John saw this as an attack. He heard her out, then took his pipe out of his mouth and said, "The trouble with you, Irene, is that I'm a great artist and you're just an accountant."

Irene went white with rage. Years later she was still angry. "And who was he to talk to me about accounts when everyone in town knew he couldn't even cover a two-dollar bar bill?"

Gene Biesecker, president of the board, cleared his throat and suggested further discussion be tabled until the next meeting and another report from the reading committee that screened proposed scripts. He asked for a motion to adjourn and got one immediately. Irene hurried out into the hall, but I overheard her say loudly to Gene, "What is that *nice* girl doing with that *monster?*"

John had never been close friends with Irene, but he had never before been so rude. That he deliberately estranged her was not an isolated incident that summer. At one point after his fall in the driveway we stood in the kitchen talking about some help we needed with the garden, something for which ordinarily we could have called on neighbors. "It's too bad I alienated the Rodriguezes," he remarked.

Later that summer, Jan Quackenbush was visiting. Jan had been away for several weeks in Vermont; once he returned he was eager to see John, telephoned us, and came out to the house. Earlier, Jan and John had collaborated on Laurel Street productions. In the fall of 1979, John had proposed a contest; they would each write a one-act play and see who could finish first. The plays, *Days of Vengeance* (by John) and *Eden's Rock* (by Jan), duly premiered to a sold-out house. John always said Jan had finished his play first; Jan maintained that John had.

In the summer of 1982, Jan had agreed to take a part in a comedy to be presented at the theater entitled *Divorce Me, Darling*. This play avoided dark issues and found humor where none exists; John thought it execrable. We talked about it that evening as we all stood in the kitchen. John looked directly at Jan, took his pipe out of his mouth, and said, loudly and clearly, "Jan, you're a brilliant playwright, but you're a fool," and put his pipe back in his mouth. Jan stared at him, stricken. John made no effort to soften or explain this wounding remark. I was surprised but kept my mouth shut. Later Jan said to me, "I kept standing there, waiting for him to take back the *fool* part." Taking things back wasn't John's style.

After Jan left, John looked at me. "I guess we won't be seeing as much of the Quackenbushes anymore."

As always, I took my cue from him. Jan was a friend of three years' standing, someone who quite clearly adored John and would do anything for him. However, if John no longer wanted him in his life, my position was not to argue.

One hot, sticky noon we woke to hear a car in the drive. It pulled in, the door opened and slammed, someone got out. John got out of bed and went to the window. "It's Peter Dzwonkoski," he announced.

"Who?"

"From the University of Rochester. We're all having lunch."

John dressed and went downstairs. I scrambled into my clothes and came down to see Peter and his wife standing in the kitchen, watching as John shaved rapidly in the bathroom, talking to them through the open door.

We did indeed go to lunch, at a local diner where dying flies buzzed in hanging yellow strips of flypaper and the food was so bad I could barely gag it down. Peter Dzwonkoski's wife kept up a steady flow of cheerful conversation with me while John and Peter talked business. Peter was the rare books curator at Rush Rhees Library at the University of Rochester; he wanted to buy John's papers, and John wanted to sell them.

Once he realized that *Mickelsson's Ghosts* was not going to be the financial success he had hoped, John began to cast about for other ways to satisfy the IRS. He had heard of similar deals whereby living writers sold their papers to a research university; for years John had saved everything, rough drafts, class lists, even the blank white sheets he used to cushion the paten of his typewriter. Peter Dzwonkoski was interested in the deal because of John's background in western New York and was surprised no other university had approached him.

Later we brought Peter and his wife back to the house, where Peter exclaimed over the books in John's personal library. He was

especially pleased with a paperback made from the Australian an-
imated film of *Grendel,* and John gave him some copies. "Look,"
he told his wife, "ephemera!" I was amused, and John was pleased
that the negotiations went so well. Peter agreed to purchase the
papers for $250,000. Next, John signed two contracts with Knopf,
one for his novel in progress, *Shadows,* and the other for his text
on writing, *The Art of Fiction.* Those two contracts would make
up the rest of the debt, and the half-million dollar obligation to
the IRS could be paid off. Meanwhile, we could live on his salary
at the university, $50,000. I felt that a great cloud had begun to
lift from our lives.

"They don't want to agree to it," he told me, meaning the IRS.
"They're hesitant to make an agreement with a dying man." I
found this ridiculous. Of course he'd had cancer five years previously, but I'd never seen anyone more alive, more energetic, more
future-oriented, more committed to his present life. What was this
"dying" nonsense?

On John's birthday we planned a party. He turned forty-nine on
Wednesday, July 21, and I prepared two birthday presents. The
first was a pair of motorcycle boots. He drove the bike constantly
in his soft, costly, Italian tassel loafers, which quickly caked with
mud and began to split at the seams. I examined them only to note
the size and contrived to find enough time apart from him to drive
to Ben's Harley-Davidson dealership in New Milford and buy him
a pair of motorcycle boots. This was no easy task, as we were
constantly together. It was a forty-minute drive each way over the
winding two-lane macadam roads into New Milford. I came up
with some excuse, jumped in the car, and hurried to the dealership.
The shop was filled with various motorcycle paraphernalia, spread
out in well-lit counters under the fluorescent light; once there I
chose a pair of black leather motorcycle boots with a silver ring,
leather strap across the instep, and a solid heel. His feet were so
small I could almost wear the boots myself.

Next I made him a small book. With a Polaroid camera I took

photos of Teddy around the farmhouse and put together a mock children's book telling the story of a day in Teddy's life. With a handful of dry food I enticed the dog into poses I wanted him to take, nosing at our bedroom door, snuffling under the edge of John's typewriter, exploring the gazebo John was building. I snapped a photo of John in the living room, leaning forward in his chair, holding his pipe in his hand, and got him to take one of me, standing on our porch, wearing my jean jacket. I put the photos into a folded paper book with hand-lettered captions, introducing Teddy, John, and me and explaining Teddy's duties—patrolling the yard for woodchucks, helping John with the gazebo—and how comfortable he found our bed. Then I bound the book together with thread and inscribed it *One (1) copy of this book has been prepared and signed by the author.* To this I added a drawing of a dog footprint.

When we woke up that hot July morning, I brought John his presents in bed. He unwrapped the boots immediately, pleased, and then turned to the book. He enjoyed it hugely, laughing out loud as he turned each page. He especially enjoyed the laconic text: "Hi, I'm Teddy. I live with John and Susan. They're OK."

That evening we hosted a picnic dinner and birthday party, in which Liz and David were included. The guests arrived; we brought food out to the picnic table John had slapped together in the back yard. John sat down in the center of the bench, and Liz sat down directly across, with David on her left. I hesitated, thought, Oh, what the hell, and plunked myself down next to Liz. John sat across from us and beamed. The two women in his life were behaving themselves. Anne Ryan told me later, "Frank and I just couldn't believe it. I told Frank that seemed to call for a degree of civility I certainly didn't have."

Close contact with Liz and constant interactions with Liz and David was just another part of my life. No one outside could understand it, and few people knew how much time we spent together.

*　　*　　*

One humid afternoon Liz came out to the house with a new pair of slacks for John, and I was stung. This wasn't her job, it was mine. On a day-to-day level, John had little interest in his clothes; indeed, he seemed to wear whatever was handy. He did on occasion dress up, and for those times had his banker's suit or the extravagant blue velvet blazer. I decided I could shop at the mall just as well as Liz could, but I didn't know his size. He was working in his study when I went in one morning announcing I intended to buy him some slacks. "What size do you wear?"

"I don't know," he said, concentrating on his typing.

I went away and came back with a tape measure. "Can you please stand up?"

Nothing doing. The typing continued. I reached around his waist with the tape measure, pulled it taut, and peered at the number, dodging his moving elbow as the steady typing continued. I found a number, wrote it down, and left him to his typing. He hadn't even looked up.

At Montgomery Ward I bought some men's slacks in the waist size I'd measured and brought them home. He was pleased and tried them on; of course they didn't fit. He wore them anyway, cinched in with a belt.

Liz and David were looking for a new apartment; Liz telephoned and asked John and me to meet her and David to see what John thought, to give the space his approval. I was tired that day and had no wish to drive up to Binghamton for a visit that would surely turn into supper and a long evening. We met Liz and David on Chestnut Street on Binghamton's west side, went up the hill to the house, then climbed the stairs to the empty apartment, a second-story flat overlooking the tree-lined street. It looked fine to me. John and Liz walked into the bare room that would serve as the master bedroom. David watched them go, then turned to me, inclining his great curly-blond head. "What if they come out of there and tell us it's all over, they decided they're going to make a go of it after all?" His voice was tense, his tone urgent; this was clearly not a casual question.

I felt a sudden panic. Did he know something I didn't? My sustaining belief all that winter and spring had been that John had chosen me, and when he spent time with Liz he was doing so out of the goodness of his heart, to be kind, to be accommodating. I looked at David's face. He was clearly worried; he was not making this up. What if it were all a sham? What if John and Liz *did* recommit, as they had in December? After all I had gone through, all I had put up with, even my miscarriage, would he after all this time really discard me? David seemed to think it might happen, that he and I both were at real risk. I burst into tears.

John and Liz came out of the bedroom. "Golly, David," Liz asked. "What did you *say* to her?"

I glanced at David, panicked. There was no way I wanted to explain what had just happened. David saw my look and understood it. He assumed a comic tone, falling into a broad Bronx accent. "All I said was, *How about them Yankees?*"

I was able to laugh and wipe away my tears. Liz looked at us oddly, but she didn't say anything more.

At last, on a sunny day late in August, Liz and David came down with a truck, and Liz packed her things and carried them out of the house. It was an emotional day for both John and Liz as she went through each room, choosing what she wanted to take and what she wanted to leave. Clearly they both felt pain at this tangible evidence of the end of their marriage; David and I were less sympathetic. We felt pain, but pain of a different kind. We stayed in the kitchen while Liz and John stood in the driveway, talking, hugging, embracing; Liz was weeping in John's arms. They walked farther and farther away from the house, down the gravel drive. "What are they doing now?" I asked.

David flipped aside the curtain in the kitchen window. "They're still hugging."

"Oh, God."

He turned to face me, angry. "Should we go out there?"

"No, David, that's not a good idea."

He turned back to the window, lifting up the curtain, looking out, and chewing his lower lip. "But they keep *hugging!*" He stayed at the window, watching.

At last Liz and John came walking up the drive toward the house, not touching, John resolute, his face carefully neutral, Liz still tearful. David and I went out to the driveway. All at once Liz turned to John. "I forgot my wedding dress."

John said, "I'll get it," and started for the door.

"No, don't," Liz said. "Just give it to Goodwill." She burst into tears again.

I turned away. David put his arm around Liz's shoulders and hurried her to the truck.

Now that Liz had taken her things the house looked empty; John had offered her the better of the sofas and most of the furniture they'd chosen together; the cavernous living room was now even more bare. We acquired another couch, took some chairs from the prop room at the Laurel Street Theatre, and patched up the living room as best we could. Liz had at last taken her books and personal papers from the ground-floor room she'd used as a study. I planned to change everything around and make my study in the upstairs spare room.

John invited Liz and David to our wedding. On a visit to Rochester I guilelessly informed my mother, and we had a painful discussion. "Oh, Sue!" she exclaimed, in a tone I remembered from my childhood. "I'll have to talk to your father about this." Mother's face, always patrician, became more and more stony and her eyes basilisk as I stammered out defenses and rationalizations for John's behavior. In the end, Liz and David declined the invitation.

Mother and I had planned an afternoon wedding at St. Paul's Episcopal Church on East Avenue, near my parents' home, with a garden reception for about one hundred and fifty guests. I had been a lifelong Episcopalian and this was my home parish, where I had been christened and confirmed. A church wedding was important to me for spiritual reasons.

John commissioned Warren Benson, then on the faculty of the Eastman School of Music in Rochester, to write a wedding march for us, and Jeanette Robertson designed our wedding announcements. We planned no honeymoon; instead, John had committed to a four-day visit to Southern Illinois University in Carbondale, where he would read, teach, and lecture. He didn't offer a wedding trip and I didn't even ask. His work always took precedence. We would be married on Saturday and leave Sunday to drive to Illinois.

John had little or no patience for discussion of wedding plans and details such as caterers, clothes, and flowers. When I pressed him for an opinion as to some minute point, he leaned forward in his chair, drew his index finger down his cheek, and said, "Maybe we should just scarify our faces."

19

"Better than Solzhenitsyn"

In August we kept up a hectic schedule. From a letter I wrote to Sue Watkins:

> August 4. . . . We're on the road a lot. Today in Batavia. This weekend in Susquehanna, then Tuesday next week at Chautauqua—want to come? Then Wednesday to California (expense-paid trip for John and me) and back in time to go to Bread Loaf till the 29th.

Our trip to California had been arranged by George Mitrovich, who had met John when he spoke at San Diego State University. He asked John to come out to speak at the San Diego City Club and said he could bring me as well; we could stay at his beach house. John accepted readily, and I looked forward to the trip. Here was the opportunity I had longed for: to play "the merry fool," as John had described himself in a letter to me, to travel and see new places, meet new people, be at John's side. I was perfectly suited to this kind of life. He'd gone on several trips that spring where I had reluctantly stayed home; either the fee for the lecture wouldn't cover my travel costs or he wasn't willing to make a declaration that his marriage had broken and he had a new partner. The trip to San Diego was perfect.

Here again John was looking for changes, reaching out in new directions. And here again he worked to help unpublished writers, as he always did, obsessively.

At a reception after his City Club talk he met Tom Bradley, then mayor of Los Angeles. John took to him immediately, and I over-heard him offering to write speeches. We talked about coming out to San Diego to live; I was intrigued by the idea and hoped it would give us a chance to make a new life, on our own. We spent several evenings with Leslie and Larry Kapiloff, who were clearly pleased to see John again.

A photograph from this visit, taken by George Mitrovich, shows all four of us under an enormous tree on his property: me, John, Leslie, and Larry. John is happy, relaxed, sitting next to me, hold-ing my hand in his warm grasp on my knee. I'm next to him, full of mischief and getting ready to hold up my free hand in rabbit ears over his head. This moment shows as clearly as possible the happiness I felt in our best moments. My face is radiant as I plan my little joke; when he turned to look at me, realizing something was up, I found only affection in his gaze.

That six-day trip was our honeymoon, a time when we could be free of all the accelerating pressures of our life. We were away from Binghamton, from his history, from Liz and David and Liz's de-mands; free from his parents and the sadness and obligations he felt for them; free, for a time, of the round-trip of 350 miles we made every week to Batavia to be of help. In San Diego we could relax, for the first time that summer. At one evening party arranged by friends of Leslie and Larry, the hostess caught John and me hugging in her kitchen. "All right, break it up, you lovebirds." She was smiling.

Even for those few days, John couldn't put away his desire to be of service, his sense of obligation to help every struggling writer who came his way. George arranged an afternoon on a friend's cabin cruiser with a congenial group of people. I reveled in the salt spray, the chance to be once again out on the ocean. Was John up with me on the deck in the sun and the wind? Not a chance. Where was he? Down in the dark airless galley, hunched over a manuscript, pencil in his fist. One of the guests had brought with him a manuscript by a friend, an immigrant Russian, who wrote of his privations and struggles in four hundred pages of densely typed faulty syntax and fractured English. John pored over the pages and by the end of the day had agreed not only to edit this text line by line but also to champion it with one of his publishers in New York. I gave him a skeptical look. He was already way overcommitted with work—his teaching, the completion of the *Gilgamesh* translation, the two-book contract he'd signed with Knopf, editing for *MSS*, speaking and reading requests—a thousand and one demands, pleas, requests, and whining solicitations blanketed his desk at the university. He became defensive. "Look, it's better than Solzhenitsyn," he insisted. "He's got details in there that are just terrific, for instance, how the guy brushed his teeth with his finger. I mean, it's wonderful."

On the plane going home I sat next to him, leaning against his shoulder, working my needle and some white wool, making a decorative needlepoint pillow with our initials and the wedding date. John wrote a long letter in pencil to Joanna Higgins about a story she had given him to critique. Now and then he looked over at my needlework. "You like doing that?"

I nodded. "You like watching me do it?"

"It's restful. It's like watching television."

As soon as we returned to Susquehanna we went to the kennel to fetch Teddy, unpacked, and did laundry, and, as always, John and Liz talked on the phone. "We're thinking we might go out to San Diego to live," John said. She responded instantly. "David and I will move too." I was filled with despair. I doubted that David would actually agree to go; however, nothing in my life with John seemed normal or predictable, and I had no idea what to think. I telephoned a married friend and asked her advice. "She can't be such a thorn in your side after you're really married, can she?" I was unconvinced and concentrated on packing to go up to Bread Loaf, which ran that year from August 17 until August 29.

Before we left, we had a letter from our new friend in San Diego, thanking John for his offer of help. Here again, John was eager to help a stranger, a Russian émigré he had not even met, but he could not sort out his own situation and save himself.

20

"I'm Not Really Interested in Writing Anymore":
Bread Loaf Writers' Conference, 1982

While we were packing in our bedroom, John looked over at me, a stack of folded shirts in his hand. "Maybe this will be my last Bread Loaf conference," he remarked. I didn't argue. I was beginning to have doubts myself about keeping up this constant summer obligation. Maybe we were both starting to feel the strain of our hectic schedule.

Carol Knauss had again asked me to manage the bookstore and I had agreed. I liked the job, I wanted to have some autonomy at the conference, the stipend paid for the books I wanted to buy, and I looked forward to having something to do.

John and I were housed in Maple, and at last I could relax. I was legitimately his partner. I was wearing the diamond solitaire engagement ring he had bought for me in Manhattan; our wedding was less than three weeks away; I was surrounded by old friends, the "real friends" John had mentioned in his letter. We had Teddy, John's IBM Selectric typewriter, and his *Gilgamesh* manuscript. In addition, my dear friend Dayv James-French, the Canadian writer, was there as a contributor; I looked forward to twelve days of happiness.

*   *   *

When I saw Dayv across the lawn I hurried to him and clasped his arm. He wore jeans and a linen sport coat with an eccentric pin: a ceramic teapot. "So when do I get to meet your little honey?" he asked me. I smiled and squeezed his elbow.

Dayv came to our room that first morning and we all went to breakfast at the inn. In the line to the dining room Linda Pastan said hello and asked if she could find us a place to sit. "Sure," I said. "Find three spots." She looked askance. Three spots. Maybe she thought Liz was with us. Beside me, Dayv beamed.

After breakfast I hurried off to finish stocking the bookstore. My assistant that year was Karen Andes, a recent Vassar graduate.

Teddy, now fully grown, highly energized, and weighing in at about one hundred pounds, was a vivid presence at Bread Loaf. No other faculty members brought pets; with his usual disregard John was breaking every rule in the book. Some were distressed by this, others enjoyed it. I heard more than once, in irritated tones, "Get that dog away from me!" However, Stanley Elkin's son, Bernie, then eleven or twelve, had fun with Teddy. In the enormous barn, where the sunlight filtered in through long cracks in the barn boards, a small snack bar was hidden away. Bernie Elkin looked past Teddy's fearsome appearance, discovered his gentle, tractable nature, and decided to have some fun. From a well-dressed grown-up he cajoled a necktie, fashioned it in a Windsor knot around Teddy's neck, then snuck him over to the snack counter. As Bernie crouched underneath, Teddy, smelling the cooking beef, needed no encouragement to get up on his hind legs, put his massive forepaws on the counter, and open his great jaws in anticipation. When the counter person looked over and gasped, from beneath the counter came a male voice, trying hard for deep, stentorian tones: "I'd like four hamburgers, not too well done, please."

As before, John settled into a routine of reading, drinking, and holding forth during late nights at Treman. Unlike previous years but in character for the last months of his life, he engaged in burning bridges and in extending one flirtatious relationship so deeply into apparent lovemaking that I was alienated and wracked with jealousy.

John's lecture that summer at Bread Loaf was the first bridge that he burned in public. For years he had lectured carefully about fiction, trying to cram into one hour the information he labored semester after semester to impart to the students who flocked to his classes. John understood he was a draw for the conference.

However, the conference in 1982 was different. Both Carolyn Forché and Terrence Des Pres were on the faculty. Each had been at the conference before, but this summer each brought a new seriousness of purpose. Carolyn was young and beautiful; she looked quite fragile. She had only recently returned from El Salvador, where she had been a human rights observer for Amnesty International. Carolyn's book of poems, *The Country Between Us*, spoke eloquently to the conditions she saw in El Salvador and to her own experience. Archbishop Romero had urged her to leave the country. "What about you?" she had asked. "You, me, we are all dead men," he had told her, spreading his hands. She took him seriously and fled. Two weeks later he was killed while celebrating Mass at a hospice for the poor.

Terrence Des Pres was the author of a terrifying book, *The Survivor*, which detailed memories of the Holocaust. He was on the faculty of Colgate University but hardly a typical academic, stalking the Bread Loaf campus with his dark leather coat flapping around his ankles, gunning his Harley up and down Route 125.

Both were passionate advocates. Both made many conference-goers uncomfortable.

Carolyn's poems dealt with war atrocities and their aftermath. One prose poem, "The Colonel," describes a dinner party where her host shocks her by bringing a grocery bag to the table. He spills out its contents: severed human ears. I was not familiar with this poem before she read it. John was, and as we sat in the audience in the Little Theatre, John glanced over at me and reached for my hand. The late-night talks at Treman took on a new seriousness as writers began to question what they were writing and why. Was it enough to write poignant novels of divorce when poets were exiled from their home countries, men and women suffered terrible tortures in prison, and children in Central America lacked medicine and doctors in badly supplied clinics? The night before his much-anticipated lecture, John announced that he did not intend to give it. Instead, he'd talk about politics.

"Don't do it, John," Ron Hansen advised. "People come here to hear about writing. Don't harangue them."

John didn't reply; he pulled on his pipe and looked thoughtful.

Word got around—Gardner was up to something—and next day at 10 A.M. every seat was filled in the Little Theatre. Those who'd come too late stood outside, peering in, leaning on the doorjambs. Five minutes after ten, people shifted in their chairs. Ten minutes after. A buzz began. Where was he? What was happening? Was this notorious bad boy of literature late again because he'd been up all night drinking?

At last John trudged across the lawn, wearing the same black Harley-Davidson T-shirt, torn fisherman-knit sweater, and blue slacks he'd worn for three days running. His face was swollen and his eyes puffy. At the doorway he hesitated, as if taking a breath, turned to kiss me, then stepped to the podium.

As soon as he took his place the crowd stilled.

Other speakers gave carefully prepared lectures, started on time, spoke with authority, were fortified by eight hours' sleep and breakfast, or at least coffee. John had no written speech, looked like hell, and spoke spontaneously, stopping now and then as if to find the words.

"I'm not going to do a lecture about literature," he began, "because I'm not that interested in literature anymore. I'm not really interested in writing anymore.

"I'm sort of interested in politics now. I think that's what all of us writers should be interested in now."

I heard a shocked intake of breath. A woman in the front row turned to stare at her companion, then back at John. Whispers started in the last row.

John ignored this and continued. "I've lectured here about writing for eight summers. Two of my books on writing are going to be published this fall. Everything I know about writing is in those two books: *The Art of Fiction* and *On Becoming a Novelist*. So I don't want to talk about writing. Instead I want to talk about politics.

"For example, something I've been thinking about lately, there's an equation between hunger and business. Do you know how many tons of lettuce American farmers dumped in the Pacific Ocean last summer? How many tons? Seventeen *thousand* tons. Because of a labor dispute. And people are starving all over the world. It's a sin. We could save millions of lives if we irradiated food and shipped it to Third World countries. But we can't. People are afraid of it, for no good reason. And it would work!"

Now there was a louder, generalized hum of protest. "Irradiated food? Is he crazy?" "What does this have to do with writing?" Members of the audience craned their necks, put down their notebooks, stared at their neighbors, and shook their heads. Chairs began to squeak.

John used up about fifteen minutes of his allotted hour and concluded, "If you're not writing politically, you're not . . . writing." Then, head down, he left the podium and went out to stand on the lawn.

A stampede followed.

John stood by the door as people from the audience in the theater lined up three and four deep to yell at him.

"I spent six hundred dollars to attend this conference and lost two weeks of work and you want to talk about irradiated food?" a man shouted, separated from John by the crush of people.

"What do you mean, politics? Are we all supposed to write novels set in Washington?" A tall, thin woman frowned and bit on her pen.

"I don't know anything about politics," came another voice. "Does this mean I'll never publish?"

"Does this mean we all have to be liberals?"

"Do Republicans count?"

The questions went on and on. The angry man who'd spent six hundred dollars climbed onto a chair. "I came here to advance my career, and I'm not getting my money's worth. And don't try to fight me because I'm bigger than you are," he warned.

"No, you're not," John observed. "You're standing on a chair."

At the far edge of the crowd, I saw Georges and Anne Borchardt, keeping a safe distance from their beleaguered client.

Discussion continued on this issue, and John's outrageous performance, for some days. "Well, that does it, he's lost it," remarked Bob Pack, the director of the conference. "I'm not inviting him back next year."

"But isn't it a privilege just to hear what a great writer like that is thinking about?" asked one calmer, more philosophic soul. "I mean, it's important to know how someone like that thinks and what motivates him. You don't get that anywhere else."

John, meanwhile, puffed his pipe and kept his own counsel. He'd succeeded in his objective, which was to shake people up and get them to talk about something more than how to get an agent or whether a new acquaintance wrote fiction or poetry. He knew he was burning bridges. He knew he'd disappointed his audience, broken his unwritten contract.

John added fuel to the fire one afternoon at a cocktail party on the west lawn. When Bob Pack strolled over to speak with John and his companion, Lars-Goran Bergquist of Radio Stockholm, John stepped forward, clapped Bob on the shoulder, and introduced him to Lars-Goran as "The stupidest man in America."

Bob drew back a step and blinked. He didn't say anything, but he was not pleased.

Lars-Goran, who directed arts programming for Radio Stockholm, had come to the Bread Loaf conference primarily to see John. He showed up at the counter of the bookstore one morning at ten to purchase *Mickelsson's Ghosts*, and I noted his perfect accented English. Later that afternoon he went up to John at a cocktail party on the lawn, and John embraced him like a long-lost brother, effusively moving to introduce me. "We've met," I said, "at the bookstore."

John and Lars-Goran hustled off to the side of the lawn. Lars-Goran had gifts for us, editions of poetry in Norwegian, fulsomely dedicated to John in a language I could not read, other pages of poetry handsomely mounted, arresting black-and-white postcards. He followed John around as close to his heels as Teddy. When he found out we were to be married on September 18 he telephoned his fiancée in Sweden to tell her he was changing the date of their wedding to match ours.

His adoration irritated the younger writers at the conference. "Who is that guy," Tim O'Brien asked me, "Lars Boring?" One afternoon Tim ambushed John on the porch of the inn. "Make him go away," Tim said. "He's the biggest phony in shoe leather."

"Look," John said, "I named a character in my book after him." The knight who battles the devil in *Freddy's Book* is named Lars-Goran. "Would I have named a character after him, a character who is good and noble, if *he* wasn't good and noble?"

Tim shook his head, unconvinced.

John had agreed to an interview with David Stanton, a contributor from California. David had first written to John eight months before and now persisted in his request, which John finally granted, telling him, "This will be my last interview." The transcript of their conversation was published posthumously in *The Croton Review*, and John's odd comment proved to be prescient.

John spoke of his views on politics, his sense that writers need to think and act greatly, that technique is not as important as heart. These were issues he'd touched on at earlier conferences; here he spoke them more openly. He also expanded on his sense of horror that hunger was used as a tool of war, a tool of business, and on his conviction that as Americans we had a moral obligation to end world hunger. He also spoke movingly about his teaching and its importance to him, giving the feeling that it was even more important to him than his published work.

What stands out for me now in stark relief is his statement, "We're on a hell course."

He said this about the United States and seemed to mean it politically. To me now it has a personal resonance. Political beliefs, any beliefs, are always personal. Many people have commented to me about the unhappiness and desperation they saw in John in the last weeks and months of his life. I took this personally, as if they were telling me I hadn't taken good care of him. Also, I doubted it. He told me privately, over and over, how happy he was with me. "I'll be so happy I'll never write again," he insisted. However, the extent of his drinking, the progress of his disease—he was sliding down a precipice and he knew it. *We're on a hell course.* This isn't the remark of a man who's looking forward confidently to a new life and a new marriage. This is the remark of a man grasping at straws. He had written to me the previous fall that he felt tumors growing. It wasn't cancer he should have feared, it was alcohol.

My college friend Sally Johnson came down from Burlington to visit the conference and write a feature story for the *Burlington Free Press*. We said hello and I invited her back to our room at Maple, where I introduced her to John and the three of us talked. She looked around at our room, its spare furnishings, the dog food in a bag on the floor, the tobacco tins, the typewriter on the table, the manuscript pages of the *Gilgamesh* translation. In her article she includes a detail I'd overlooked; she mentions that John was drinking Wild Turkey from a tumbler and that he sang for her, "The Ballad of Frankie and Johnny." I remember that song and John's plaintive, soul-filled tenor. What astonishes me is the Wild Turkey. If I hadn't read her article, I would have sworn that John didn't drink during that interview.

During our talk with Sally, she asked about his brother Gilbert. The pain of this was always overwhelming, and John could never escape it. After he published his short story "Redemption," the accident was fodder for every journalist, every casual inquirer. Rather than refuse to talk about it, John would attempt to answer questions and thus reopen the wound. I can't calculate the pain this must have cost him. On that afternoon, he turned to me with tears in his eyes. "I killed my best friend. I killed my best friend."

I had never thought of it before, but of course John would have been delighted to have a little brother, would have loved him as a person and enjoyed being the big, strong, older brother. I looked at John's tears and understood his pain in a new way.

In a family where a child dies, the siblings bear a tremendous burden, even if they don't feel responsible for the death. John coped as best he could, by drinking, which only added to his emotional pain. That he achieved as much as he did, in publication and in the national notice he attracted; that he taught so generously and so well; that he reconnected to his parents and tried to be a good father to his own children; that he made lasting friendships—these are his real accomplishments.

In his last year, John was reaching for escape. He sought it in constant work, in alcohol, in love affairs. None of these efforts succeeded. To solve his life problems by changing his marital partner was not a solution. What he needed was to deal with the alcoholism first and then, sober, seek to lay to rest the early trauma, and only later to sort out his life, decide whether he wanted to be married or single and, if married, which wife he wanted.

At any moment he might have seen the danger signs—after realizing that his second marriage had indeed failed, after vomiting as he left the home of a woman with whom he had engaged in casual and loveless sex, after falling and cutting his head in the driveway, after punching me when I was pregnant. Any one of these events might have been a wake-up call. His tragedy is that he didn't seek the treatment he needed for the disease that was killing him.

*   *   *

Page Edwards remembers a conversation at Bread Loaf in 1982 where John asked him, "Do you think you'll become one of those writers who can't write without alcohol?"

"I hope not," Page replied.

"Well, I'm one," John told him. "I made my choice to write even though I've become a drunk. Some writers need alcohol."

In his book *On Becoming a Novelist*, John says casually, "Or the writer may slide into alcoholism, the number-one occupational hazard of the trade."

In interviews, explaining his decision to divorce and remarry, he repeated over and over, "Liz is ten thousand volts of electricity." As he said this he opened and closed his grubby fingers, imitating the flash of a lightning bolt. Then he would say, "Susan is peace. And I need peace in my life now. I need it for my work. Susan is peace."

However, John couldn't live without his own peace, his own serenity, the kind that can come only with treatment for alcoholism.

A photograph taken by his son, Joel, in that summer of 1982 is telling. Joel caught him in an unguarded moment: in his banker's suit and his motorcycle boots, sitting in his study chair, which we had brought out into the gazebo. His face is not composed for the camera; he is wearing a look of utter devastation, utter weariness, utter despair. It is the look of a man who knows he is dying, who knows something terrible is going to happen, and who can't stop it, can't save himself. The accident was hurtling toward us like a freight train; we couldn't see it coming.

And yet, and yet. One day we left the conference and drove north to Burlington to see Joel. On the contact sheets of the photographs he'd taken in Susquehanna, I saw a different picture of John in the gazebo with Teddy. John is holding out his hand to stroke Teddy's ear and looking at the dog with a sweet, gentle look;

his other hand holds his pipe on his knee. His pose is relaxed, his face full of love; it's a beautiful photograph.

As I looked at it I felt as if a window opened in my soul and I was pulled through it suddenly, to stand in a difficult place, a lonely future, looking back, seeing that John and I would never have the life together we had planned. In a profound way, I *knew* a chapter in my life was about to close. Its ending had already been written, and what would come to be was not what I wanted or intended. As soon as I had this feeling, it passed, as a sudden gust of wind will pass. I was shaken and looked again at the photo. Now it was just an image, a beautiful, touching photograph. I didn't say anything to John; he was standing so close to me I could feel his warm breath on my shoulder.

Another memory: in early September of 1981 I wrote to John about a dream. "I was walking across the street from Treman to Cherry Cottage. The leaves of the trees were wet and brushed against my face. We were all there, but you had left a day early."

Now I remember the verse my father taught me from the *Rubaiyat of Omar Khayyam*, translated by Edward Fitzgerald. My father and I had been speaking about his friend, Art Elliott, a World War II veteran who had survived fierce fighting in the Pacific theater only to be felled at home by a heart attack at forty-eight. My parents mourned this loss intensely. My father looked at me with his kind brown eyes and recited from memory:

> For Some we loved, the Loveliest and the Best
> That from his Vintage rolling Time hath prest,
> Have drunk their Cup a Round or Two before,
> And One by One crept silently to Rest.

*   *   *

One night at the Bread Loaf conference, I became convinced that John was with a woman. He had worked closely with her on her fiction, and she had a crush on him that was only too apparent. At one-thirty he disappeared from Treman. It was much too early to call it a night. The woman disappeared also. I checked our room: nothing. I remembered the party at Jim's: "He went home." I left Treman and hurried over to Dayv's room next door to the inn. I knocked, then quietly pushed the door open. He was sound asleep. I sat on the edge of his bed and shoved his shoulder. "Wake up."

"What, what is it?" He was groggy. "Susan, what are you *doing* here?"

"Never mind. You have to help me with something." I went out in the hall while Dayv dressed. "What's going on?" His face was puffy but good-humored; he tucked his shirt into his pants with the flat of his hand.

"Come with me." He saw the look on my face and didn't argue. With Teddy we went to the inn.

"What are you *doing*, Susan?"

"Shh. Never mind."

"If you're going to be so mysterious, you might as well let me take a picture of this occasion, whatever it is." Dayv had me pose under the clock in the hall: the time was 2 A.M. Teddy prowled up the stairs, looking oddly like a kangaroo. I waited until Dayv had the photos he wanted, then led him up the stairs. We walked along the corridor in silence until we got to a door. It was the room of the woman I suspected. I knocked. Nothing. Beside me Dayv shifted his weight from one foot to the other; Teddy whined and licked at my hand. I knocked again. Were two people in there, trying to be quiet? The inn doors had no locks; I turned the knob and pushed the door open. The room was innocent, empty. Dayv let out his breath and looked at me sideways.

Back at Treman, John sat in front of the fireplace. He looked up, startled, a guilty expression on his face. "*There* you are," he said, as if it were all my fault.

Two days later I left Treman at about three-thirty in the morning. I didn't want to leave, but I had to open the bookstore the next morning at nine and needed to get some sleep. I left John, holding forth in the kitchen. He stood, back against the drainboard, and watched me, with an expression on his face I couldn't read. A year before he had watched me hungrily, angled for a chance to leave with me, enticed me into leaving early. Now he stayed in the kitchen, watching me leave alone. I dragged my feet in the pebbles edging the macadam. Treman was quiet. I listened for the bang of the screen door and didn't hear it; he wasn't going to follow me. I thought about Liz. Now I was in her shoes. I patted Teddy, who sighed and thumped his tail, climbed into one of the twin beds, and fell asleep. Bright sunlight in my face woke me later that morning at eight. I was immediately uneasy—I was alone in the room.

Teddy whined at the door, turned his head, and came over to the bed to nose me, making sure I was awake. I got up, dressed, let Teddy out ahead of me, and headed back over to Treman. The house was quiet, filled with that smell of all-night party; spilled booze in the carpet, overfilled ashtrays, and stale tobacco. Dust motes danced in the air. There on the carpet in front of the fireplace lay John, in all his clothes, his arm around the shoulders of the woman I had stalked in the halls of the inn. Teddy leapt joyfully over to John and licked his face. John waved his arm, to indicate, *Go away. Don't bother me.* I looked at the two of them, the woman still deeply asleep, also fully dressed, her long dark hair fanned out and disheveled, and my heart just tore. It wasn't in my nature to kick them, shout, or make a scene. I couldn't face talking to either one of them, so I left them where they were. On the way to the bookstore I began to rationalize. They were both still in their clothes; maybe it wasn't too serious.

Half an hour later John came rushing in. They'd been woken by the hapless cleaning lady, who'd dared to intrude with her vacuum cleaner. John had vented his wrath on her, run over to Maple, then hurried to the bookstore. He related all this and many incoherent apologies as he hugged me and we stood by my desk. I felt many conflicting emotions, among them embarrassment, as Carol Knauss and other staffers were gathered in the office just the other side of the connecting door, only too obviously eavesdropping on all these apologies and protestations of love.

*   *   *

A friend once told me about a woman whose husband was unfaithful to her on their honeymoon, yet she was so obsessed she stayed with him. I knew my line: I was supposed to say, "Isn't that awful! How could a woman degrade herself like that?" I couldn't say it. I turned away so my friend didn't see the look on my face; it was like that for me with John. No matter what he did or how he hurt me, I had no intention of leaving him.

I forgave him, but I kept a close eye on girls who seemed to be too friendly, and I hoped the incident wouldn't spark any conference gossip. That I would find him on the floor of Treman with his arm around another woman, three weeks before my wedding, was just something else I had to accept.

As we talked about plans for our life together, we discussed various possibilities. One plan was to move to California. John also suggested moving to Batavia. We could take the nicer of the two apartments in his parents' house, the front duplex. John would give up his teaching at SUNY-Binghamton and teach instead at Genesee Community College in Batavia. He would continue to write, to travel, to lecture. I would stay home, help John and Priscilla as they needed it, and take care of the children we both wanted to have. As far as living with or near my in-laws, my only request was to have my own kitchen; I knew I couldn't cope with Priscilla's ancient gas stove.

We talked about these plans at Bread Loaf and at odd moments when we were together; our life was so fluid I had no idea what might transpire. I was ready to say yes to anything, as long as it meant being with John.

On the last night of the conference, I felt an atmosphere like that of the last night of a really good summer camp, a camp where individuals have made lasting friendships and where new understanding has flowered, a camp where nature and nature's beauties come to life in a piercing, indelible way. My sense was, not only for me but also for many others, that the conference that year had been memorable, important. The meal the last night seemed to reflect that. Ordinarily the long trestle tables were bare; this night each table was covered by a crisp white tablecloth and adorned with bouquets of cut flowers; candles flickered in the breeze that blew sweetly through the curtained windows. John Gillespie, a contributor from Connecticut, had taken the extraordinary step of contributing wine for each table. New friends exchanged addresses; in the excited buzz of voices I heard repeated promises to write and to call, and no one could believe how quickly the time had gone. We all knew it was a celebration.

Outside the windows, across the road, ran a low stone wall, and beyond that stretched an open field, expanding into the beauty of the wooded hills beyond. The late summer light was luminous, the road empty and quiet.

Karen Andes remarked to me later on the extraordinary atmosphere of love in the room. "It was significant, I think. It wasn't just the end of any writers' conference; we all felt it: the sense of promise, of hard work rewarded, the sense we'd been part of something special, an era." I sat across the table from John, wearing my red cotton dress and beaded sweater. I remember reaching across the table for his hands and feeling an electric current flowing over and between us; I was transported with love and happiness.

After the meal was concluded, as guests were beginning dessert and requesting coffee, in those moments before the group would disperse, John let go of my hands, pushed back his chair, and strode to the front of the room. The light flashed on his glossy white hair; contributors and faculty watched expectantly. "What's he up to now?" my seatmate hissed in my ear.

John startled a knife against a glass to get everyone's attention and, standing next to Carolyn Forché, announced that we would sing "Amazing Grace." The wait staff gathered in the doorway to the kitchen; the cooks came forward, wiping their hands on their aprons. Those of us who had been primed by late nights at the barn or in Treman, to whom John had taught the words, knew we were salted in the audience for a reason. One by one, we stood up.

Other diners looked at us; then I heard one chair and then another pushed back, scraping on the floor. At all the tables across the room, people pushed back their chairs and stood, looking to the front of the room. Then John and Carolyn began to sing, his tenor voice blending sweetly with her clear soprano.

> Amazing Grace, how sweet the sound,
> That saved a wretch like me.
> I once was lost, and now am found,
> Was blind, but now I see.

Like Pete Seeger of the Weavers, once he had the group singing the well-known first verse, John began to lead the chorus, speaking the words of each line aloud as the singers needed them. With his head lifted and his arms raised, he had everyone in the room standing and most of them singing.

> 'Twas Grace that taught my heart to fear,
> And Grace my fears relieved.
> How precious did that Grace appear,
> The hour I first believed.
>
> Through many dangers, toils, and snares,
> We have already come.
> 'Tis Grace that brought me safe thus far
> And Grace will lead me home.

The entire kitchen staff filled the doorways. The wait staff in their white coats stood at the front of the room with John and Carolyn like a leading chorus, singing loudly, clearly, their throats and hearts opened. John smiled at Carolyn and raised his arms again, heading into the fourth and fifth traditional verses of the hymn, verses so unflinching in their faith they are often neglected by believing Christians, omitted from some hymnals as too harsh, too mysterious in their doctrine.

Must Jesus bear the cross alone
And all the earth go free?
No, there's a cross for everyone,
And there's a cross for me.

When we've been dead ten thousand years,
Bright shining as the sun,
We've no less days to sing God's praise,
As when we first begun.

John raised and lowered his arms on the last words, drawing our voices out in the concluding note. Everyone in the dining hall was standing, poised, on the edge of powerful feeling. On each table candles burned, casting a warm glow over the upturned faces. John's face was serene, smiling, as open as bread; his blue work shirt clung to his chest. He put his arms at his sides, and the last note died out into silence. From the open windows a breeze, like spirit, came floating in from the wooded hills, to flutter the lacy curtains in the window and make the candles flicker, as if it too were grace.

21

"I Wrote Her that I'd Leave You"

We left Bread Loaf planning to see our friends soon again. John had entertained listeners with stories of the pigs he was raising and promised a November pig roast. I looked forward to that, pleased. First would be our wedding and the trip to Southern Illinois University in Carbondale.

As soon as we arrived home, John continued his work on the *Gilgamesh* translation, driving himself to finish, working late each night in his study, squinting at the photocopied text and the pictures of Assyrian stone tablets with their cuneiform markings. Six nights in a row he worked from 11 P.M. to seven or eight in the morning. In that time he completed a translation of nine tablets, a vast body of material.

His raw material was badly photocopied pages of photographs of Assyrian and Babylonian clay tablets. "Sometimes I can't tell if I'm reading a character or an impression of a leaf," he told me. He told my mother that staring at the blinding sheets of paper under the glare of his study lamp gave him a headache so piercing that he wanted to gouge out his eyes.

One night he went to bed early, for him, at twelve-thirty and got up again at three. As he got out of bed and dressed to go downstairs, he looked at me and said, "It's time to do God's work." Later, he told me something odd. As he was attempting to translate the Old Babylonian, he suddenly became aware that he could read this language with perfect clarity when before he had not understood it. His eyes were opened, and from some mysterious source he was given what he needed to complete his work.

The *Gilgamesh* epic, the oldest poem in the world, is a poem of death. The gods give to Gilgamesh the gift of a friend, Enkidu. Enkidu dies and Gilgamesh weeps and mourns over the body, holding it in his arms and shaking it until a worm falls out of the nose. He then begins the long journey to the underworld in search of his friend. John told me that the first eleven books of *Gilgamesh* tell the reasons why life is not worth living and the twelfth tells why it is.

When Gilgamesh braves the underworld and finds the spirit of his dead friend, he asks him questions. "What of the one who died a sudden death. Have you seen him?" Enkidu answers, "I have, / He sleeps at night on a couch and drinks pure water."

Gilgamesh then asks, "The one whose spirit has left no one alive to love him. Have you seen him?"

Enkidu answers, "I have, /The leftovers of the pot, the scraps of bread thrown in the gutter (what no dead dog will eat) / He eats."

Saturday, September 4, was a hot night and I couldn't sleep. I sat up, reading, while John worked in his study. Teddy lay curled at my feet, now and then making a small *wuff* as his paws twitched in a dream. I went to the back door to look out at the sky, crowded with stars above the dark, enclosing hills. The air was still and hot. I turned back into the house, ready to go up to bed at last, when John came out of his study. "Let's go see Jeanette," he announced.

"It's one in the morning."

"She won't mind."

I shrugged, held the door for Teddy, and we all got into the car. It seemed a mysterious drive over the shadowed mountains in the dead of a hot late-summer night. We pulled into the long drive at

Jeanette Robertson's house, waking her dog, who barked and barked. She answered the door wearing a satin wrap. John hugged her. "We came to wake you up."

"I'm so glad you did." She laughed and invited us in. I sat on the sofa while she changed and then decided I was sleepy. Jeanette proposed a boat ride on her pond and I told them to go ahead. I lay down on the couch and fell asleep.

Later, after John died, Jeanette told me what he had wanted to talk to her about.

"He was sad. So sad. I would have to say . . . despairing. I rowed out to the center of the pond and then kept the boat still. He talked about death, about Gilbert, about a young man he had seen killed in a motorcycle race when he was young. He told me he was afraid he was going to die. He said he was so happy with you, but he had this fear that it wouldn't last, because *he* wasn't going to last."

"Did he think it was the cancer again?"

"He didn't know. He didn't say *what* he thought it might be. Something beyond his control. He just said he had this feeling, and he said I mustn't tell you. He thought if he told you, you would be devastated, and he didn't want you to feel pain."

"He should have known he could have told me anything."

"He *begged* me not to tell you."

At home, after this night, John looked at me and shook his head. "My life is changing in ways I can't predict."

I didn't press him. I sensed that he was speaking about something large, something spiritual. It seemed he was talking about more than divorce and remarriage.

We were discussing art and music. "It's all just play," he said. "Beethoven, Mozart, even Rossini, who's goofy, you know. But the great art is play. The greatest play in the universe, but play." He was silent a moment. Then: "I'm lonely. There are no other great artists around for me to talk to." I took what he said at face value. It was true that while he surrounded himself with creative, interesting friends, there was no one in our circle who was at his level of achievement. I didn't know what to do with such a comment, except listen to it.

He told me he had an uncle who always knew when someone in his town, or in his family, was going to die. "He would dream of an open field," John said. "And if he saw someone he knew walk into the field, he knew they would die soon."

"What about you?" I asked. "Do you ever have experiences like that?"

"Sometimes I have a dream," he said. "I dream I'm up in the attic, where you keep the old trunks, you know?"

I nodded.

"Like the trunks where you store away camp clothes, things like that. And I open one of the trunks and there's a smell, a smell of infinite decay."

Early the next week John woke me up at five in the morning. He stumbled into the bedroom, drunk, triumphant, jubilant. He'd received a letter from Liz that "freed us."

I sat up in bed. "What?"

He sat down heavily next to me. "I wrote her and told her if she really wanted me back, that it was all over, that I'd leave you."

"What!"

"No, it was the best thing, you see," he explained, swiping at his upper lip, his face puffy, eyes half closed. "I told her that if her heart was really broken or she was really going to kill herself or something because I'd left her, that you and I would separate and I'd go back to the marriage.

"And, see, it worked; she's written me a letter saying she's committed to David, really committed, and she doesn't want me back; she's letting me go. See, see, it means we're free now."

He was elated, nearly incoherent. I was furious, frightened, incredulous.

"How could you do that without telling me?"

He waved that off.

"Let me see that letter."

I snatched Liz's letter from his hands and read it over rapidly. I saw nothing of what John described. Instead I saw only an intent to hang on as long as possible, under whatever circumstances. She spoke of her supreme love for John, of their eternal connection; he was always her best self; since their separation she felt like one of the living dead, cut off from the ground of her being; they could never really be parted in this life. To me it read like a love letter. None of it seemed fair or rational or even well thought out. That they still corresponded on such an intimate level made me furious.

Suddenly I realized he was smiling; he was enjoying this, his plan, his secrecy, his letter writing, and the response it had engendered, and he was enjoying my consternation and rage. It was so like a novel, the same event interpreted differently by two participants, worked out sentence by sentence, paragraph by paragraph.

I imagined him sitting down in his study, below me, getting drunker and drunker as I slept, unheeding, until he could work up the courage to open the letter from Liz which she had given him earlier that day. That he had taken such a risk without telling me . . . was I nothing in his life after all? Only an interruption in his ongoing marriage? The divorce was proceeding; they had filed all the necessary papers; all that was left was their final signatures and the granting of the decree. I began to rationalize. Maybe I could see the logic of it: maybe this was the only way he could think of to manipulate her, to force her to leave us alone, to make her admit she would. Maybe he thought that by giving her a final chance, so late in the game, to undo the divorce they had begun, she could then accept their final separation, and he could say, "But Liz, you wrote me that letter; you agreed. I gave you a chance to back out at the last minute and you didn't take it." Still I distrusted it. Rhetoric didn't seem like enough to me. Her letter didn't read to me like a renunciation, a "freeing."

Since I was on campus that semester, I used to go to John's undergraduate lectures. I was now fully committed to the Master of

Arts program in English literature, had begun my course work and my teaching fellowship. John taught two classes, one on writing, and one, a team-teaching effort with two other faculty members, a continuation of the class he had already begun on the epic. It was for this class that he was translating *Gilgamesh*.

One afternoon I sat in the back row of the sloping seats, listening. I already knew most of his lecture, from the talks we had at home, but I still sat in on his class. Only much later did it occur to me that I never broke out of the student role.

I looked over the crowd of students and realized Liz was sitting down front; she too was taking on a student role. I hadn't seen her come in. She listened intently, her dark head bent, the lights gleaming on her glossy hair. John concluded his lecture, stepped away from the podium, and took out his pipe. "Any questions?" He tipped his head to the side and concentrated on filling his pipe.

"I have one," said Liz.

John put his pipe in his mouth and rocked back on his heels, his arms crossed over his chest, looking at her sideways.

I was startled and listened closely. The substance of her question and his answer didn't concern me, only the tone of their voices. It was a puzzling scene. Their relationship had begun as teacher and student. He became her mentor and guided her carefully along a professional path. Her own career was well under way with teaching credits, awards, publications. Their marriage was formally ending; the divorce proceedings were going ahead, and here she was, in the second row, pretending to be a student again, asking incisive, interesting questions, and he was answering her.

This seemed shocking and sad. I focused my distrust on Liz. Her action was public, private, daring, open, and hidden at the same time. It looked honest and wasn't. She wasn't a student, she was an assistant professor, a junior member of his own department. Their affection and regard for each other was real and public, open for all to see and yet expressed inappropriately. John let her play it out; he didn't stop it, he led her on; and there I was in the back row, watching. I did not fully realize what I was seeing. I knew, I saw, I shut my eyes.

Her questions seemed to go on for a long time. The students began to reach for their backpacks, rustle their papers, and move in their seats, and at last Liz said "Thank you" and sat back in her chair. John gathered his notes and walked up the aisle toward me; Liz left by a different door.

Their interaction seemed to me like a tangled web. The connection was far from ended and would never be cut off neatly. I was moving toward the center of John's woven web, and Liz was moving toward the edge, but each of us was caught by sticky strands. I blamed her for this attachment and denied that John encouraged her, that he couldn't let go.

In the months that had passed, John had made no real progress in defining a new relationship with Liz. He did not draw any limits, he did not treat her only with the courtesy due an ex-wife, a colleague; there was always something more. As we moved closer to marriage, John seemed to involve Liz more rather than less in the personal details of our lives. I had shared with him my delight in the perfect dress I had found for our rehearsal dinner: a shimmering black cocktail dress whose full skirt was shot through with red, blue, and orange threads, like fireworks. To go with it, I was obliged to purchase a dark slip, something I'd never had before. I confided this to him in a lighthearted way, then was shocked when later I saw Liz and she teased me. "Susan, how come you never had a black slip? I can't believe it." I was distressed that he had shared the information with her; nothing was private.

He had what he wanted; he had us both in his life. It meant so much to me to deny this truth that I have not been able to look at it or think about it for many years. I treasured those moments when I was alone with John. I denied the strands that still bound him to Liz, the strands he would not cut. I was hanging on for dear life, bound to him by my own hopes, my own desires, my own love.

In the meantime, I had done little or no planning for our wedding. I had left most of the details to my parents. As my life was so chaotic, it was all I could do to get from day to day. At Bread Loaf, Blue Argo had asked what we wanted for a wedding present. What was our china pattern? I thought hard. I could picture the dinner plates with a bold band of red and gold, as different from the china Liz used as possible, but I could not recall its name. Blue was astonished. "I can't believe a bride who doesn't know her own china pattern!" I shrugged. I knew it was pretty and I liked it, but had little time to dwell on it. I didn't think about my wedding because I half feared it wouldn't happen. I wasn't at all sure Liz was going to sign the divorce decree.

However, during those first days of September, the papers were delivered separately, to Liz and John, and each signed them, and on Wednesday, September 8, John's divorce from Liz was final.

Thursday night John finished his *Gilgamesh* translation. Friday he would take the pages up to the university so the English department staff could photocopy them for him to distribute to his class.

That night my mother telephoned. This was unusual; mostly she waited for me to take the initiative and call her, but that night she couldn't wait any longer. "Susan, you have some very worried parents up here. *What* is happening?" She meant with the divorce; all her plans for the wedding were on hold and she was justifiably upset.

"It's OK," I told her. "Everything's OK. The divorce went through yesterday."

"And you didn't call me?" She became momentarily sharp.

"I'm sorry, John's been working so hard. . . ."

"Never mind, never mind. Now, about the rehearsal dinner." My godmother, Catherine Elliott, Mom's girlhood friend, had offered to host this dinner for us and needed to make her final reservation. "About the rehearsal dinner," Mom went on. "Is John planning to be there?" She was icy, ironic, and I knew how angry she really was. I attempted to mollify her, but when we hung up

257

she was still angry; the rehearsal dinner and the wedding, were after all, only eight and nine days away, and I had been negligent in not calling her.

I put the phone down with relief and went back to join John in the living room. He at least was not angry with me, he was jubilant that he had finished this major body of work.

He was waiting for me impatiently. "I'm going to teach you how to write poetry," he said. "The secret in poetry is that everything is red meat. Every line. Nothing extraneous." He proposed that he would write a line and then I would write a line and in that way he would teach me how poetry worked. I was glad for a joint project and readily agreed to this game.

Neither of us mentioned the sonnets I'd written for him. I expect he wanted to shake me out of that form. In any event, I began, by writing "The tree was green." As John wrote lines and I wrote lines, alternately taking the pencil, we created a poem which included images of a dog, and a child reaching toward light. This first attempt satisfied neither of us.

John took the pencil and wrote a new beginning line about an elephant that had killed a little girl.

I looked at this sentence and added some descriptive material about how such an incident would happen. Impatient, John crossed out my words and tried again, with a stanza where Christ insists the elephant think harder about what had occurred.

I looked at what John wrote and thought about everything I knew about him as a man and as a teacher. What could I write next that he wouldn't cross out in his impatience?

I wrote:

I thought for ten thousand years and a day.

John wrote in parentheses *A+*.
I continued to write:

And began to walk toward heaven.

I had more in mind, but John took over and added some lines to the effect that a little girl was not as important as an elephant. Now I became impatient and wrote:

(Heaven grew farther from that instant)

I hadn't finished my thought, but John took the pencil and wrote a line about guilt.

I shook my head, frowned at him, took the pencil and wrote:

> *I stopped walking to heaven and*
> *began to look for a man more*
> *guilty than I.*

Over my shoulder, John read, breathing into my ear, but not reaching for the pencil. I kept going. By now, I had realized what was going on.

> *I came to Caesar in his tent.*
> *He looked at me and said, "Elephant,*
> *Why do you weep?" He would not*
> *say more, so I left him.*
> *I came to Judas, who ignored*
> *me, tying a knot to a tree.*
> *I came to a woman crying*
> *in a field, holding a letter.*
> *I came again to Jesus, who*
> *said, "Elephant, are you satisfied?*
> *Come with me to Paradise."*

John looked at what I'd written, reading as I composed it, steadily and without stopping, and we didn't say anything more about poetry that night. We both knew that the exercise had changed. He had begun by teaching me about poetry, and we had ended by writing about Gilbert.

*   *   *

I always knew when John was going over 95 mph on the Harley because my feet wouldn't stay on the footrests. The Saturday before he died we took the motorcycle down Route 17 to New York City. That sunny afternoon, I clung to his back and hid my face from the wind tearing past his shoulder. My feet bucked and jerked against the sides of the bike as if they didn't belong to me. On the back carrier of the bike we had two crates of the magazine *MSS* which we had picked up at his office at the university. John wanted to sell them at the Strand in the Village in order to give more exposure to the young writers he championed. He was driving fast because we were late; we had a dinner date with Liz and David in New York.

We got to the Strand just as the clerk was locking the door. He stared at us in disbelief. Was this small man in blue jeans with a motorcycle helmet dangling from his hand *the* John Gardner? And if he *was* John Gardner, what on earth did he want? And who was this girl with him, in the cotton jersey summer dress and sandals, wearing no makeup, her hair flying all over the place? He made us wait while he hunted down the manager, who peered at us with suspicion. We explained our errand and opened the boxes; the magazines looked awful. Every cover was smudged. They looked as if Teddy had been playing with them in ankle-deep mud. In their crate on the back of the bike they had vibrated against one another and the ink of the cover—a bold design of a messenger angel— had run. The manager of the Strand said he was sorry; he would take them, but not at full price.

We locked the bike and went to meet Liz and David, who were staying in the city. Outside the restaurant, John and Liz walked a little away from us. David leaned over to me and out of John's hearing said, "Well, there's the motorcycle and I know how to drive it; you've got the ring, let's get out of here." David's tone was jocular. I laughed. That night he was relaxed. We both knew the divorce was final and John's and my wedding would now happen. We ate in a Spanish restaurant, had wine with dinner; then John and I got on the bike to go back to Pennsylvania.

Around midnight, coming over the Delaware Water Gap, I felt the bike waver. At 55 mph I knew John was falling asleep. I tightened my arms around his waist and the bike straightened out; he pulled off the road to a motel. We were still two hours from home. In the motel room we switched on the television and found an old episode of *The Twilight Zone.*

The story shows an elderly widow who is terrified of Death. A stranger in need is at her door, beseeching her for help. She won't open to him. At last his gentle voice and kind manner win her over—she opens the door to Robert Redford, young and boyish; it must have been one of his earliest roles. Because he is so handsome, she is disarmed; he is Death, and leads her out of her hovel into a glorious garden, flooded with bright light and blooms. John looked at me with a knowing smile.

Sunday morning we got up, checked out of the motel, and rode home. We stopped on the way through the town of Jackson to say hello to Dave Biesecker, a carpenter who had done some work for us out at the house. He and his wife were on their way to church. "Well," said John, "say hello to them for me."

That afternoon we rested. Monday began the second week of teaching at the university. John had a full schedule of classes and appointments and spent the entire afternoon in a meeting of the English department.

Monday evening was our meeting at the Laurel Street Theatre, a casting call for the play, *Marvin's on "The Distant Shore."* One friend remarked on John's evident exhaustion. "He was white with fatigue. Didn't you see it too? He looked like he needed to go away somewhere and sleep for a month."

We were hurrying to get this musical play up and rolling by mid-November, only eight weeks away. The rehearsals, the production itself, were a hobby, something fun. John already had a full teaching schedule, two book contracts, speaking engagements, and travel plans: a crowded calendar.

At that meeting we assigned parts and property masters and designed a rehearsal schedule. So many local people had come out for the casting call that John determined to write more parts. The play was a cooperative effort involving several authors: John, Liz, Sue Biesecker, and Frank and Anne Ryan. Both Frank and Anne contributed music and lyrics, as did John. Others contributed ideas and scenes. John structured the play as a revue to allow for flexibility and concocted a fantastic, deliberately unbelievable plot to keep the pot simmering and include all the action.

The title song of the show is "The Distant Shore," for which John and Frank Ryan wrote lyrics. Frank wrote the sweet and tuneful melody; it's easy to remember, light and lilting. The verses read like a testament of faith, a certitude that another world, a distant shore, an eternal life do in fact exist.

22

"Is Mrs. Gardner There?"

When our meeting was over at the theater, we went out to get in the car. With a wave of his arm, John invited a group to follow us home. It had been raining when we left the house, so we had the Honda, not the motorcycle. He opened the car door, and Teddy leaped out to lick his face; he smiled, roughed Teddy's ears, and the dog vaulted in again, joyous for a ride. Several cars pulled out of the parking lot and reconvened at our farmhouse.

Once home, we put music on the stereo and brought out whiskey and gin. It was a comfortable group; most were to be guests at our wedding that coming Saturday. Jeanette was there with the wedding announcement we had asked her to design: an oversize card, showing a procession of musicians carrying instruments and flowers. Jim Rose, John's bosom companion, was in rare form, leaning forward over his glass, telling improbable, obscene, and funny stories—I laughed until my face hurt, gasping for breath, the tears running into my collar.

It got to be midnight and then a little past; the party began to wind down. Jeanette left, Jim stayed, and then a car pulled up, seeing the lights and a car still in the drive. A couple came in, the man already drunk, the woman with him not his wife. I cringed as

I heard his slurred hello, saw his weathered hand on the doorjamb. "Come in, come in," John called, and dived into the kitchen for more ice.

I cornered him in the hall. "It's after midnight. Make them go away. The party's over."

He rocked back on his heels, looking at me in some surprise. "The party's not over. They just got here."

"Make them go away." I insisted. "You don't even *like* these people."

His eyes got wider. I realize now that he liked them perfectly well; it was I who harbored the dislike. He shook his head and went out to join the party.

I had to go into the university the next day to teach; my house would be full of people drinking and doing God-knows-what till all hours. I remembered the awful evening when he fell and cut his head, only six weeks earlier. What if something like that happened again? I ran upstairs in a fine fit of pique. In the bedroom I hesitated. To go to sleep in our double bed seemed tacit approval; I wanted to show my displeasure in a stronger way. I continued through the connecting bath into the small spare bedroom at the head of the stairs. The bed was a mattress and boxspring on the floor. I fell down on it to cry myself to sleep.

Downstairs, Jim overheard our exchange and my angry feet on the stairs. When John came back into the living room, he said, "Not even married yet and already in trouble."

John waved that aside. "I've been working really hard. I deserve to have a little fun."

Below me I could hear music, the clink of glasses, conversation, laughter. He'll know I'm really mad, I thought. We had only once before slept apart if we had the opportunity to be together.

Much later I found out that, after I fell asleep, John and Liz talked on the phone for some time; just before he hung up he said to her, "I love you desperately."

Deep into the night, I woke up. It must have been three-thirty or four. The house was quiet. For a minute I wondered why I was in the spare room, sleeping on the mattress on the floor. Then I remembered. I sat up, my heart beating fast—John wasn't there; where was he?—then I saw that he was there after all, asleep on the floor in his clothes, with his head facing the foot of the bed, without even a blanket.

I scooted down and touched his shoulder, lifted up a corner of the bedclothes; he got up and crawled into bed under the sheets to lie next to me, and we both fell asleep. That John came upstairs and did not find me in our bed but in the spare room, that he lay down on the floor in his clothes, not disturbing me, is emblematic of his good qualities, his sensitivity, his love. As well, it illustrates his sense of the theatrical. If I would deny him, he would show me how faithful he was by lying at my feet, equating himself with Teddy. The gesture was at once endearing and annoying.

In the morning I got out of bed quietly, not waking John, changed in our bedroom, and went down to the kitchen to fix something to eat. I had a morning class to teach. I had no idea of John's schedule for the day; we seldom discussed daily plans in advance; mostly the mornings were for sleeping and the nights were for staying up and writing. I knew he remembered I had my class, but I didn't want to leave without saying something. I went back upstairs and sat on the edge of the mattress.

"John," I said. He was still wearing his blue work shirt, khaki pants, and socks under the bedcovers. "I have to go in to school now to teach my class."

His eyes were shut. I waited to see if he'd understood. He nodded.

"Don't wake up and miss me."

He shook his head no. He didn't open his eyes. I went back downstairs. We had made up our quarrel as we made up all our quarrels about his drinking, by gesture and without saying anything about it.

*   *   *

I drove to school, parked, and went in to teach my class, which ran from 11:20 to 12:50. After class I stopped by the English department office, checked my mailbox, took an armload of student work, got in the car, and headed home, at about 1:15. Carol Fischler and others on the faculty had told me about this great store in Johnson City called Philadelphia Sales. I hadn't been there, but everyone raved about it. I decided to stop on my way home. I'd never paid attention to directions in Binghamton and became totally confused. Philadelphia Sales, as I was later to discover, was on Clinton Street; I had been looking on Main Street. After about twenty minutes or so I recognized a road I knew and followed it directly to the highway. By then I was hungry. It was a lot later than I had planned, and I was impatient to get home. If I hadn't taken that detour, I would have arrived at the house before John left.

I drove down Route 81 south, a four-lane highway, to Great Bend, Pennsylvania, where the Susquehanna River makes a 90-degree turn. There I cut off onto the two-lane highway, Route 171, that leads from Great Bend to Susquehanna.

When John left the house that day, he rode into Susquehanna, crossed the bridge and turned right onto Pennsylvania Route 92. Later I learned that John had had an appointment to meet the author Ted Hower at his office in Binghamton. When Ted arrived, John wasn't there. He telephoned John at the house and they agreed to meet at a restaurant in Windsor, just off New York Route 17. John was probably planning to continue on to the university after his meeting with Ted, then return to Susquehanna for an evening appointment with Jan Quackenbush at the Laurel Street Theatre.

I was coming from the west, John was leaving to the north, our paths wouldn't cross.

A mile or two outside Great Bend, I had a funny thought. It entered my mind almost as if it had been placed there by a power outside myself. It was: *If I died, it would kill him*. I was surprised by this thought as I wasn't driving dangerously; if anything, I drive conservatively, and I'm not prone to morbidity.

At that moment, John was on Route 92 maybe even downshifting and leaning into the curve he never came out of, on the freshly oiled gravel surface.

I got to the bridge leading to Susquehanna, turned right, went into town, parked, went into Freddy's market, and came back out to the car. As I got in, an ambulance siren sounded in the distance.

I drove home, noting as soon as I turned in the drive that the motorcycle was gone. Teddy leapt up to greet me, scratching my forearm with his long nails, wagging his furl of a tail. I had just missed John; he had washed the dishes before he left, and warm dishwater still filled the sink.

I was fixing a snack when the phone rang at two forty-five. An East Indian voice asked, "Is Mrs. Gardner there?"

"This is Mrs. Gardner." Our wedding was four days away; it seemed the simplest answer.

"Your husband has been involved in a very serious accident."

"A motorcycle accident?"

"Yes."

"I'll come right to the hospital."

"Yes, I wish you would."

Teddy jumped through the broken screen of the door and squirmed into the car behind me. I tried to shoo him out, but he didn't pay any attention. Instead, he sat bolt upright in the back seat, ears pricked forward. What did the doctor mean by "very serious accident"? I did not understand that John was dead. The thought went through my mind, *Well, we can postpone the wedding; maybe it's a compound fracture of the leg.* Then I had a more immediately frightening thought: *I don't know where the hospital is.* It was like a nightmare, where you have to do something vitally important and you don't know how. I trod on the gas, ground the key, and jumped at the awful noise. Teddy whined and nudged my shoulder with his cold wet nose. I backed out the driveway and headed down the hill into town. Once I got there I aimed for the theater, the only part of town I knew. Then I realized that was crazy; no one would be at the theater. On the corner was a dry cleaner—Home Town Cleaners. I parked the car, ran into the shop, and demanded, "Where's the hospital?" The man behind the counter, startled, said something, and I ran out to the car again. I continued up the street until I saw what had to be a hospital building at the top of the hill.

I parked in the lot and ran in the back door, looking for the emergency section. "Where is he? Where is he?"

A nurse stepped forward. "The doctor wants to see you." She steered me out of the hall into a small room and the East Indian doctor came in. He stood with his hands in the pockets of his white coat and began to talk. I heard only three words: "No vital signs."

I began to feel like I couldn't breathe. "Not *my* John Gardner," I said, "who lives at *our* house." I was desperate for it not to be true, for it to be some mistake. The doctor left the room. The nurse looked at me. "If I go and get his wallet, will you believe us?"

I couldn't think of anything else to do, so I nodded. She left me alone and came back a few moments later to hand me a brown leather wallet, still warm and molded to the shape of a man's hip pocket. I opened it and drew out the driver's license. When I saw the photo, I was filled with horror. It was John's license, with the photo that made him look like an old woman, like his mother. With one part of my mind I remembered how awful I had thought the photo. With another part of my mind I began to realize they were telling me the truth.

If the nurse could bring me his wallet so quickly, he must be close by. "I want to see him," I insisted.

The nurse hesitated. "There were head injuries."

I thought it over. Could I bear to see him if he had only half a face? I decided that I could.

She took me by the elbow and guided me to the small room where John's body lay on a gurney. He still wore the blue work shirt and khaki pants I had seen him in that morning. He wore his helmet; I saw at once that there were no head injuries; the nurse must have said this to discourage me. The body was unmarked except for a scrape on the left shoulder. A ridged plastic tube protruded from between his teeth; his eyes were shut. Except for the tube he looked just as I had last seen him: the same blue shirt, the same face, the same white hair; the eyes were still shut. The nurse helped me to remove his helmet. I touched his torso, bare where the ambulance crew had ripped his shirt open. It was still warm. I touched his hands—the fingers were starting to turn yellow. I bent over his face and opened his left eye—dirt was caught in the lower lid. I slowly pushed the eyelid down.

When I saw the dirt in the lower lid I knew this was real.

I wanted to lie down on the gurney with him, to hug and kiss him, make him wake up. I leaned forward and moaned and cradled his head in my arm. The nurse had had enough. She took my arm and pulled me away. She led me to a small room off the emergency ward where I sat alone, holding his wallet.

As I had sat on my couch in December, when I thought I had lost John, that he had ended the affair and pushed me out of his life, when I retreated into myself in my grief and shock, so I reacted at the hospital. I had the childish thought, *If I don't tell anyone, it won't be true.* I turned inward, into myself. I didn't cry. I was with a nurse who had lied to me about head injuries, pulled me away when I wanted more time with John's body, and seemed cold and unsympathetic. If either the nurse or the doctor had been more warm and giving, I might have broken down. As it was I hid in silence and pride, horrified by what had happened and unable to take it in, to understand what it might mean.

A younger, prettier nurse came into the room. She sat down next to me and spoke kindly. "Do you want a shoulder to cry on?" That was the last thing I wanted. If someone comforted me, if I cried, then it would be real. I twisted the diamond ring on my left hand. "We weren't even married yet," I said. "We were going to be married on Saturday."

The nice nurse left and the first nurse came back. "I need his wallet," she said. "The state trooper wants his license." I gave it to her. Now I didn't even have his wallet. She left and came back again. This time she was holding a telephone book. "You have to call someone. Isn't there anyone you can call?"

I shook my head. "I don't know anyone. I only came out here because of him." I felt totally isolated. That the previous evening I'd been with a party of friends never entered my mind. I could not think of one person to help me at that moment. I didn't even think about my mother or my father. All I wanted was John, and he was gone.

"How about your next-door neighbors?"

I remembered that awful night in June. If I said something practical, something I felt was the truth, maybe she would leave me alone. "They're no good in a crisis," I said coolly.

She looked at me as if she couldn't believe what she was hearing, but she didn't leave. My training to be polite ran so deep I decided to cooperate. I had to come up with someone's name to please this insistent person. At last I thought of Jim Rose. She looked up the number. "Is this it? Rose Art Studio?" I nodded, and she placed the call. Jim answered right away. "Jim Rose? Just a minute." She handed me the phone.

I thought about what to say. I knew Jim loved John. I didn't want to tell him what had happened over the phone because that seemed too cruel. It was a twenty-minute drive from his house to the hospital, over curving narrow roads. I didn't want him to be in danger driving while he was overwhelmed by emotion. I decided to be ambiguous.

"Jim?" I said. "This is Susan. John's been in an accident, and I need you to come and get me."

"You're at the hospital? Barnes-Kasson?"

"Yes."

"I'll be right there."

While I waited for Jim, I finally put my head down on the shelf next to the telephone and began to cry. But even as I cried it felt false, like it was something I was obligated to do. The nurse put her hand on the back of my neck. "That's better," she said.

When Jim arrived I went out in the hall to meet him. I surrendered, almost self-consciously. "Oh, Jim, he's dead." Jim looked into the air over my shoulder. I think he already knew. I had told him without telling him. If John had been living when I called, I would have said, "John and I need you. Please come right away."

We hurried out to the parking lot and Jim drove me home in the Honda, ignoring Teddy in the back seat, who whined and nosed us as we got into the car. As soon as I got there I tried to get through to Liz on the telephone, terrified that she would hear the news of John's death through the media. I dialed her home; no answer. I dialed her office. Again no answer. I telephoned the English department office. If I could get Carol Fischler, the English department secretary, maybe she knew where Liz was.

At first I got the receptionist. "Good afternoon, English department. How may I direct your call?"

I was still polite, controlled. It didn't occur to me to be anything else. I was putting my emotions on hold until I could contact someone I trusted. I was in shock, and my protective mechanism always reverts away from hysteria.

The screen door banged open and Anne Ryan came into the kitchen; she had heard the news and was clearly frightened for me, afraid of what she might find if I had been alone in the house.

I looked at Anne and turned back to the phone. "May I speak to Carol Fischler, please," I said, trying to keep my voice as steady as possible.

"Hello, Susan." Carol's voice, always pleasant. "What can I do for you?"

Now I decided I could tell the truth and be direct. "Something bad happened. John was in an accident, and he's dead."

Carol gasped.

I let my control slip a little bit. "I can't find Liz. Someone's got to find Liz."

"Have you called his mother?" Carol responded. Then, more urgently, "Have you called *your* mother?" I had not. My first thought had been of Liz. I had not considered John's parents, his children, his brother and sister, or his first wife, Joan. There was now almost no time. I found out later that as soon as Carol put down the phone someone in the office found a radio and turned it on; the news of John's accident was already being broadcast.

I hung up the phone. I couldn't face making the call to Priscilla and made Jim do it. He reached her at once. "Mrs. Gardner, this is Jim Rose, a friend of John's."

"Yes, yes," she responded happily. "Oh, yes, you're going to be in the wedding, aren't you? I'm so glad you called—" Jim was forced to break into this flow of good cheer with his news: She began to weep immediately. Then Jim was sobbing, too, clutching the phone. Anne scribbled something on a piece of paper and thrust it into my hand. The note said, *Will she call his children?* I got on the line and asked Priscilla to telephone Joel and Lucy.

Jim got himself under control and we discussed calling my mother. "If I call her, she'll think it's something about the wedding," I said. I didn't realize that just the sound of my voice would tell her something terrible had happened. I remembered only too well that the last time we had spoken on the phone she had been angry at me, with that icy anger I recalled from my childhood. Jim called her, spoke briefly, and then handed the phone to me. "Oh, Sue," she said. "Oh, Sue." Like me, she did not break down in tears; furthermore, she and Dad would have to get in the car and drive the four or five hours down to Susquehanna to be with me; they couldn't afford to lose control. She said they would leave right away.

Then the phone rang. It was Ted Hower. He had been waiting at the restaurant in Windsor for John to meet him. As John missed the appointment and the time passed, he had begun to worry and had telephoned the house several times. This was the first time someone answered. When we heard the phone ring, Jim picked it up immediately. Ted asked for John and Jim said, bluntly, brutally, "He's dead."

John and Jeannie Rodriguez came down the hill. Jeannie stood by the door, her face white, her hands shaking. More people came over. The kitchen was crowded and now the phone began ringing as more people heard. I found out later the story was broadcast on the CBS six o'clock news with Dan Rather. The phone rang and rang as friend after friend called. "Susan, what happened? Susan, what happened?"

Jan Quackenbush came over. He led me solemnly out of the kitchen and into the living room, where he sat me down on the couch. He put his arm around my shoulders and said, "Susan, you are going to have to be strong."

I was in no mood for platitudes. "Are you telling me I can't cry in public?" I was almost flip; I was trying desperately to retain some sense of myself, some sense of who I was as a person, yet feeling as if the earth was collapsing under me.

Sue Watkins called; she said later I was so composed it was scary. A college friend called from Washington. "Susan, how are *you*?" "I'm fine." "Oh, *Susan*," she said, with despair in her voice. I didn't understand her response.

23

"I'd Like Him to Be Buried with My Ring"

That evening many friends came out to the house, including those who had been there the night before. Jeanette and Jim were there; Susan Strehle and Bill Spanos sat on the couch, their faces masks of misery. I put Mozart on the record player. "He wouldn't want us to be sad."

Then Liz and David arrived. As soon as I saw Liz's face, I knew her question. We walked a little apart, out the front door, and down the path that led to the road, the two of us, alone. "What *happened*, Susan?" Liz asked me. "What *happened*?"

"I don't know," I said.

"Were there any last words?"

"No," I said. "He was dead when I got there."

Then she said, "Susan, I'd like him to be buried with my ring." She meant his wedding ring. He no longer wore the wedding ring he had put on when he and Liz had married. John had teased me with that ring over and over during the winter, now wearing it, now taking it off, like a novelist creating rough drafts—how does it feel without it? how does it feel with it? At last he took it off for good, but I knew he carried it in his wallet. After the trooper had taken the information he needed from John's license, the nurse had given the wallet back to me, and I had it with me at the house; I'd put it in John's study. As well as the license and the wedding ring, it held a single crumpled five-dollar bill.

Liz said, "He promised me he'd continue to wear my ring on his right hand as a friendship ring."

This was the first I had heard of such a promise, a promise that totally erased me, even as John and I married. Had he made such a promise? How could he? Yet I knew how he wanted to please, his weakness for saying what he knew the other person wanted to hear. I knew he had lied to Liz before, lied about me. Or was *she* lying?

It was too much for me. I was still in shock. I had so seldom confronted anyone in my life, and I had no energy to spare. I had lost all I cared about; all my vital force was employed in holding myself together. Politeness had always worked. It seemed safe to me at that moment. I had been passive all that winter and spring, even into the summer, taking my cues from John, swallowing my anger, pretending I didn't care that Liz was such an enormous part of our lives. I shrugged. "Do what you want." I watched her go in and out of the room where the wallet was, I saw her look at me and nod, I watched her leave.

My parents arrived, well after dark. Mom embraced me, as best as she could. Her left arm was still in a cast from shoulder to wrist, for the break had refused to heal, even after surgery. As I hugged her I felt her frail frame and the hard plaster of the cast. Dad stood behind her, his face a study in misery, grief, fatigue. The crowd that had been at the house now dispersed; I realized they had been waiting with me until my family arrived.

I helped Mom make up a bed for herself in the spare room and a bed for Dad on the couch downstairs. I went to my study and gathered up all the letters John had written to me and took them up to the bedroom with me, where I spread them out on his side of the bed. Then I lay down in my clothes on my side, holding one of the letters in my hand, and fell into a fitful sleep.

In the morning when I woke up I looked at the place where John usually slept and saw the letters and was filled with horror at what I had done. John was dead, and the idea that I had tried to fill his absence with love letters he had written now repulsed me. To think that a living, breathing human being could be replaced by pieces of paper . . . I could hardly bear myself. I gathered up the letters and put them back in my study. For the next two nights I couldn't sleep in our double bed upstairs but lay down wherever sleep or drunkenness overtook me: on the couch, on the living room floor, wherever.

Dad had to go back to Rochester that day. He had an appointment at Strong Memorial Hospital for radiation therapy for prostate cancer. Jim arrived, late, to take Dad to the bus station in Binghamton. Mom and I watched them drive away.

I was filled with a sickening fear. We were so vulnerable, my mother and I, she, tiny, frail, seventy-one years old, and me, distraught and unprotected.

Then I remembered the office. Some of John's papers, the papers with which he hoped to buy his way out of the IRS mess, were in his study at the house, not organized or cataloged in any way. The rest of them were in his office. I had the keys to the office; the nurse had given them to me at the hospital. Who else had a key? I was frantic. Had John given a key to any student so they would have a place to work? Would they now become curiosity seekers, souvenir hunters? There was no way to know. I couldn't ask anyone; I didn't trust anyone but myself. I knew the office was unsecured, I knew the papers were very valuable. Liz had a key. I trusted her least of all.

Mom tried to calm me down but I wouldn't listen. I opened up the folding staircase to the attic and looked among the boxes stored up there. I left Liz's papers, which I identified at once, and brought John's papers down to the second floor. Every few minutes I telephoned Jim's house, desperate for him to get back from taking Dad to the bus station.

At last he answered, sounding harried, tired. "Jim, it's Susan. You've got to come back over here and take me up to the university." I had to have him take me, partly because I didn't trust myself to drive and partly because I wanted his help; I didn't want to be alone.

"OK," he said. "I'll be right over."

I called another friend to come over and stay with Mother. "Bring your shotgun," I told him. I didn't think even Teddy would be enough to protect my mom and the house. I thought I was being perfectly rational; I didn't understand that I was hysterical.

Jim came out to the house. I got in the car and he drove me to the university. We parked in the restricted lot and entered the building. I didn't see anyone. I didn't want to see anyone. No one would have expected me to be there, on the day after John died. I didn't even bring a box. I let myself into the office with John's keys and, in the hushed, quiet space, looked for the valuable papers. Over and over I made Jim carry bulky armloads to the car. Manuscripts, loose galley proofs, packets of typed pages, letters from agents and publishers, more manuscripts, folders of lecture and class notes, bound galley proofs, correspondence from writers all over the world, philosophy books heavily annotated, more manuscripts. At one point Jim looked at me and at the piles of papers in dismay. "Can't I get some boxes?"

"No," I snapped. I didn't want him to leave me. I worked feverishly. The corridor outside the office was quiet. All John's colleagues were stunned by his death. Classes were canceled. Everyone thought I was at home. But I was in his office, reading, sorting, collecting, shoving armloads of paper at Jim, hardly breathing until he came back to the office again. We filled the trunk of the car and the back seat with unsteady, sliding towers of papers and books, the bulk of the collection now at the University of Rochester. At last I told Jim we could go. As we pulled out of the parking lot I looked at my watch. It was two-thirty, just twenty-four hours since the accident.

*   *   *

We hit a cat on the way home. It darted out, a narrow black shape, under the left front wheel of Jim's car. Jim glanced in the rearview mirror. "It's dead." He turned to me. "Should we stop?" I shook my head. I could not cope with a housewife grieving her dead cat.

Those first few days had a dark, mysterious quality, making me think of Irish legends. On the front path to the house I found a dead bird; it was as if death were an atmosphere that visited like weather, like rain, was present and all-pervasive.

It filled me, too, death, for in spite of all the activity, all the demands, all the people, the things I had to do, the decisions I had to make, I was suicidal. This was like a force that overtook me from both inside and outside myself. That day and for several days afterward, I felt that John was at my elbow but unreachable. Over and over, I turned my head to the right, sure that if I were quick enough I could see the presence I was convinced was there. I was filled with rage against my own healthy body. If I could only discard it like a worn jacket, torn at the elbows and cuffs! All I wanted was to be with him. I had never known such pain existed; it was like an amputation through every nerve. Family and friends took turns being with me, standing at the bathroom door, knocking if they thought I was alone too long. "Susan, are you all right in there?"

"I'll see him again on the day I die," I told my mother. Now I understand how chilling she found those words.

I made Jim stop at the site of John's accident. At the hospital I had pictured him plunging off the road into the river, dramatic, turning end over end, but it was not like that. Instead, the accident happened on a relatively flat bit of land along the river, where the road made a series of gentle curves, a shaded ribbon of asphalt leading out into verdant meadows. Jim kicked at a smudge of soot. "The state police put up flares."

I paced and wept.

Jim, angry, turned to the car. "Let's go look at the bike." I had asked to see the motorcycle.

I shook my head. "Let's just go." Later, I saw the bike, undamaged, unmarked, as if perverse. The front tire was coated with a smear of dirt. I imagined John braking, reacting to the accident, clenching his hands, trying to stay alive.

We took the papers to Jim's house and unloaded them in his living room. I knew they would be safe. No one would expect anything important to be in Jim's remote house, on the edge of a ghost town of only two hundred residents. I began to relax.

In the meantime, Teddy grieved too. He nosed about the house, whining, looking for John. At one point I caught him lying on the couch, worrying one of John's leather gloves; it tore at my heart. Instead of taking the glove away or reprimanding him, I left the room.

Mom found me upstairs in the spare room. I was lying face down on the mattress where I had slept Monday night and where John had joined me in the early hours of Tuesday morning. I was weeping. Mom sat down gently on the edge of the bed and put her good hand on my shoulder. As she touched me, I quieted down. "You've had something wonderful in your life, my dear," she said, in her soft voice. "Something many women never have, not in forty-five years of marriage." I stopped crying; I understood she was speaking about herself. I was touched. She had never before really spoken to me, woman to woman.

That afternoon, Wednesday, Bob Reiss came out from New York to see me. He made the trip because he would not be able to attend the funeral; it coincided with the High Holy Days and he had family obligations. He arrived just after I had the phone call telling me that I was not mentioned in John's will. The attorney who handled his divorce had not asked the obvious question, "Have you changed your will?" John had not. While he was married to Liz he had made up a simple document dividing his estate in half; leaving half to Liz and half to his children. This meant I had no legal standing, in his life or in his estate. I did not quite grasp what this would mean to me, but I knew it was bad news.

I came out from the house to where Bob was sitting on the floor of the unfinished gazebo and said, "Everything's going to be all right." I heard the falseness of my own tone and burst into tears in Bob's arms. I wept so desperately that I could tell Bob was scared. Teddy heard me crying and raced out from the house. He thrust himself between me and Bob, frantically licking my face, pawing my arm, whining. I remembered John licking my face when I cried and became convinced John's spirit was in the dog. I let go of Bob and hugged Teddy around the neck, burying my face in his fur.

I sat up and collected myself and then said something that frightened Bob even more. "If it gets too bad," I remarked, offhand, "I'll just kill myself."

He looked at me, shocked. "Would you call me first, if you were seriously thinking of that?"

"No," I said, surprised. "Why would I want to call you?"

Bob shifted his weight from one foot to the other, the gravel of the driveway crunching under his feet. His family was expecting him back in New York. "I don't want to leave her," he said miserably, to my mother.

"Just go," I said. "I'll be all right." I was nowhere near all right and had very little understanding of how far I would have to journey to be "all right" again.

Now I began to let down my guard. Once I'd acted to protect John's legacy, I could begin to feel my feelings. That night, Wednesday, I was sitting on the couch. My mother had her arm around my shoulders. We were talking about what had happened and about Liz. Suddenly I burst out with "And she wants him to be buried with *her* ring!"

"Well, *that's* not going to happen," Mother said.

I began to think of a way to prevent it. I called Jeanette Robertson and asked her to come by the house early the next morning. I didn't trust myself to drive, and I wanted my mother to stay at the house if I left it for any time.

The next morning, Thursday, Jeanette came to the house at

seven and we went to the funeral home. I had told her only that I wanted to say good-bye to John's body. I knew timing was crucial because the body was to be transported to Batavia for the funeral and I knew I had to do something before it got there. As I opened the car door, Teddy shoved past me and leaped into the back seat of Jeanette's car. Jeanette was afraid of him. He was a big unmanageable creature with dirty paws; her car was brand-new. "I don't want Teddy in here, Susan."

I wasn't in any frame of mind to drag him out of the car. I knew I was being selfish and I didn't care. "Let's just go," I said.

Jeanette put the car in gear and drove into town. We entered the funeral home by the door from the parking lot in back. The undertaker came rushing out. "What are you doing? You can't go in there." I pushed past him and hurried down a hall. "You can't do that," he kept saying. "You can't go in there."

John's body was in a white room off to the right, lying on a narrow table; it was the only body in the room. A sheet was drawn over it up to the chin—the face wasn't covered. The body was naked under the sheet. All I knew of morticians was what I had seen on television and in the movies; there someone pulls a sheet over the face of the dead. I was surprised and gratified to see that his face was uncovered; it seemed more friendly, in an odd way. As if from another world, I heard the undertaker on the phone upstairs. "It's going to be a hell of a day."

For a few moments we were alone, Jeanette and I, with John's body, and I felt this was as it should be; we loved him and wanted to mourn him in our own way and had been prevented from doing so by the custom that kept the body at the funeral parlor and the family at the house. It was a primitive feeling. I wanted him to be at home, I wanted to be the one to wash and dress his body; it didn't seem right that strangers should do this last personal service.

The autopsy had found that John died of an internal hemorrhage. In biker's language, the bike had "high-sided," or flipped. This happened on the straightaway after he came around a slight bend in the road; the state police estimated that he had been traveling at 55 miles an hour. John had been thrown from the bike and lost consciousness when he hit the ground. As he was thrown off, the handlebar had hit him hard enough in the abdomen to cause massive injuries. He bled to death internally and lost his pulse in the ambulance, without regaining consciousness, just minutes before it arrived at the hospital.

John may have swerved to avoid an oncoming car that crossed over too far into his lane; he may have braked to avoid a woodchuck scuttling across the road; he may have been so sleep deprived that he fell asleep for a microsecond. He had been drinking the night before; the autopsy showed a blood alcohol level of 0.075; the legal limit now for driving is 0.08. The combination of sleeplessness, his exhaustion of the last few weeks, the alcohol in his system—all these factors might have slowed his reflexes, affected his judgment. While the curve doesn't look that bad, two years later there was another motorcycle accident at the same place. This time the driver and his passenger were injured but survived.

John's sudden death has in its circumstances a mystery, an unknowable quality, questions that will never be answered. Also, there is a coincidence. Years later I was startled when I looked at my hardcover copy of *The Sunlight Dialogues*. The last page is a death certificate for Taggert Hodge, made out in John's hand, dated September 13, 1966. John's own death was September 14, 1982.

I took John's hand from under the sheet; the ring was on the ring finger of the right hand. I covered his hand with my own. When Jeanette wasn't looking I removed the ring, shoved it into the pocket of my jean skirt, and put his hand back alongside his body.

His beautiful silver hair was pushed back from his forehead—it had been combed, but not the way he combed it, with a part; instead, it fell straight back to the sheet. As I touched his face the tears came again. I traced the scar on his nose and forehead from where he had fallen in the barn that night in June. "That didn't turn out so badly, did it?" I meant that the wound had healed and the scar wasn't terrible, it was just there, a scar.

"No," Jeanette said. She knew what I meant.

"I wish I had a lock of his hair," I said.

"I'll get it for you."

She turned away and came back with a pair of medical scissors, the kind you cut bandages with, and separated a lock of his hair and cut it for me and wrapped it in cotton gauze.

I put my hand behind the back of his head and scratched his scalp. When we had gone for long rides in the car he had liked me to do that—he would be driving and I would put my left hand at the nape of his neck just above the hairline and scratch his scalp; he would lean his head back and give himself over to the sensation. Now it didn't feel right. The skin was icy cold; there was no response. I took my hand away, filled with a dread I didn't want to feel.

Jeanette had told me of a dream she had, a dream that seemed to her to presage his departure from this life. After we came back from the undertaker's she said, "In the dream that was the way his hair was—pushed back from his forehead, falling back like that."

What she said gave me comfort. There was no escaping what had happened, I felt. It was fated, it was written; it couldn't have turned out any differently.

We had those few moments where time seemed to stop—moments of silence, of blessing, of mourning—and then time began again. I said, "Let's go." Jeanette walked with me down the hall. I heard the undertaker behind us. He stopped and went into the room, came out again, and called to me, "You can't do that. Come back."

"What is it, Susan?" Jeanette was alarmed. "What did you do?" I wouldn't answer her or look at the undertaker. I hurried to the car and jumped in.

The undertaker followed us out to the parking lot; I had the ring in my fist shoved into the pocket of my blue-jean skirt; Jeanette got into the car and turned the key in the ignition, but hesitated, seeing the undertaker pursue us. By now she realized I had done something reckless, but she didn't know what to do. "Just put the car in gear," I demanded. Teddy's head hung out her window, and he barked at the undertaker. His white teeth gleamed, dog spit flew from his dark mouth, growls rose from deep in his massive throat. The undertaker stepped back from this assault, but called out, "I'll have to get legal redress."

Teddy continued to bark and I continued to demand, "Let's go." In her confusion and pain, Jeanette did what she felt was kindest for me; she took her foot off the clutch and put the car in gear, telling the undertaker, "You'll just have to do that, then," and backed rapidly out of the parking lot.

At home we stood in the kitchen and waited for the police, Jeanette, me, and my mother. I was prepared to go to jail rather than to surrender the ring. Teddy pressed against my knees as I leaned on the kitchen counter. I patted his fur, hugged him around his bulky neck. He licked my ear with his warm pink tongue, nosed at my chin. I had put the ring in the glove compartment of my mother's car, reasoning that it was not in the house, not in my possession, but was in a safe place. As I did so, I glanced at it. Liz had taken it to a jeweler and had it engraved. The word ALWAYS in capital letters was now crowded onto the inside surface.

After a while Pete Janicelli, the town's policeman, and the undertaker arrived. Pete Janicelli is tall, balding; the look on his kind, expressive face was a mixture of compassion and apology. The undertaker did most of the talking, desperately explaining that he had a legal responsibility. "If people tell me to bury a body with a million dollars in cash in the casket, I have to do it."

No one seemed to remember that Liz wasn't family, that the divorce had been final. "I don't want him buried with it, I don't want him buried with it," I kept saying. Finally they asked if it would be all right if they sent the ring up to Batavia with the body and let John's family deal with it. I was reluctant. At last Jeanette looked at me and said, "Go and get the ring." I went out to the car and got the ring, and Pete and the undertaker took it and went away.

24

"Amazing Grace"

That same day, on Thursday, late in the afternoon, Carol Fischler called me, hesitant, afraid of my grief, and said, "We need to seal the office, to keep out souvenir hunters and protect the papers." "Yes," I said, "go ahead." The important papers were already protected, hidden at Jim's house.

During this time John's daughter, Lucy, called. She wanted all the papers sent up to the University of Rochester, and after the funeral she and John's business manager, Willard Saperston, would be coming to Susquehanna to collect all the papers and personal effects. Lucy was direct, businesslike, firm, sounding much older than her twenty years.

Liz meanwhile had demanded to be named literary executor, a position she would hold from 1982 until 1984. I understood I was less than nothing in this picture.

I had taken steps to save all his papers; this was something I had wanted to do for the man I loved. Now the papers would be taken away and sent to the University of Rochester. That was all well and good. I approved of that part; the body of work would be safe. My problem was I didn't know what John had done with the letters I had written to him from Cambridge. If Lucy and Willard packed up the study and took all the papers to the University of Rochester Library, I would never get my letters back; they would be part of the permanent collection and anyone could read them. I was desperate to protect what little I had left that was mine.

There was hardly any time and I was exhausted. The next day was Friday, and Mother and I would be going up to Rochester and then to Batavia for the calling hours. More calling hours were scheduled for Saturday, and the funeral for Sunday. John's parents and children had made all the arrangements; there was already a cemetery plot. They didn't ask me what I thought, but I didn't take offense; I wouldn't have had anything coherent to contribute. The only request I made was of the undertaker. He had asked me to bring clothes for John to be buried in, as at the hospital the nurses had removed and discarded the clothes he wore at the time of the accident. Jim Rose and I took John's pinstripe suit, his banker's suit, which he had had cleaned so he could wear it for the wedding, and I added the motorcycle boots and insisted he be buried in them, because he had "died with his boots on."

It took me a long time to find my letters. John had hidden them very well. I stood in his study and thought hard. If I were John, where would I hide them? I looked on his desk, through all the loose papers. There I found a letter to Susan Strehle and her husband, Bill Spanos, dated February 25, 1982. As I read it, the words blurred before my eyes and I could not believe what I was reading. John had written it shortly after I had moved into his house.

> So Liz left the house for a couple of days or perhaps forever. For two days I lived my life, writing all night long, and drinking— because Liz wasn't there to disapprove—and fucking Susan Thornton to my heart's and hers content. . . . The beast couldn't be more happy than with Susan Thornton: I mean, she's fantastic, beyond all human hope. . . . But my heart crashes for Liz, only Liz.

I was shocked and sickened. The paper shook in my hand. What was I to do with this? I felt a moral obligation to keep the collection of papers as he left them at the moment of his death. I did not want to be judged as had been the widow of Sir Richard Burton, the Victorian explorer and translator of *The Arabian Nights*, who destroyed her husband's legacy by burning the work she found "obscene." I owed John the courtesy of letting history judge him as he had lived; it was not my place to edit and select. But this letter I kept, partly out of spite and partly out of self-protection. Years hence I did not want some "scholar" reading it and misunderstanding me and my situation.

I still hadn't found the letters I had mailed from Cambridge. I looked carefully among the books that lined the table, facing the typewriter. There was the snapshot I had given John—me, Blue, Betsy Sachs, and Joyce Renwick surrounding him at Bread Loaf. He is in the center of the group and I am at his right; he had slipped the photo between two books that faced him as he worked at the typewriter. He could take it out at any time and look at my picture.

Going through his papers in that way was a rare privilege. I wished I had more time to savor and understand. It was like an archaeological dig, through layers of deep, rich, enriching soil. I found parts of the rough draft of *Marvin's on "The Distant Shore,"* the play we had begun to cast on the night before his accident; drafts of an unfinished TV drama about Dr. Johnson; galleys of *The Sunlight Dialogues*; notebooks filled with his script; letters from publishers; contracts; many many drafts of the typescript of *Mickelsson's Ghosts*. That small room was packed, lined with his creative genius, the fruits of all his years of hard imaginative labor; it was a rare glimpse into the processes of his mind, and it was evanescent; soon enough it would be packed and gone, and the study would be a bare room in an empty house, put up for sale.

At last I found them, my letters, seven of them. I had to stand on a chair and reach way back into the shelf of the closet off the study. I glanced at them hastily. I had no idea how many I had written. Later, Liz found six more in John's desk at the university.

*   *   *

Now my desire to commit suicide came back in full force. I'd done all that I felt needed doing. I'd protected John's papers, and I'd found and claimed my letters. They would not be part of the collection. I'd prevented John from being buried with Liz's ring. I had nothing left of importance to do, and now I could die. It seemed so simple. If only I could die, I could be with him, and this nightmare would be over.

I still wasn't sleeping, wasn't eating. It was more than I could do to choke down food; to get through those long dreadful evenings and nights, I was drinking. Intense grief can look and feel a lot like psychosis. My hands and whole body shook continually; I was always cold, yet bathed in sweat. I thought I heard John's voice in my ear; I hallucinated, so I couldn't trust my eyes. If I looked at a farmer plowing a field, the entire landscape looked flat and I wondered why the tractor didn't fall off the vertical surface. At one point, Mom and I had to drive to Binghamton. I directed her up a narrow country road. I saw something and made her stop: I'd seen a rabbit, crucified on a tree stump, legs dangling, chest cavity red and gaping, blood-soaked flesh showing under the torn white fur. A crow strutted nearby, preened his brilliant wing, cocked his head, and returned to the corpse. He pinched a piece of fur in his jet beak, tore it loose, and cast it aside, then regarded me with the insolence of death itself. I stared wordlessly for such a long time that Mother became frightened. "Sue, what is it?" I blinked and the image vanished.

I was in this state when Jeanette came over to the house Thursday and proposed a walk to a local waterfall, a scenic spot she and Jim had liked to paint. For a long time John had had one of Jim's paintings that depicted this spot. At first it was a relief to get out of the house, but the beauty of that autumn day seemed to mock me. We walked in silence through the sunlit field until we got to the roaring stream and the precipice, with its tumbling flow of water. Jeanette and I stood balanced at the edge and I saw my chance. I could dive over the edge, head first, a hundred feet down.

I could do it. I could make it happen. If I could get out of my body, I could find John. It would only take a running jump. . . . Instead of rushing forward, I grabbed blindly for Jeanette's hand and stepped back. She saw her mistake at once and pulled at my hand to get me away from the edge. We hurried away from the waterfall, neither of us speaking.

There was one more night in Susquehanna, and then it was time to leave, on Friday morning, to go back to Rochester for the funeral service, which I dreaded, which would take place the day after we had planned to be married.

We arrived in Rochester on Friday, and that evening Mother and I drove out to the funeral home in Batavia for the calling hours. It was the evening that should have been my wedding rehearsal dinner, planned for the Maplewood Inn in Rochester. It was a warm and humid night, the air close and damp. I was wearing the same blue jersey dress I had been wearing for three days running. John's Aunt Lucy greeted me at the door and encircled my waist with her narrow arm. "Well, dear, this isn't what we had planned for this weekend, is it?"

The casket was open for family viewing only and stood in a carpeted room off a hall. I walked in to look at John's hands. There was no ring.

Later John's cousin approached me. "I'm Bill Gardner," he said. "Will Hodge, Junior, in *The Sunlight Dialogues*." Quite a few of John's family and friends introduced themselves to me in that way, as characters from this novel, which was set in Batavia. Bill and I walked outside to the parking lot for some privacy. The calling hours were crowded, Joan, John's first wife; Lucy and Joel; Liz and David; friends, relatives, students, colleagues, flowers, books to sign, demands—I was glad of a breath of air. Bill came right to the point. "John's going to be buried without the ring."

"I know," I said. "I saw the body."

"Liz was wrong."

I nodded. "Who has the ring?"

"The family."

"I want it returned to Liz."

He shook his head. "Not now. In a year, eighteen months, when things cool down."

"Now," I said. "Give it to her now. I want her to have it now."

"No." He reached into an inner pocket of his suit coat to remove something.

My nerves had reached their breaking point. I held up my hand. "I don't want to see this particular piece of jewelry."

He raised his eyebrows, startled, his hand in mid-gesture; he had been going to give me his card. He held it out, between the tips of his index and second finger. "William Gardner," I read, and an address in Buffalo, an attorney's office. "Call me if I can do anything for you." A lot of people said that to me during that time.

I nodded and took the card, we went back into the funeral home, and I watched Liz from a distance.

Saturday, the day John and I would have been married, was clear and cool. I wore a cotton dress and my jean jacket with the Harley-Davidson emblem. I felt a cool wind rushing against my body as I walked across the parking lot in Rochester to meet my friend Olivia Lovelace. I had asked her to be my maid of honor, and she came from New York City to be with me.

Olivia has blunt-cut blond hair, bright blue eyes, a lovely smile; we had sailed together on the *Regina Maris*, five years before; we'd forged a friendship through fierce gales off the rocky coast of Labrador as we sailed north to the Arctic Circle, haunted by the Northern Lights, the midnight sun, the never-ending twilight of those mysterious latitudes.

I asked Olivia to take me to the conservatory—an elaborate glass pavilion—at the center of Highland Park. This garden spot was my favorite place in Rochester; I felt it would be healing to sit in the presence of the fragrant plants under the glass panes. As we got out of the car we saw a bridal party cross the lawn, going into the Conservatory for wedding pictures. The bride smiled and picked up the skirt of her wedding dress so the hem wouldn't touch the grass. I looked at Olivia and we got back into the car.

This coincidence is not so remarkable. The Conservatory at Highland Park is a popular setting for wedding photos. My interpretation of this chance meeting shaped my life for many years. I began to hate God. I felt I was being ridiculed. I decided God hated me, too, and would do whatever He could to destroy me. If God controls everything, the extraordinary timing of John's death, only four days before our wedding, must be meant to send me a message about myself and what I could expect from life. As I looked at this bride, lifting up her skirt so the dew wouldn't drench the hem on the day that should have been my wedding, I decided I'd survive just to show God how tough I was. If God intended desolation and despair for me, I would live it out, however long it took, until I died and could be with John again. My attitude was one of defiance and rage. Life became something to be mastered or endured.

At the calling hours, Lucy told me she intended to come early to the church. "There will be music at the funeral tomorrow. Gardners always have music. I'm going to get there early to rehearse the musicians." She was joking; I took her literally and said I would meet her there. At that point I would have done anything for Lucy. I wanted to make a connection to her and to Joel. I knew I had failed them both by not telephoning them with news of their father's death, yet Lucy had greeted me at the funeral home without rancor. She had taken both my hands and looked into my face with her open, frank one, so like her father's. I was trembling all over, in the constant shaking I was unable to stop. "I only want what you want, I only want what you want," she repeated. She was referring to the safety of her father's papers, of his body of work; she understood their vital importance and must have seen how deranged I was by grief and shock.

Fans of John's work had seen my name in the local paper and telephoned the house; I remember one long incoherent conversation with someone I didn't know who insisted he had to come to the funeral, and my insane promise that he could stay at my parents' home. Fortunately, he never appeared.

Sunday morning I tried to write a letter to a friend John and I had made on our trip to San Diego. I had only his business address and sat for more than an hour staring at the envelope. I knew there was a word you could write on the envelope so that only the addressee would read it. At last I remembered the word: *Personal.* I began to write it, but as soon as I'd made the letter *P*, drawing it as carefully as a child might, I realized that it didn't look right. I looked at the address I'd written. I couldn't read it; the letters were a meaningless jumble. I understood in a distant way that I'd lost the ability to read and write and wondered, without much caring, if I'd ever be able to again.

After the scene at the calling hours, surrounded by a crowd of strangers, acquaintances, family, trying to speak in a meaningful way to Lucy, pushed up against Joan, and constantly seeing Liz clinging to David, I knew the funeral was the last place I should be. I was goaded into attending by my certain knowledge that, if I didn't go, people would say I hadn't loved him. What should I wear? I didn't own a suitable black dress and Mother hadn't wanted to leave me alone long enough to go shopping. I chose a simple skirt and blouse and borrowed mother's brown velour jacket. It was an effort even to brush my hair. My parents asked friends to stay at our house while we were gone; since our name had been in all the papers we were afraid of a break-in while we went to the funeral. I telephoned Priscilla and advised her to do the same.

I asked Olivia to drive me out to Batavia early, well before the service was to start. She and my parents were uncomfortable with this plan, but I insisted. "Lucy said to meet her early." I would not listen to anyone. Olivia and I drove the forty-five minutes to Batavia and she dropped me off in the empty church parking lot. My parents were to follow later in their car. It was an hour before the service was scheduled.

"Are you going to be all right?"

"I'm fine," I insisted.

She said, I believed, "You know I have to go back to New York now. Don't you want me to stay with you until the service starts?"

"No," I said. "Go along."

She left.

I clearly remember Olivia telling me she had to go back to New York, although years later she told me she never said this and was indeed in the church, sitting in a back pew with Jim Rose. But I also clearly remember being alone in the church parking lot.

I went into the church looking for Lucy. John's coffin stood at the intersection of the aisles before the choir stalls, all by itself in that empty church. I hesitated at the back of the cavernous, echoing space. An older lady in a dark blue coat and scarf lurched down the aisle toward me and asked me when the service was to start. I told her and then abruptly left the sanctuary.

A bride waits with her attendants in a small room off the main aisle from the church. Her maid of honor makes final adjustments to her hair, her veil, another bridesmaid smiles, touches her hand. A photographer requests one more pose and then is sent away. The bride's mother smiles with tear-bright eyes. Her father stands ready to offer his arm. In the church, the organist adjusts the bench, squints at the stops on his instrument, gathers his breath, lowers his hands, and begins to play a joyous, resounding march; the groom steps forward.

I went out to stand at the far edge of the parking lot and watched the cars arrive. Eventually Lucy, Joel, and their mother pulled up and got out of their car. Lucy was wearing a slim, tailored black dress. Her long blond hair was spread over her shoulders, and she looked quite beautiful.

I watched from a distance, as if I were observing an event that didn't concern me. It didn't occur to me to go up and speak to Lucy; I really didn't feel I knew her that well, and I had no desire to go inside. It felt much safer watching from the margins. If I had

seen my parents I might have gone to them, but they hadn't arrived. By asking Olivia to bring me out early, and by sending her away, by not riding in my parents' car with them, I had cut myself off from the people who loved me the most and would have given me the support I needed. I felt as I had at the hospital. The only person I wanted was gone, and I could think of no one else.

I might have stood in the parking lot for the rest of the afternoon, but John Rodriguez saw me. I watched him approach. His suit hung off his thin bony frame. He inclined his curly head. His face was lined with the deep wrinkles of the outdoors man. "What are you doing out here all by yourself?" he asked, horrified. He took my hand; his whole body was trembling. In a halting voice I explained. He kept my hand in his large trembling one and led me into the church.

The Gardner family was gathered in a large sitting room near the sanctuary. Priscilla was seated. John Senior was standing up, one hand on his cane, the other on Aunt Lucy's arm. When I walked into the room he burst into tears. I realized it was the shock of seeing me alone; always before I had been at John's side.

Liz and David came in. Liz was dressed all in black and was carrying a pot of mums, which she held out to Priscilla. As soon as she arrived, John's family stood up and embraced her. No one spoke to me. I sat alone on the chair.

Sue Watkins, who, with Olivia, had been going to stand up with me at my wedding, sent me her memories of that day:

> I drove to Batavia and found my way to one of the anterooms of the church, where you were sitting in an overstuffed chair, staring at the floor, surrounded by John's parents and a conglomeration of people all dressed to the nines. The room was a hubbub of voices and perfume, people rushing in and out. You focused on me for a small moment and then someone said something to you and you unfocused again. Liz came in and the entire Gardner family stood up to greet her. You looked up at me with an ex-

pression that I've seen on the faces of mortally wounded animals who only wish to die. I thought—I've got to get her out of here.

Someone came in and said we should all go into the church now. You got to your feet and reached out for me, but someone else took your hand and led you out through the hall and into the sanctuary. I trailed along behind in the crush of people. The church itself was absolutely packed, way back to standing room only and out the door onto the sidewalk—I could see the blue autumn sky outside the big doors, and people standing on the steps. I ended up sitting about five rows back from you, next to a man who treated me with disdain. I have no idea why, and didn't care. He might have been "somebody" who thought he ought to be sitting up by the coffin—that was his attitude. But the second the minister began to speak, this man put his face in his hands and wept.

A bride processes up the aisle on her father's arm; her mother has already been seated by an usher. The groom stands ready at the foot of the steps, with his best man, who holds the ring. The groom smiles as he sees the radiant face presented to him, crowned by flowers, illumined by hope.

I came into the church from the wrong direction, separated from my parents. Instead of a wedding dress I wore a simple cotton skirt and blouse and a brown velour jacket. My head was bare. I had no flowers. The organ music was funereal instead of joyful. Instead of a groom, at the foot of the steps was a coffin.

At last I saw my mother and father walking up the aisle toward me. My mother was carrying her folded raincoat over her arm. She had a grim look on her face; I knew she had been waiting for me, trying to find me in that crowd. I blindly took a seat in the first pew and then realized someone was tugging at my arm. It was John's Aunt Lucy. "You can't sit there," she whispered in my ear. "You can't sit there." I was reluctant; how far back was she going to make me move? The old lady wouldn't give up; her nails poked into my arm like birds' claws. At last I stood and she pulled me out of the first pew and down next to her in the second; I realized I had been sitting next to Joan Gardner, John's first wife.

My mother sat on my other side, next to my father. The service began with a hymn sung by the congregation; then there were words from the minister. I was told later that he looked out over the congregation and said that John had been many things to many people: a son, a father, a husband, a fiancé—looking at each family member in turn and then at me. Then music began again, the hymn "Amazing Grace" played on a tape—a tape of a duet John had played on the French horn with Joel.

As the first notes sounded I felt a pain more intense than any I have known before or since.

To hear John's breath on tape—knowing it was the breath of a man who would never breathe again, the breath of the man who had died so suddenly five days before, the breath of the man I would never see anymore in this life—was more than I could bear. It went right to my heart, piercing it as if with a red-hot needle. I remember sobbing; then, horribly, as if it were happening to someone else, I remember laughing: high-pitched hysterical laughter that rose and rose until I feared everyone in the church would hear it and know what I now knew, that I was going mad at last, that my mind had broken and would never return to me. I felt the fear I had known as a college girl, that if I swallowed the next pill, if I stayed up all night one more night, I would black out and wake up in a white hospital room, not knowing where six days, six months, six years had gone. I felt the fabric of my mind begin to rip like old silk, strained beyond the limit of its strength, irrevocably torn at last. As the music started, Mother knew immediately what I would feel hearing it. She gripped my hand and hissed into my ear, "Oh, that was a dirty trick!"

I pushed up from the pew and headed blindly out of the church, back the way I had come in.

Sue Watkins and my parents followed me out and took me back

to Rochester. I was so emotionally disorganized I thought that
John's family had chosen to play the tape of "Amazing Grace"
deliberately to drive me insane.

The interment in the Batavia cemetery was scheduled for Monday. I couldn't face it; I couldn't imagine standing at the grave site
with John's parents, with Joan and her companion, with Liz and
David. I didn't go. I had had enough.

*A bride leaves the church in a hail of rice and good wishes. She
tosses her bouquet to her bridesmaids and travels with her groom
on their honeymoon. They return together and she arranges her
household, unpacks wedding presents, writes thank-you notes,
places china and crystal in order on her shelves. She sings as she
works, making a home for herself and her husband, for the child
or children who are to come.*

After John's funeral I went to my parents'. Within the week I
was back at the farmhouse in Susquehanna, petitioning his estate
for permission to keep memorabilia, competing for household objects and furnishings with his ex-wives, hearing other people decide
what to do with his clothes, packing my own possessions, and
moving out of what had been my home. I was now, quite literally,
homeless.

25

———

"It's Not Awarded Posthumously":
Sweden and the Nobel Prize

"This is the bridge people come to when they want to jump off and kill themselves." My host in Stockholm, Lars-Goran Bergquist pointed to a lofty pedestrian bridge looming over an arterial highway. I looked at the span, some sixty feet above the roadway. I looked at Lars-Goran to see if he was serious. His face showed no understanding of what I might be feeling. It was three weeks since John's death.

After John died, Lars-Goran telephoned. He wept. He put his wife on the phone. She wept. Then he called again. He called my mother and tracked me down in Dundee, New York, in the Finger Lakes where I had fled to be with Sue Watkins. One morning at six-thirty she answered the telephone, cinched her terry-cloth bathrobe tighter around her waist, and handed me the phone. "It's the Nobel Committee."

Lars-Goran had noised it about the Bread Loaf conference that he was in close communication with the Nobel Committee. Blue and I had listened avidly as he told us that John's name was on the short list for the prize.

On the phone Lars-Goran kept asking me to come to Sweden. I decided to go. My mother paid $1,300 for a round-trip business-class ticket to Stockholm, and I went when the house in Susque-hanna had been emptied out, as soon as I could. I went because I wanted to see Lars-Goran and he wanted to see me, and I went because I wanted desperately to connect to the person I had been before John had come into my life. I wanted to recapture the spirit, the courage, the daring I had had. I wanted to regain a sense of myself beyond pity. I wanted to go somewhere where no one knew what had happened. And I wanted to go because I had a plan.

Lars-Goran met me at the airport. I had brought gifts I hoped he'd treasure: an empty tobacco tin, one of John's pipes. Lars-Goran was disappointed. "No whiskey?" I hadn't realized how prohibitively expensive it was in Stockholm and that duty-free whiskey was the only gift from travelers that most people wanted.

Even before we were back at his apartment, Lars-Goran demanded to know the safety of John's manuscripts. "And *Shadows*? What about *Shadows*?" He named the novel John had planned to turn to next, a work that had been in progress for some years. I told him all the papers were safe.

Later in my stay I got up the nerve to ask him about the Nobel Committee. My plan was no less grandiose than to save the estate for Joel and Lucy. The debt to the IRS was one half million dollars. While John had negotiated with the IRS to pay it off, he had died before the sale of his papers was complete. The debt, as I understood matters, would consume the entire estate. The Nobel Prize translated roughly into $300,000. I thought if John were awarded the prize, Joel and Lucy would achieve some kind of legacy from their father. I asked Lars-Goran what he thought. He shook his head. "It's not awarded posthumously."

I could have found that out in a transatlantic phone call. But I still think I did the right thing. My journey gave me something to do and gave me hope, however fantastic or unrealistic. I began to retain a sense of myself as someone who could do something, an actor, not a victim. And sitting in a park in Stockholm, I began to write a short story. I decided that writing could give me a path out of recent events and into the future.

26

"I Could Hurt You Very Much"

Mother wanted me to make a clean break, come back to Rochester, and live with her and my father for a while. I didn't want to do that. I also felt I couldn't go back to Cambridge. The flashy, fun life I had had there now looked empty and meaningless. At first I gave up, and then demanded back, my assistantship at the university. An apartment in Sue's building in Dundee became vacant, and she put a deposit on it for me. I determined to go back to SUNY-Binghamton and finish the master's degree, even though the university was a two-hour commute from Dundee.

This gave me a place to start, and I moved into the small duplex apartment on Seneca Street with Teddy and my typewriter.

As promised, eighteen months later, the family sent John's wedding band, the ring I had taken from his corpse, back to Liz. Liz and I were in intermittent contact. My feelings toward her were a tangle of thread I couldn't straighten. I liked her, I hated her, and I depended on her as if she were the only person who could validate my experience. At times I turned to her for comfort, which she gave. I resented and mistrusted her. I was lonely, grief-stricken, often confused, and didn't trust my own instincts.

I had the use of a large ground-floor office on the corridor where

John's office had been; Liz's office was around the corner. Late one evening there had been a fiction reading we both attended, and we walked down the stairs together afterward, back to the corridor where our offices were. As we headed to the stairs, she said something offhand. "I've heard from John's family. Priscilla sent me an odd letter. And something strange: she sent me back John's ring." Her tone was casual; she didn't suspect my part in this.

She went over to the soda machine, singing to herself, "Amazing Grace, how sweet the sound. . . ." As she bent down to get the can, she said, "I don't understand what happened. Joan must have prevented his being buried with the ring. It's something Joan would have done." She turned down the hall.

I hesitated; then I knew I had to speak. I followed her. I took a breath. "Liz, it was me."

"You!" Her eyes were wide with surprise. "You."

I know where her surprise came from—I had been so gentle, so docile, so accepting, so sweet and quiet for so long. She got angry and turned away down the hall. I took a step after her and grabbed her arm, spun her around to face me. "He *divorced* you, Liz," I said. "He *divorced* you."

She wrenched her arm from my grip. "Don't push me, Susan. I could hurt you very much. Just don't push me."

I went into my office and shut the door. *Her*, hurt *me*? I didn't think it was possible. I stood by the door, shaking with rage and frustration. Then I heard footsteps. They approached the door and stopped, someone bent down, and a sealed white envelope came sliding under the door. I looked at it as if it were a snake. It was from Liz. The footsteps went away. I sat down in my office chair and looked at the envelope for a long time. Teddy, sleeping in his usual place on the office floor, kept me company. Then I put my gloves on, picked up the small envelope, put it in a larger one, and sealed that. I waited some more. Then I looked out into the corridor. All was quiet. Convinced that Liz had gone, I walked to her office door, slid the envelope under, and went back to my office, got Teddy, went to my car, and drove home.

*   *   *

I returned the letter to Liz not because I was afraid to read it but because it was as deliberately rude as I knew how to be. I knew that to return one of her letters unread was an insult so large it would push her definitively out of my life. It was my divorce from Liz.

What was in the letter I didn't read? Was it an apology? Was she sorry for her momentary lapse, her harsh words? Or was she still angry? Would she have recounted the times she and John had made love after I thought he was committed to me? Would she have cited some wounding remark, some comment that I really wasn't all that bright, after all, and he didn't know why he had left her? I already knew he had said terrible things about me; after he died she gave me a photocopy of a letter he had written to her while I was pregnant. He had remarked that when he said disparaging things about my sensitivity and intellect he was very mistaken.

In the end we both lost him. A certain clock stopped when he died, and Liz and I remain stuck there, parts of us, as if caught in amber. We've each gone on with our lives, but we have in common our separate loves for this difficult man, his connection to us, his sudden violent death. We both live in the city to which he brought us, separately, within walking distance from each other's homes, and we both live not twenty-five miles from where he died.

When Liz found six of my love letters in John's desk at his office, she had a choice. She could easily have destroyed them, out of anger, out of jealousy, out of spite. Instead she was generous; she returned them to me. She wrote me a note, handwritten, on a piece of *MSS* magazine stationery that says in part that she read the letters and refused to feel guilty about doing it. I couldn't blame her for that; I would have done the same thing. Her note said she had known in her heart what my letters contained, that no one else had seen them, and she concluded that we had both loved him, and that this love tied us together in good ways. She signed her note, "Love."

Liz also gave me a sheet of paper, written on both sides. It's something John wrote. On one side is a typed draft of a love poem he wrote to me, on the other side is a penciled draft of a poem to her.

"Why don't you and me—and Liz—have a really brilliant short life?" This brilliant short life always included the triangle that was never resolved.

27

"The Woman I Want to Marry"

After the funeral, I had to return to Susquehanna so I could move my personal items out of John's house and his estate could put it on the market. I didn't want to make the trip. Sue Watkins drove me and I lay on the back seat of her car, pretending to sleep. At last I gave it up and asked her to stop and got into the front seat. As she drove, we talked. She asked me again what John's plans had been for us after our marriage. "Well," I began, "he wanted to move back to Batavia, take the nicer apartment in his parents' house, and live there so he could look after them. And he wanted me to have a baby, to try again to get pregnant."

"What was he going to do?"

"He was going to write, teach at the local community college, and travel around and give readings, like he always did."

Sue pulled the car over to the side of the road and stopped on the gravel verge. Outside the car stood a tangle of staghorn sumac, dark red against the green of the surrounding foliage. She put the car in park and turned to face me. "He was *what*?"

I repeated what I had said.

She continued to look at me as if I had lost my mind. Then she hesitated.

"What?" I asked.

She decided to jump right in. "That would have been death for you. *Death*. For you, for your writing, for everything—for the person you are. What did you say to him?"

"All I said was, if I had to live with my in-laws I wanted my own kitchen."

Sue shook her head, as if I couldn't hear myself. "That would have been death for you," she repeated. "You know that, don't you?"

It had only been two or three days since the funeral. I was exhausted, bereaved, distraught. What were my feelings? Did I want to rail at her, to accuse, to deny? To shout at her that she was insensitive, foolish, wrong? To ask the obvious question, "How can you say such a thing at a time like this?" I didn't do it. I thought it over carefully and said, "I know. But I would have done it."

Sue put the car in gear and drove back onto the highway.

"You remember meeting him, don't you?" I asked. "Do you understand me at all?"

"Yes," she said at last. "I do."

My recurrent nightmare since John's death wakes me from a sound sleep with a pounding heart and sweaty temples. This nightmare comes twice, maybe three times a year and has not changed in substance over all the years that have passed.

The nightmare is not about speed, not about accidents, not about motorcycles. It is not about weddings, wedding dresses, or being left at the altar.

In my dream, John is alive. He has been alive all these years. He has been hiding from me with another woman.

I wake with a sickened stomach. If John is alive, the awful grief I walked through is meaningless. If he has been hiding from me, he never really wanted me. If he is with another woman, he is totally faithless.

Sometimes there are embellishments on the dream. The woman

305

is a student; I hear about this because she comes to me with a paternity suit related to her baby. John never appears in these dreams directly; instead, he is offstage. I never confront him.

After John died I fell into grief as one falls into a pit. I experienced rage so overwhelming I feared it would disorganize my personality permanently. All those months and weeks where I had swallowed anger and accepted an unacceptable triangle at last came pouring out. But I was not angry at John. I was angry at God, for taking my lover. I was angry at Liz, for having been his wife. I was angry at friends who tried to console me, at my mother when she tried to calm me.

I should have been angry at John. I could have been enraged that he died and left me. I denied even that, telling friends, "He wouldn't have gone and died like that if he didn't think I could handle it." At the same time I felt his death was an accident, something he could not control, did not intend. My thinking was like a tangle of torn webbing, impossible to live with, so I drank to avoid thinking, to dampen, so far as I could, my feelings of bereavement and loss.

When, after eleven years, I began to work on this memoir, my husband asked me, shaking his head, "When are you going to get to the anger?"

"What anger?" I was genuinely puzzled.

"The anger for everything he put you through."

It has taken me a long time.

In November 1982, about seven weeks after John's accident, I was unpacking in my apartment in Dundee and came across a long narrow box from Bloomingdale's. I turned it over and saw a cartoon John had drawn. I remembered a comment by one of his colleagues. "John drew a cartoon at our last department meeting, the one on September thirteenth. Did you ever find it?" Here was that cartoon. The line drawing—a parody of Picasso's *Guernica*—shows a pyramid of unhappy people, some scowling, some looking down or away, one reaching out from the crowd in a futile gesture, another looking quite amusingly mad, others looking resigned or bored. I recognized John's friends and colleagues. On top of the tallest head perches a tiny, skeptical bird; John's signature creature. Some of the cartoon faces have balloons coming from their mouths: "Polish thy chains." "Be a joke unto thyself!" The tag, in John's hand, reads ENGRISH DEPT. MEETING.

I looked at the box and smiled, pleased to have this silly sketch, glad to have to put together a piece of the puzzle, reverent to have something personal. Then I turned the box over and opened it. Underneath the white tissue paper lay an extravagant silk necktie, silver gray with a figured design in pink, exactly the tie he would have chosen for himself. But where had he gotten it? We hadn't gone shopping.

I sat in my study chair transfixed. Liz had bought the tie when she and David were in New York on Saturday, September 11, and had saved it to give to him at the department meeting. He would have worn it at our wedding. I, willfully blind as I had been, would not even have noticed that he had a new tie.

Was I more angry at Liz for buying the tie or at John for accepting it? I sat frozen in my study, looking at this box and what it held, knowing I should be furious and not knowing what to feel.

I remember now the scene where I sat in on John's lecture, so soon before he died, and Liz sat in the front row and asked her questions. Whenever I was angry about my situation, about our triangle, I blamed Liz. I felt she was grasping, intrusive, that she overstepped. I was never angry with John, but I should have been. He led her on. He refused to draw lines to separate cleanly from her and begin a new life with me. He had no intention of excluding her from his life, from our lives. In living with him I was entering a tangle of emotions, evasions, and lies as deep and dark as any medieval thicket or mythological maze. He enjoyed having both of us in his life, manipulating, prodding, keeping us both at a high emotional pitch. As well as his addiction to alcohol, he was addicted to adrenaline and high drama. He told each of us what he felt we wanted to hear. He told me he had chosen me. His last words to her were, "I love you desperately."

His charm, his charisma, his psychological power were so present that I lived within them like air and never questioned them. I thought I was happy; I thought I was getting what I wanted and denied in my heart how difficult it was, living with a man who wouldn't decide which woman he wanted, living with a man who was alcoholic and reckless. Every moment was uncertain, was indeed like walking on broken glass.

And when it was over there was a bottomless grief.

I feel now that if the triangular relationship with Liz had at last been resolved, another would have replaced it. This is what my dream has been telling me, the truth I could not face. At the Bread Loaf conference in 1982 he spent the night at Treman on the floor with a woman who dearly loved him, yet he couldn't give her the commitment she wanted, as he could not give it to me. The qualities I had found attractive in him as a lover—that he lived without boundaries, took chances, courted risk, and included many friends and lovers in his life—served as barriers to establishing a true, intimate partnership. I would have had the trappings, the engagement ring, even the wedding ring, but not a real marriage.

Liz was not the villain I wanted to paint her. In the grandiosity of his alcoholism he was unfair to both of us. He liked to set up close, incestuous love relationships where the women involved knew each other, were kept off balance, were expected to bow to his demands. In his pain and his disease he had become a moral monster, confused, compelling, grandly manipulative.

I look back on the turbulent, brilliant months with John and I'm grateful, first that I survived and, second, for the happy times I do recall.

Sometimes I wonder where I would be had I not met John at Bread Loaf and accepted his offer of love, as difficult and as fraught as it was. When I do, I picture a brittle lady intellectual, still making the rounds of Cambridge parties, first-run films, trendy coffee-houses, careful in her clothes and opinions, lonely in her heart. I am glad I escaped that fate. It was John's gift to me to shake me out of that life.

It is only one of many ironies that I have found domestic happiness not with John but instead with a man to whom John introduced me.

In July 1982 I went with John to a meeting of the board of directors of the Laurel Street Theatre. The board met every month, in the green room of the theater, a former classroom in the elementary school building the theater occupied.

That night I was afraid to look at anyone. John had told me so often how much everyone loved Liz and how I couldn't compare to her that I just figured they would all hate me.

One person loved me on the spot.

It was Gerry.

"I saw you walk into that meeting, like a little brown wren in the shadow of the famous figure, and I thought, There she is, the woman I want to marry, and I'll never get her because she's with Gardner."

Gerry was the secretary for the board of the Laurel Street Theatre, and in the summer of 1982 he was recuperating from a broken back. He had been helping his father in his painting business, and they had a job at IBM. In April, Gerry had fallen thirty feet from a collapsing scaffold inside one of the vast IBM complexes in Endicott, New York. On his way down he hit a pipe and fractured two vertebrae, narrowly escaping a paralyzing injury.

Gerry's parents have a summer cottage on the bank of the Susquehanna River. For therapy, Gerry was required to swim great distances in the river every warm day. September 14 was a warm day, 82 degrees, and Gerry was at the cottage, resting on the dock after his swim, at 2 P.M. when John rode by on his motorcycle. Gerry heard him. A half hour later, he heard the siren and thought, I guess the motorcyclist didn't make it.

That evening he went up to SUNY-Binghamton, where he was taking classes for a master's degree in public policy administration, and heard the news of John's death.

At the funeral Gerry sat in the row behind me; I didn't see him. "That Gerry Hough," my mother remarked. "He didn't worship at John's feet the way the rest of them did."

Mother had been worried about me and my choice of John as a husband. At first there were the obvious considerations: his wife, the seventeen-year age difference, the drinking, cancer surgery, a half-million-dollar debt to the IRS. Mom also saw the hero worship in those who surrounded John. She looked at Gerry and saw something different. She was right; Gerry observed John, kept his distance. Gerry is not a writer; instead, he was involved in the theater as actor, set designer, producer. When John moved to Susquehanna, Gerry was borough manager, a position like that of mayor. He observed John with a skeptical eye, wondering about this well-known writer who had adopted his town, and one by one checked John's books out of the library and read them.

In my desolation after John died I clung to his friends in Susquehanna. Jan Quackenbush invited me into the Laurel Street Theatre, and I began to work behind the scenes on plays; then I was offered a seat on the board. I got to know Gerry as we worked at the theater. He sent me a card that first Christmas, in 1982, and it was the only one I didn't throw away unread. He quoted something John had written for a comedy the Laurel Street Theatre had produced: a line to the effect that life should be a glorious joke. In the summer of 1983 we all produced the play John had helped to write, *Marvin's on "The Distant Shore"* and later another play, *The Dreamers*, by Joanna Higgins, which Gerry directed and in which Jan, Anne Ryan, Jeanette, and I had parts.

I began to realize Gerry could be a true friend. In the meantime I was working my way through the master's degree and then the Ph.D. and applying for college teaching jobs. I was awarded the Ph.D. in 1986, and Gerry and I married in June of 1987.

* * *

For many years, I avoided Liz. I took a teaching job in Syracuse, New York. Gerry and I stayed in Binghamton, and I commuted ninety miles each way. I felt this gave me an opportunity to get away, to make a new start. It didn't work. Most of my colleagues knew Ray Carver and asked me about John; one colleague had taught with John years before at Skidmore. I was polite, noncommittal, turned questions aside.

I would not shop in the bookstore David opened in Binghamton and built into a thriving business. If I ran into Liz in a restaurant I left abruptly.

All this time I wrote: a novel for my master's thesis, a different novel for my Ph.D. dissertation, two more novels after that, two collections of stories. These books were not formulaic as my first book, the mystery novel, had been. I read and reread my notes from John's classes, strove to create literary fiction according to his advice, listened to my teachers at the university, wrote and rewrote with genuine devotion. The fiction I had written for John's class in 1982 was quickly accepted by small literary magazines; all my new work, except for two short stories, was turned back. I submitted to agents and publishers and was rejected time after time: an apprenticeship of sixteen years and one million words, all unpublished. At last one friend said to me, in my despair, "These are good, Susan, but you're not writing with your heart, only with your head."

In the meantime, I still drank. An outsider would not have perceived a problem. Gerry and I had a lovely duplex apartment. We each had a car, a job. I devoted many hours to lesson plans, student papers, steady hours at my own writing. Gerry knew there was a problem when I emptied a bottle and collapsed into our bed, but he didn't know what to do. The crisis came as a direct result of my despair over my failure to publish.

Dayv James-French came to see us for a weekend. His first book of short fiction had been published in Canada; a friend from Bread Loaf, Carole Glickfeld, had published her first collection of stories and was speaking at the university; Gerry and I invited both of them to come and planned a dinner to celebrate their work. I tried to be genuinely happy that both had succeeded in publishing. Each had worked hard, had experienced many rejections; each had produced wonderful work. In my heart I couldn't be happy. I was envious, despairing, hopeless.

The dinner was a great success. I masked my feelings of envy and disappointment all too well. By the next day I was emotionally exhausted from this effort. Gerry and Dayv sat chatting in our kitchen. I was drinking liquor as if it were water. At last I realized I was going to pass out, which had been my plan, because I could not bear my bitter feelings. I excused myself and staggered up to our bedroom, where I passed out on our bed, lying on my back.

I came to just as vomit rose in my throat. I made it to the bathroom and then knelt on the cool floor, shaking all over. I might have aspirated my own vomit and died that afternoon, died as I lived, quietly, politely, with my job and my car and my marriage and my quiet misery, and Gerry and Dayv wouldn't have known anything was wrong until they found me.

For more than two years I tried to abstain from alcohol. I could last about three months, and then my feelings would overwhelm me, I would reach for a drink, telling myself it would be "just one to ease the ache in my throat," and I would drink until there was no alcohol left in the house to drink. This happened over and over.

At last I sought help from a group of sober alcoholics in a structured program. With God's grace, I have stayed sober, one day at a time. In my first year of sobriety, I conceived our daughter. Three different doctors had told Gerry and me this would never happen. Eleanor's birth opened a new life for both of us, and when she was three months old I began to write this memoir.

Gerry and I have worked hard to build a partnership. Early in our marriage I idealized John, wished he had not died, yearned for his charisma, his charm, the sense I had with him that anything was possible. It has been very difficult for Gerry to live with a woman who yearned after a lost, perfect partner. Until I became sober, I could not see the unmanageability of John's life, how his drinking damaged him, how it twisted his thinking and his relationships, how my drinking damaged me. In our married life, Gerry and I have faced genuine hardship: the decline of his parents, the deaths of mine, unemployment, financial ruin. For a long time I lost hope. I felt I would be unable to use the gift God had given me, the gift of expression in writing, that I would ultimately fail at what I had felt so strongly was my life's purpose.

I yearned for the sense I had had in those months with John that I could indeed make a contribution in the world of letters, could be of service.

As I became sober, I began to think about my feelings about Liz, about John, about those turbulent months. Binghamton is a small town. When my path crossed Liz's, once or twice a year, at a supermarket or on the university campus, we acknowledged each other, waved, smiled, said "hi" but didn't speak at length.

At a retirement party for Carol Fischler, we had a chance to meet for the first time, face-to-face, in some years. I saw Liz across the lawn and decided I could not go through the entire party without speaking to her. I took a deep breath and went over to greet her, and brought her back to say hello to Gerry and meet our daughter. "What a beautiful red-haired baby!" she exclaimed. Eleanor was fourteen months old, riding in her pack on Gerry's back. I complimented Liz on her second book of poetry and she thanked me. David and I spoke about the birth of their son. It wasn't exactly a reconciliation, but it was cordial.

Some years later, in 1998, Liz and Jan Quackenbush and I were featured speakers at the First Annual John Gardner Conference in Batavia, sponsored by Genesee Community College. Jan presented a paper about John's interest in theater and opera, Liz read a poignant essay about her life with John, and I read a paper about John's last lecture at the Bread Loaf Writers' Conference.

When I saw Liz I went right up to her. "Can I have a hug?" I asked.

She embraced me warmly. "Oh, Susan, you can have all the hugs you want."

We sat together in the last row of chairs, chatting briefly, and were interrupted by an elderly lady bearing a photo album. Marge had been a close friend of Priscilla's and had family photos of John, Gilbert, Sandy, and their youngest brother, Jim. She approached Liz with the album and the two of them conferred. I looked at the faded images of John and Gilbert as children and had no idea which was which. Beside me, Liz was more confident. "This one's Gilbert," she asserted. "Look at that sweetness around the mouth; it has to be Gilbert." Marge looked at her skeptically. She had known the boys as children; Liz had not. Yet Liz was so sure of herself. A scholar approached and sat on her other side. Making conversation, he asked her if she had visited the collection of John's papers at the University of Rochester. "I've never gone over there." She laughed. "I keep being afraid I'll find my underwear or socks mixed in with the collection." I drew back in annoyance. Here it was again, that terrierlike persistence, her continual staking of a claim in John's life. I could have said, "Gee, Liz, I don't remember packing your underwear when *I* packed the papers," but I let it go.

As I sat next to her on the cheap folding chair and watched her face, so familiar and yet so unknown, the intent tilt to her head, the bright encouragement of her look, the tiny parallel lines around her nose that show only when she laughs, for the first time I considered how difficult it must have been for her. John had driven her into divorce through his actions and his words, yet he had clung to her. I wondered what it must have been like for her, to have the divorce finalized but the relationship unresolved, indeed, still entangling, at the moment of his death, only six days afterward. A piercing chunk of ice that had been lodged for years in my heart began at that instant to shift, to melt.

After the talks on John's life and work had been presented, amid the general milling around, a man approached us. Betsy Sachs had joined Liz and me, and we all sat in the back of the room. This novitiate neared us hesitantly. He had come to academics late and was about fifty. His love and admiration for John's fiction and the soul it expressed shine through on every page of his careful, stu-

314

dious book about John. As this man looked at the three of us sitting on our folding chairs, tears welled in his eyes. "I can't tell you what it means to me," he began, "to meet all of you here today, to meet those of you who actually knew him—" His voice broke. I looked at his shaking hands, listened to his tremulous voice. "To me," he continued, "it's like meeting the apostles."

28

―――――

"Mommy Misses You"

On the fifteenth anniversary of John's death, I went to look at his grave for the first time. On a fine September day, with the domed crystalline sky swept by shining, high-flying clouds, I drove out to Grand View Cemetery in Batavia.

The cemetery lies just outside of town on a section of level ground next to the road. Twin stone pillars guard the entrance, reminding visitors that this is a place of seriousness and sorrow. I stop first at the office; it is locked. I get back in the car and drive around and around the winding paths through an atmosphere of whispery loss. A polished stone with the inset photograph of a smiling child; a legend: MOMMY MISSES YOU. No other living being but myself. Feelings of annoyance compete with sadness. If I really believe in eternal life, what am I doing here? One might as well put up a monument to a discarded winter coat. The words *Mommy misses you* catch at my throat. I look to the right and to the left. How will I ever find the plot? I drive some more and at last end up back where I started and turn off in a new direction, this time to the left, and look to my right and there it is: a stone pillar reading GARDNER and the names JOHN and PRISCILLA, John's parents. I park the car and walk over.

It's so small, really, this plot—how could it hold that immense coffin I remember?—and totally flat, grass-covered, with a small stone: JOHN CHAMPLIN GARDNER IV, and the dates: 1933–1982. To its left is another stone: GILBERT DAY GARDNER: 1938–1945.

I kneel on the grass for a long time. A car engine: I look up to see an older couple, not that much older than I, really, in a small American car. They hesitate, and I realize they are wondering if they can get by my car on the narrow path. I stand up. "Shall I move my car?"

"No, no, we can get by." The man wears a turquoise cotton T-shirt; he might be fifty-six, hunched over his potbelly, big pale hands on the tiny wheel. His wife has glasses with clear plastic frames; frown lines crease her forehead. Have I found the care-taker? they ask. Can they get help finding a grave? No, I say, no one's here, you just have to drive around. "We're looking for a thirty-year-old grave," the man says. I nod. The woman peers at me, purses her lips. "Sorry to disturb you."

I nod again. "You just have to keep looking," I say. "You'll find it." At last they pull around my car and leave, and I go back to the grave.

I had pictured a garden cemetery, Victorian in design, with wind-ing paths, high exposed places crowned by angel monuments, and secret, shaded dells, perhaps a pond. Instead here is a functional space, a stone's throw from the main road, a level plot of ground in which to put the dead, as much a part of life as tract housing. Across the path for cars is a sugar maple, to my right is a beech; at the edge of John's parents' monument lists a pot of geraniums, now wilted, past their prime.

After some time I see the woman from the car pacing through the graves, looking at her feet, reading, looking, reading again. Then she turns away, gets back in the car, and they drive to another part of the cemetery.

A high-pitched siren—I look up. A rescue vehicle flies down the road, siren wailing; then another, and another; fire rescue, ambu-lance, sheriff's car, then a civilian car with blue light attached flashing above the driver's side; the noise of the sirens rises and falls as one vehicle after another hurtles down the road out of town.

I look around and realize I'm alone. I lie down on John's grave, fit my shoulders into the grass, feel the coolness of the earth beneath my shoulder blades and along my spine, align my feet, spread my fingers next to my sides, then cross them over my torso. The diamond he gave me rests in the hollow of my throat; after ten years I had it reset from an engagement ring into a pendant I can wear on a chain. The sun warms my face. At my feet stands the sugar maple, above me wave the broad flat leaves of the beech. Beneath me the earth is spinning in its orbit, revolving around the sun, soaring through the universe within the swirling galaxy. I clench my fingers in the cool green grass.

At this very moment my daughter, Eleanor, is lying on a blue cot at day care, eyes wide open, waiting for the other children to settle down so she can get up and sit at the table and color. At age four she no longer naps, and the teachers allow her to get up as long as she remains quiet. She murmurs to herself, making up a story for her doll, Baby Annie, a constant companion, pressed to her heart. She brushes Annie's forehead with her lips.

At this very moment Gerry is at his desk, phone to his ear, the computer screen brightly illuminating the room; across the cubicle his work partner laughs huskily into the telephone. "You can't mean it. They didn't?" Later in the day he will get in the car to pick up Eleanor. They will have supper together, he will help her with her bath, they will choose her clothes for the next day, he will read to her and tuck her into bed.

In the crypt below the altar at St. Paul's Episcopal Church rest two small rectangular boxes in their niches next to each other in the wall: the ashes of my father, Knight, and my mother, Virginia.

I lie on John's grave and cling to the earth spinning beneath me, the grass cool under my fingers, the sun warming my eyelids on this fine September afternoon. Above me, unseen in the domed crystalline sky, burn the luminous stars, wheeling and soaring in their immutable, impromptu patterns. I lie on his grave, borne through space like the earth, with its beech trees, sugar maples, messages of sadness and loss—"Mommy misses you"—sirens wailing in their rescue errand along the road. I lie on his grave under the unseen filigree of stars, luminous, patterned, as, sailing aloft, they outstrip the solar winds, lacing through our life like bright music, bearing their twin themes: their messages of endurance and hope.

Acknowledgments

A great many supportive friends have helped me as I worked over the last seven years to write this book. Initial support and encouragement came from Susan M. Watkins, who shared memories, read drafts, and returned my letters to me. Her wisdom and cheerful support at just the right times has kept this project going. Richard Kendall spent many hours reading, compiling bibliographic information, and giving valuable advice. Without these two individuals this project would never have succeeded.

Dayv James-French returned to me my half of our voluminous correspondence over the last two decades and provided a steady flow of supportive e-mail. Olivia Lovelace also saved and returned my letters from this period. I am grateful to the staff at Creighton University in Omaha, Nebraska, who made copies for me of letters I wrote to Ron Hansen in September and October of 1982. These letters are part of their permanent collection of Ron's papers.

Individuals who read, commented on, and helped me with this manuscript in its various stages are numerous. I owe a great debt of gratitude to the late Barbara Moore, the late Joyce Renwick, the late Terrence Des Pres. Other readers who contributed time and editorial skills include Betsy Sachs, Shona Ramaya, Dorothy Argetsinger, Sheila Purdy, Donna DeVoist, David Stanton, Michael Pavese, Ernest Stephenson, Arlene Walsh, Karen Andes, Barbara Remington, Mary Pat Tigue, Anne Ryan, Leslie Reynolds, Jill Smolowe, Susan Watkins, Dayv James-French, Jeanette Robertson, Sally Crossley, Alexis Khoury, Kim Robinson. I received help and encouragement from Kevin Huffman and Allan Duncan, and from Noreen Suriner.

For sharing memories of Susquehanna and the Laurel Street Theatre I thank Anne and Frank Ryan, Jeanette Robertson, Irene Allen, Jim Rose, and Mary Pat Tigue.

I thank Blue Argo, Ron Hansen, Ambrose Clancy, Bob Reiss, Norton Girault, Page Edwards, Barbara Schiappa, Karen Andes, Betsy Sachs, David Stanton, Arlene Walsh, Tom Miller, Barry Sanders, and others for sharing memories of the Bread Loaf Writers' Conference with me. For reference, I turned to David Haward Bain's book about the conference, *Whose Woods These Are: A History of the Bread Loaf Writers' Conference from 1926 to 1992* (Ecco Press, 1993) and to *John Gardner: A Bibliographical Profile* by John M. Howell (Southern Illinois University Press, 1980).

Charley Boyd of the John Gardner Society in Batavia, New York, helped me get in touch with several old friends. His group's website, The John C. Gardner Appreciation Page, proved a valuable resource.

I would like to thank my friends in the Southern Tier Writers' Guild for their support and good fellowship.

My agent, Susan Raihofer, believed in this project and saw potential during its intermediate stages. My editor at Carroll & Graf, Martine Bellen, asked many careful questions and helped me refine and improve the manuscript. Janet Baker provided valuable editorial help as well.

My husband, Gerry Hough, has not read this manuscript in process. We have talked it over at length and he has been unfailingly supportive during its difficult composition. At times when I have wanted to abandon it, he has encouraged me to continue. For many years he says he has felt the ghost of John Gardner in our house. As the manuscript drew to its completion, he had this feeling less and less. To Gerry I owe my second chance at life. He was patient with me while I was alcoholic and unsure and has supported my efforts to achieve and maintain sobriety. His situation, of marriage to a woman who still yearned for a charismatic, dangerous partner, has not been easy. I respect his grace and treasure his love. To him and to our daughter, Eleanor, I owe my present day-to-day happiness.